STUDIES IN FRENCH INTONATION

LONDON AGENTS
SIMPKIN MARSHALL LTD.

MADE AND PRINTED IN GREAT BRITAIN AT THE WORKS OF
W. HEFFER AND SONS LTD.,
CAMBRIDGE, ENGLAND.

STUDIES IN FRENCH INTONATION

26847

BY

HÉLÈNE N. COUSTENOBLE

AND

LILIAS E. ARMSTRONG

LECTURERS IN PHONETICS AT UNIVERSITY
COLLEGE, LONDON

CAMBRIDGE
W. HEFFER & SONS LTD.
1934

PREFACE

WE should like to express our gratitude to those mentioned below who have very graciously permitted us to reproduce the extracts referred to under their names.

Madame Alphonse Daudet for the passages chosen from *Lettres de mon Moulin* and *Contes du Lundi* by Alphonse Daudet; Monsieur Louis, Paul Dubois (who owns the author's rights) and the Librairie Hachette for the passages chosen from *La Fontaine et ses Fables*, by H. Taine; La Librairie Plon for the passages chosen from *Mon Oncle et mon Curé*, by Jean de la Brète, and from *Mon Petit Trott*, by André Lichtenberger; Messrs. Jérome and Jean Tharaud for the passage from *La Fête Arabe*; L'Illustration for the passages taken from *L'Illustration* and from *La Petite Illustration*; La Nouvelle Revue Française for Extract No. 21, page 242; Le Mercure de France for the passages from *Le Vigneron dans sa Vigne*, by Jules Renard; Messrs. Calmann-Lévy, Editeurs, for the passages from *Voyage autour de mon Jardin*, by Alphonse Karr, from *L'Enfant à la Balustrade*, by René Boylesve, from *Pierre Nozière*, by Anatole France, and from *Eve Victorieuse*, by Pierre de Coulevain.

Very special thanks must be given to Monsieur Jacques Maurice-Vallis and to Mademoiselle V. Lacroix, who have enlivened our collection of texts with dialogues specially written for this book. Monsieur Maurice-Vallis has given us *La Petite Ville du Midi* (in collaboration with H.C.) and *Jour de Pluie*; Mademoiselle Lacroix *Une Emplette Peu Ordinaire*.

We acknowledge our indebtedness to Klinghardt and de Fourmestraux, the pioneers of all studies in French intonation, for help received from their work, *Französische Intonationsübungen*; and to H. O. Coleman, whose article *Intonation and Emphasis*,[1] was the forerunner of all that has been written on this subject. We

[1] Published in *Miscellanea Phonetica*, 1912, by the Association Phonétique Internationale.

v

have tried in this book to show the significance of intensity-emphasis and contrast-emphasis by using two distinctive marks: ‖ for intensity and ″ for contrast.

Our thanks are also due to Mr. G. Noël-Armfield, who laboriously read through the proofs and sent us many suggestions.

Lastly we thank Messrs. Heffer & Sons, Ltd., for their courtesy, patience and accuracy in the very difficult task of printing this book.

H. C.

L. E. A.

UNIVERSITY COLLEGE,
  LONDON,
    July, 1934.

PHONETIC SYMBOLS

The following list of phonetic symbols[1] used in this book is given here in case some readers are not already familiar with them.

VOWEL SYMBOLS.

Key-word.		*Key-word.*		*Key-word.*	
i	livre	o	beau	ɛ̃	fin
e	nez	u	mousse	ã	temps
ɛ	fête	y	lune	ɔ̃	long
a	café	ø	eux	œ̃	un
ɑ	sabre	œ	œuf		
ɔ	homme	ə	le		

CONSONANT SYMBOLS.

Key-word.		*Key-word.*	
p	pas	r	rare
b	bas	f	fille
t	tas	v	ville
d	deux	s	ça
k	cas	z	maison
g	gros	ʃ	chose
m	moi	ʒ	jaune
n	ni	w	oui
ɲ	ligne	ɥ	cuisine
l	laide	j	rien

ʔ represents the glottal plosive, a non-essential sound sometimes used in French.

[1] Of the Association Phonétique Internationale.

CONTENTS

CHAPTER I

INTRODUCTORY

PART I

UNEMPHATIC INTONATION IN ENGLISH AND FRENCH

A. FALLING INTONATIONS (Simplest Forms)

CHAPTER II

THE FALLING INTONATION IN ENGLISH

CHAPTER III

THE RISING-FALLING INTONATION IN FRENCH

ix

CHAPTER IV

CHAPTER V

THE FALLING INTONATION IN FRENCH

CHAPTER VI

OTHER USES OF THE RISING-FALLING INTONATION

CHAPTER XV

CHAPTER XVI

PART II

EMPHATIC INTONATION IN ENGLISH AND FRENCH

CHAPTER XVII

CHAPTER XVIII

INTENSITY IN ENGLISH

CHAPTER XVIX

INTENSITY IN FRENCH

CHAPTER XX

INFLUENCE OF INTENSIVE STRESS ON INTONATION IN FRENCH

CHAPTER XXI

SHORT EXAMPLES WITH INTENSITY IN FRENCH

CHAPTER XXII

CONTRAST IN ENGLISH

CONTENTS

CHAPTER XXIX

CONNECTED TEXTS WITH EMPHASIS

CHAPTER I

INTRODUCTORY

OBJECT AND SCOPE OF THE BOOK.

1. The aim of this book is to provide teachers and students of French pronunciation with a practical method of learning French intonation. The book should be worked through with a teacher from the North of France; if possible, with one who has some understanding of the intonation of his language.

2. The analysis of the intonation recorded here is the result of several years of observation. It is an analysis of the essential characteristics of the typical intonation used by educated speakers of Northern France in conversation and in the reading of passages of descriptive and narrative prose. A study of the intonation devices used by actors and by teachers of diction in declaiming oratorical prose and in reciting poetry has not been attempted here.

3. Numerous examples are given of isolated sentences and of connected texts which give systematic practice in both unemphatic and emphatic intonation.

4. The student must be prepared to find that many of the isolated sentences sound unnatural, spoken apart from their proper setting. He will also find, by the time he reaches the connected texts, that the intonation given in each case, is not, in all its details, the only one possible. Some French readers would read the passages slowly, using many short intonation groups. Others would read them very quickly, using long intonation groups. Some would use emphasis where others would avoid it, and *vice versa*. The same reader might, on different occasions, use different intonations for the same passage. If the English learner reads the passages as recorded here, he will be using an intonation which is appropriate and which educated Frenchmen will accept as being French.

5. The book is written primarily for the use of English teachers and English students of French pronunciation; and for this reason

the main features of French intonation are compared and contrasted, where helpful, with those of a characteristic type of English intonation.[1] The comparison which is drawn between the intonation of French and English should also be useful to those of French nationality who are engaged in teaching French to English learners or English to French learners.

UNEMPHATIC STRESS AND UNEMPHATIC INTONATION.

6. When we speak, even without emphasis, certain syllables stand out more prominently than others.

7. Stress is one of the causes of this prominence, both in English and French.

8. Stress means the speech energy which is used in pronouncing a syllable. Speech energy is, of course, used in pronouncing all syllables; but the term *stressed* is reserved for those which are pronounced with more energy than their neighbours. Other syllables are said to be *unstressed*.

9. Stress is not just a question of force of exhalation; it includes also greater muscular activity of the organs of articulation, especially of the tongue and lips, greater jaw movement, greater tension in the larynx.

10. In most cases stress results in increased loudness of the syllables upon which it is expended. But it often happens that a syllable upon which the speaker has expended more energy than on neighbouring syllables is hardly audible to the hearer. For example, the final stressed syllable of a French sentence is often pronounced on such a low pitch that its sounds are wholly without voice. The prominence of the syllable is obvious to the speaker because of the speech effort he uses in pronouncing it. The hearer finds it difficult to catch the syllable at all, and is aware of its importance only by the presence of some outward sign of the speaker's effort.

11. In a simple English word of more than one syllable there is one syllable on which the speaker expends more energy than on the others. E.g. 'perfect (adjective), per'fect (verb), per'fection, 'politics, po'litical, poli'tician, 'idol, i'deal, 'realise, 'industry,

---

[1] See also *A Handbook of English Intonation*, by Armstrong and Ward (Heffer, Cambridge).

in'dustrial, in,dustriali'sation.[1] The correct placing of this stress is an extremely difficult thing for a French learner who is confused by the fact that there is no fixed place for it.

12. In English, in connected speech of an unemphatic nature, words of important meaning, whatever their position in the sentence, are generally stressed as they would be if they were pronounced in isolation. Important monosyllabic words are also stressed. The following example will illustrate this:

> The 'children are a'sleep | after an ex'citing 'day.‖ 'This 'country 'air | has 'worked 'wonders | on their 'health and 'spirits.‖ 'No 'signs of ,conva'lescence about them 'now!‖ 'Baby is the 'picture of con'tentment; ‖ and 'Teddy is his 'perky, in'quiring little 'self once more.‖ He 'finds 'life on a 'farm 'full of ad-'venture.‖

13. The stress system is very different in French. Each syllable of a French word pronounced without emphasis receives a fairly even amount of stress,—hence the rather staccato effect of spoken French. But it is generally felt that there is a little stronger stress on the final syllable. E.g. répu'blique, élémen'taire, direc'teur, sympa'thie, réali'té, fran'çais, hiron'delle, intermit'tent. One need never hesitate in stressing a French word pronounced un-emphatically: it would never be wrong to stress the final syllable.

14. A short sentence may be considered, from the point of view of stress, as a many-syllabled word: stress falls on the final syllable. E.g. Il va ve'nir.‖ C'est inu'tile.‖ Il ne regarde 'pas.‖ Ils viendront ce 'soir.‖

15. If the sentence contains a number of grammatical groups (sense-groups),[2] each of which the speaker makes prominent, stress falls on the final syllable of each group: Ils vien'dront | ce 'soir.‖ Il y est res'té | pendant trente 'ans.‖ Nous n'aimons pas beau'coup | aller en Es'pagne | pendant l'é'té.‖ Il tenait à la 'main | une lettre tout ou'verte | qu'il venait à la minute 'même | de rece'voir | de Pa'ris.‖ Au de'là | commençait la grande 'mer, | frémissante et 'grise | dont l'extrémi'té | se per'dait | dans les 'brumes.‖

---

[1] The mark ' is placed before the stressed syllable.   , denotes secondary stress.

[2] Sense-group is the name given to each of the smallest groups of gram-matically related words into which many sentences may be divided.

16. Thus, in connected unemphatic speech stress does not belong to the word, as in English, but to the word-group: the word does not bear it unless it occurs finally in that group.

17. Another and more important cause of prominence in both languages is intonation.

18. Intonation means the rise and fall of the pitch of the voice in speech. It is thus in itself an entirely different thing from stress. Generally the two work together, and in such a way that it is often difficult to decide what each contributes towards the effect produced. Many writers have hitherto considered stress entirely responsible for effects of prominence due primarily to intonation.

19. In unemphatic speech the speaker uses what may be called unemphatic stress, marked thus, ', and unemphatic intonation.

20. Part I of this book analyses the intonation used in unemphatic speech in English and French and explains its effect.

21. Another important thing which gives prominence to a word is the addition of length. Length is marked in this book only in the French examples which are phonetically transcribed. It is shown by placing : after the symbol representing the sound which is prolonged.

EMPHATIC STRESS AND EMPHATIC INTONATION.

22. Emphasis may be defined as an all-round *special* increase of effort used to convey some special or added meaning. (See Chap. XVII.)

23. In emphatic speech the desired effect is produced sometimes mainly by extra stress, marked thus ", and sometimes mainly by the use of what may be called emphatic intonation, marked thus ″. (See Chap. XVII.) Length is also an important factor.

24. Part II of this book analyses the intonation used in emphatic English and French speech, explaining its effect and also that of other devices used to express emphasis.

NATIONAL SPEECH MELODIES.

25. We are apt to think that the intonation of any language other than our own is an exceedingly difficult and complicated

thing; that there is no method in its madness; that it is impossible to analyse it, and impossible to learn it or to teach it. It is certainly difficult for adult students to catch all the variations heard in the intonation of a good speaker of another nationality; but it is neither impossible nor very difficult for a student of average aptitude to learn and to teach what may be called the *typical* intonation of another language. Some learners are capable of elaborating this typical intonation by introducing into it many details which, though not essential, are extremely effective.[1]

26. The most difficult thing we have to grasp is the intonation that people of other nationalities use when they are speaking without emphasis. Then they use their own national "tune." This can generally be analysed into a very limited number of simple themes. There is always an intonation which *falls* somehow, and another which *rises* somehow. The method of falling is usually different for different languages; the method of rising is different. These simple rising and falling intonations, with various slight modifications, repetitions and alternations make up the melody of unemphatic speech. Foreign students find this melody difficult because it *is* a national thing.

27. In emphatic speech, when we are roused to express something more than ordinary statements, questions and commands· when we want to give expression to our emotions, we show ourselves to be more akin to speakers of other nations. Then we use various devices, most of which may be described as international in character, for they are such as the speakers of many languages use in similar circumstances. Because of the international nature of these devices for emphasis, the intonation of emphatic speech offers much less difficulty to the foreign student than that of unemphatic speech. You will see in Part II that the devices used in French emphatic speech have an immense amount in common with those used in English emphatic speech, though they are not always applied in the same way in the two languages.

28. It may be pointed out here that the French use emphatic speech much more readily than the English; in fact, it may be argued that emphatic speech is *normal* in French!

[1] Many of these unessential details are omitted from this book so that the learner may not be confused by too many variations.

PART I

UNEMPHATIC INTONATION IN ENGLISH AND FRENCH

A. FALLING INTONATIONS (Simplest Forms)

CHAPTER II

THE FALLING INTONATION IN ENGLISH

29. Listen to the intonation you use in the following short assertion said without emphasis:

I 'can't re'member the e'xact 'date of it.

This statement has four important words, *can't, remember, exact, date,* the importance of these words being conveyed to the hearer chiefly by the stress which is placed on each, by the length and by the different pitch with which each stressed syllable is pronounced.

30. The pitch of the stressed syllables of these words could be represented in this way:

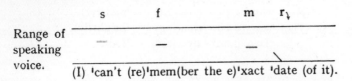

The long parallel lines represent the upper and lower limits of the intonation of the speaking voice. The range in unemphatic speech is roughly about an octave.

1. ANALYSIS OF THE FALLING INTONATION IN ENGLISH.

31. Intonation of the stressed syllables:

(*a*) The intonation is a falling one.

(*b*) The pitch descends gradually until the last stressed syllable is reached. In the assertion given above the intonation of the stressed syllables might be approximately represented in the tonic sol-fa system by s f m r↘, the mark ↘ suggesting a fall of varying depth.

9

(c) *Within* the last stressed syllable the pitch falls quickly to a low tone. This fall in pitch is quite an appreciable one, though many English people have difficulty in hearing it. The depth depends on the degree of finality intended.

32. The above statement has four important words. When there are three, as in

> You can 'look it 'up in the di'rectory,
> He 'thinks it 'doesn't 'matter,
> The 'sun was 'shining 'brightly,
> 'Two and 'two are 'four,

the intonation of the stressed syllables may be represented thus:

	s	m	r

You can 'look it   'up in the di'rectory.
(He) 'thinks (it) 'does('nt)   'mat(ter).
(The) 'sun (was) 'shin(ing)   'bright(ly).
    'Two (and) 'two (are)   'four.

33. When there are two important words, as in

> I shall 'always re'member it,
> You 'never can 'tell,

the intonation of the stressed syllables may be shown thus:

(I shall) 'al(ways re) 'mem(ber it).
You 'never (can) 'tell.

34. When there is only one important word, as in

> 'Thank you, I've 'sent it, I shall 'borrow one,

the whole fall may take place in pronouncing its stressed syllables:

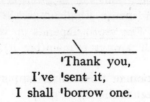

'Thank you,
I've 'sent it,
I shall 'borrow one.

35. Intonation of the unstressed syllables:

It is not necessary to go into detail in describing the intonation of the unstressed syllables.

Notice:

(a) The intonation of those syllables that precede the first stress may be either level or rising gradually in anticipation of the pitch of the first stressed syllable. In the statement *I shall always remember it*, the intonation of *I shall* may be either

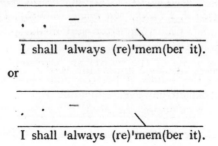

I shall 'always (re)'mem(ber it).

or

I shall 'always (re)'mem(ber it).

(b) The intonation of syllables linking the stressed syllables may be level or descend gradually to the pitch of the next stressed syllable. In the above statement the intonation of the unstressed syllables between the two stresses may be

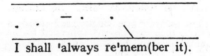

I shall 'always re'mem(ber it).

or

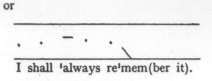

I shall 'always re'mem(ber it).

(c) The intonation of final unstressed syllables is low and level or descends slightly, e.g.

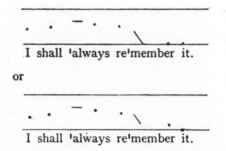

I shall 'always re'member it.

or

I shall 'always re'member it.

36.   All expressions of small significance like *he said, he explained, he added, he suggested, I think, you know, they say, I've heard, poor thing, I understand,* occurring after statements pronounced with the Falling intonation, have the intonation of final unstressed syllables, even if some of the words are stressed.[1] The pitch of words expressing the names of persons addressed is also low and level, or descends slightly. E.g.

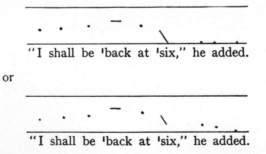

"I shall be 'back at 'six," he added.

or

"I shall be 'back at 'six," he added.

---

[1] This applies also to such expressions appended to those questions which have the Falling intonation, and to commands. Stress need not be marked in these short appended expressions.

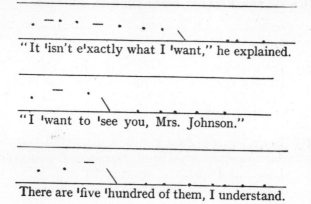

"It 'isn't e'xactly what I 'want," he explained.

"I 'want to 'see you, Mrs. Johnson."

There are 'five 'hundred of them, I understand.

2. SUITABILITY OF THE DOT AND LINE NOTATION FOR ENGLISH.

37. The dot and line pitch notation is very suitable for English where there is a considerable difference between the degree of prominence given to the different syllables. The line marks the pitch of the prominent syllables, and the dot that of the unimportant syllables to which we do not want to draw the attention of the hearer. Many French students of spoken English are tempted to treat all syllables of a sentence as of almost equal importance, with the result that they obscure the meaning rather than make it clearer; and at the same time they fail to produce the rhythmical patterns of English speech which owe their form mainly to the arrangement of prominent and non-prominent syllables.

38. The dot and line notation has this disadvantage: it suggests that the tune consists of a series of disconnected notes. This, of course, is not so. Wherever there are voiced sounds they carry the tune. And since there is in speech a much greater percentage of voiced than voiceless sounds, the tune is practically continuous, and would be more accurately represented by a continuous curve, i.e. by

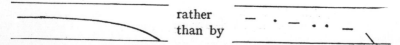

rather
than by

The writers consider, however, that the latter notation is more useful for all practical purposes.

c

3. USE OF THE FALLING INTONATION IN ENGLISH.

39. The above intonation, which we have called the Falling intonation, is used in English:

(a) In short assertions of the type given above. These are all of a final nature. We shall see later that no matter how long the assertion is, the general trend of the intonation is a falling one.

(b) In questions beginning with a specific interrogative word. In such questions the speaker is practically demanding information which he assumes the other person can give; and there is something final about a demand:

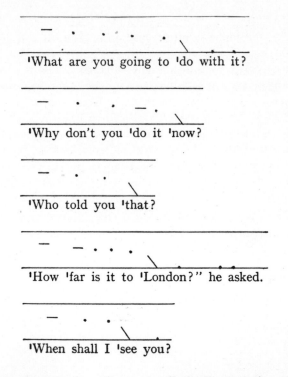

'What are you going to 'do with it?

'Why don't you 'do it 'now?

'Who told you 'that?

'How 'far is it to 'London?" he asked.

'When shall I 'see you?

(c) In Commands. These are distinctly assertive and final in character. There is no suggestion of allowing the other person to have a voice in the matter.   Hence the falling intonation is very suitable:

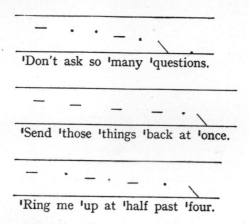

'Don't ask so 'many 'questions.

'Send 'those 'things 'back at 'once.

'Ring me 'up at 'half past 'four.

(d) In some non-final sense-groups in connected speech. (See §150(d), §151(e), (f), §153.)

Chapter III

THE RISING-FALLING INTONATION IN FRENCH

40. Now let us examine a number of short unemphatic French sentences of the same kind.

41. In the assertions *Nous ne les voulons pas, Il est midi vingt,* there are five syllables, the pitch of which could be represented approximately thus:

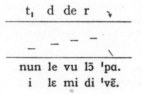

nun le vu lɔ̃ 'pɑ.
i lɛ mi di 'vɛ̃.

a notation which is more helpful to beginners than

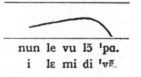

nun le vu lɔ̃ 'pɑ.
i lɛ mi di 'vɛ̃.

and which suggests the rather staccato effect of French speech.

1. Suitability of the Line Notation for French.

42. In unemphatic French, the difference between the amount of energy spent on the various syllables of a sentence is not strongly marked. It cannot be said, as of English, and especially of German, that some syllables are strong and others weak : each syllable is rapped out clearly, but not very forcibly. It is customary to regard the stress in unemphatic speech as being more or less evenly distributed over all the syllables of a short sentence except the last, which is pronounced with slightly more effort. Only this final

syllable need carry a stress mark. In the non-final syllables there *are* differences of degree in the amount of stress, differences which can be ignored for all practical purposes.

43. A short horizontal line is used to mark the intonation of each non-final syllable ; an oblique line marks that of the final syllable.

44. It is helpful to notice that in French, in unemphatic connected speech all really important words generally occur in the position of importance, i.e. finally in the sentence and finally in each important grammatical subdivision of the sentence. In English, position is not of such great significance ; a speaker stresses all words which he considers important in expressing his meaning no matter what may be their place in the sentence. Thus, in French unemphatic speech, position plays a greater part in giving prominence than in English ; in English stress plays a greater part than in French.

2. ANALYSIS OF RISING-FALLING INTONATION IN FRENCH.

45. Notice these characteristics of the Rising-Falling intonation of French :

(*a*) The intonation falls finally as in English.

(*b*) The method of falling is different. In English the pitch gradually descends throughout the stressed syllables, so that the highest pitch is generally on the first stressed syllable, and there is not a very big musical interval between the initial pitch of the final syllable and the preceding one :

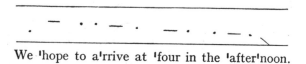

We 'hope to a'rrive at 'four in the 'after'noon.

(*c*) In a French sentence of the simple type given in § 41, the pitch rises gradually in level steps, generally until the penultimate syllable is reached.[1] There is rather a big

[1] See also Chap. IV.

musical interval between the pitch of the last two syllables.[1]
The last syllable has a falling tone, the pitch not falling
from so great a height as does that of the final syllable
in an English statement :

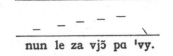

nun le za vjɔ̃ pɑ ˈvy.

In statements suggesting finality, the pitch of the final
syllable starts low and falls to the extreme limit of the
speaking voice ; it is difficult for a foreigner to hear it.
Sometimes a final syllable is so low that it is impossible
to voice it at all. In statements of a less final nature
the pitch of the final syllable does not fall to such a depth,
and is often level.

(*d*) The difference in pitch between successive non-final
syllables is a very small one, especially if the sentence
contains many syllables. Any exaggeration of these
musical intervals sounds absurd. In the early stages,
however, it is sometimes necessary to exaggerate the
intervals in order to make beginners realise that the
syllables are not pronounced on a monotone.[2] This
exaggeration should be discontinued as soon as possible.
The intonation of the sentences given in § 41 might be
represented in the tonic sol-fa system by t_l, d, de, r, ↘.
The pitch of the last syllable is marked ↘. It is difficult,
and often impossible, to represent it by a musical note :
it starts very low and drops lower.

(*e*) What should strike an English learner, apart from the
intonation, is the even succession of syllables in French :

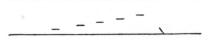

They fall regularly and with almost equal strength,
suggesting the rapid ta-ta-ta-ta of a machine-gun. In

---

[1] See also § 179.
[2] In very rapid speech there is often, of course, a levelling of pitch.

English this regularity is impossible : strong syllables and long sounds may occur *within* the various sense-groups in juxtaposition with syllables which are relatively very weak and short.

The above examples, *Nous ne les voulons pas, Il est midi vingt,* have five syllables.

46. In a four-syllabled sentence such as *Je ne comprends pas, Il ne va pas bien,* the intonation is

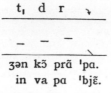

ʒən kɔ̃ prɑ̃ 'pɑ.
in va pɑ 'bjɛ̃.

47. In a three-syllabled sentence *Il s'amuse, Je l'ai vu,*

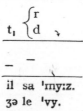

il sa 'myːz.
ʒə le 'vy.

48. In a two-syllabled sentence *Ça y est, C' est ça,*

sa 'jɛ.
sɛ 'sa.

49. In a one-syllabled sentence *Non, Bon,*

'nɔ̃.
'bɔ̃.

50. Unimportant expressions of the type, *dit-il, ajouta-t-il,*

dit-on, monsieur, madame, enfin, cependant, vous savez, par exemple, etc., appended to statements of this kind are low and may be level in pitch,[1] as in English. Stress is not marked in these short appended expressions, though it may be present to a greater degree in some words than in others. It is convenient to regard the intonation of short expressions of this type as belonging to the preceding intonation group:

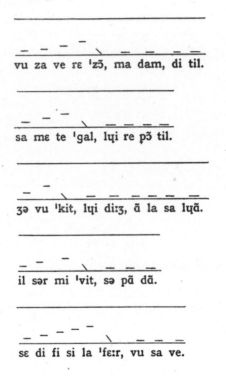

vu za ve rɛ 'zɔ̃, ma dam, di til.

sa mɛ te 'gal, lɥi re pɔ̃ til.

ʒə vu 'kit, lɥi diːʒ, ɑ̃ la sa lɥɑ̃.

il sər mi 'vit, sə pɑ̃ dɑ̃.

sɛ di fi si la 'fɛːr, vu sa ve.

3. Use of the Rising-Falling Intonation in French.

51. The above intonation, which we have called the Rising-Falling intonation, is used in French in short assertions of the type given above. Later it will be shown that no matter how long the assertion, the intonation has the same general trend as that of the short statement. (See §§ 170-197.)

[1] For the intonation of *long* appended expressions see Chap. XXVI.

52.   The Rising-Falling intonation is not the typical intonation for questions beginning with a specific interrogative word, nor for commands, though it can be, and often is, used for these types of sentences.   (See Chap. VI, §§ 80-85.)

53.   The Rising-Falling intonation may also be used for questions which may be answered by saying "yes" or "no," but it is not the typical intonation for such questions.   (See Chap. VI, §§ 86, 87.)

4.   PHONETIC SYLLABICATION.

54.   In all those French sentences and connected texts which are given with a pitch notation, and in all examples in phonetic transcription in Part I the words are divided into *syllables* so that the different pitch of each syllable can the more easily be shown, and therefore produced by the student.[1]   The division is not the traditional one of ordinary orthography.   For example, *Il est cinq heures moins le quart* is transcribed i lɛ sɛ̃ kœːr mwɛ̃l kaːr.

55.   The syllabication shown in this book is felt to be phonetically correct in the case of slow speech.   But in the case of sentences pronounced fairly rapidly, it is difficult, if not impossible, to decide whether a certain consonant terminates one syllable or begins the next.   It is especially difficult in unemphatic French because of the evenness of the stress.   For this reason the syllable division recorded here may sometimes lack consistency.

56.   Phonetic syllabication breaks up the sentence into syllables which are very unfamiliar to the eye ;[2] so that it is impossible to see the words as a whole, and impossible, therefore, to grasp the meaning of the sentence until the syllables have been pronounced aloud and the meaning brought home through the medium of the ear.   The first reading of these exercises will tend, therefore, to be rather mechanical, which is no disadvantage in the early stages : a student who speaks French with an English intonation must first attempt the new melody consciously and perhaps laboriously, note by note.   But he should not be allowed to leave it at this.

[1] In Part II (Emphatic Intonation) all examples except those given with a pitch notation are divided into *words* instead of into syllables.

[2] Phonetic transcription, even when it observes word division is, of course, unfamiliar to many.   We assume that the reader is fairly familiar with the phonetic transcription of French.

The intonation of each sentence, or of each part of a sentence occurring between pauses should give the impression of a continuous tune and not of a succession of disconnected notes.

57. Young pupils can generally imitate the teacher's example. It is often helpful to put the notation on the blackboard :

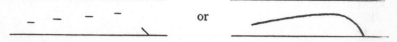

and to suggest the regular succession of the syllables by tapping. The correct tune should be insisted on from the beginning. There is no need to give formal lessons on intonation.

58. Good gramophone records of short sentences and simple connected passages are useful in the early stages.[1] The teacher could attach a "repeater" to the gramophone, or, with much less harm to the discs, he could, with a little practice, become expert in lifting and lowering the sound-box so that the pupils could hear the same sentence, or part of the same sentence, over and over again.

5. EXAMPLES OF THE RISING-FALLING INTONATION IN FRENCH.

59. Below are examples of assertions pronounced with the Rising-Falling intonation. They are arranged in order of the number of syllables.

The student must be prepared to find that many of these assertions, especially those of more than six syllables, sound rather unnatural apart from their context.

60. Assertions with 2 syllables :

il 'vjɛ̃.
il 'paːr.
il 'sɔːr.

---

[1] Many of those published by "His Master's Voice" to accompany *Colloquial French for the English*, by E. M. Stéphan and Daniel Jones, are excellent for this purpose. The Linguaphone Company also has some remarkably good records.

il 'dɔːr. ɛl 'marʃ. sɛ 'ruːʒ.
il 'grɛ̃p. ɛl 'laːv. sɛ 'gro.
il 'nɛːʒ. sa 'jɛ. sɛ 'fɛ.
il 'plø. saz 'di. sɛ 'sɛ̃ːpl.
il 'tɔn. sɛ 'vrɛ. sɛ 'bo.
il 'grɛːl. sɛ 'sa. sɛ 'lɛ.
ɛl 'ʒu. sɛ 'grɑ̃. sɛ 'klɛːr.
ɛl 'ʃɑ̃ːt. sɛ 'larʒ. sɛ 'ʒyst.
ɛl 'dɑ̃ːs. sɛ 'lɔ̃. sɛ 'bjɛ̃.
ɛl 'kuːr. sɛ 'mɛ̃ːs. sa 'va.
ɛl 'li. sɛ 'pti. sa 'bryl.
ɛl 'ri. sɛ 'blɑ̃. sam 'plɛ.
ɛl 'ku. sɛ 'nwaːr. sam 'ʒɛ̃n.
ɛl 'sɔːt. sɛ 'ʒɔːn. ɔr 'vwaːr, or
ɛl 'mɔ̃ːt. sɛ 'blø.   or 'vwaːr
ɛl 'kri. sɛ 'vɛːr.

61. Assertions with 3 syllables:

i va 'bjɛ̃.
ʒe bjɛ̃l 'tɑ̃.
san fɛ 'rjɛ̃.

i ʃɑ̃t 'bjɛ̃.   ɛl ʒu 'bjɛ̃.
i vjɛ̃d 'ʒwe.   sɛ par 'fɛ.
i sa 'myːz.   i lɛ 'taːr.
ɛl sɑ̃ 'va.   ʒmɑ̃ truv 'bjɛ̃.
i le 'kut.   ʒem mjø 'sa.
i lɛ 'ʒɔːn.   ʒnɑ̃ vø 'pɑ.
ɛ lɛ 'ruːʒ.   ɛl mɑ̃ 'nɥi.
ɛl va 'bjɛ̃.   a bjɛ̃ 'to.
in di 'rjɛ̃.   sɛ ski 'fo.
ɛ lɛm 'sa.   ʃtə le 'dɔn.
in dɑ̃ːs 'pɑ.   san marʃ 'pɑ.
san va 'pɑ.   i vav 'niːr.
is pɔrt 'bjɛ̃.   nu par 'tɔ̃.
ɔ̃ lɑ̃ 'tɑ̃.   ɛl sɑ̃ 'vɔ̃.
saz vwa 'bjɛ̃.

62. Assertions with 4 syllables[1]:

```
    ___ _  _
   _____
  __          \
  _____
```

i vjɛ̃d par 'tiːr.
i tra vaj 'bjɛ̃.
i va   plœ 'vwaːr.

ɔ̃ vjɛ̃d məl 'diːr.
ʒən le pɑ 'vy.
i va fɛr 'bo.
i fɛ dy 'vɑ̃.
ɛl te le 'fɔn.
nu tra va 'jɔ̃.
nu la vɔ̃ 'vy.
ɛl le ty 'di.
i la mɔ̃ 'liːvr.
i ne kut 'pɑ.
in rə gard 'pɑ.
i nɑ̃ vø 'pɑ.
san lɥi plɛ 'pɑ.
ɔ̃ nɑ̃ parl 'pɑ.
ɛn vø pɑv 'niːr.
i lɛ ma 'lad.
san mə ʒɛn 'pɑ.
ʒən kɔ̃ prɑ̃ 'pɑ.
ʒvud mɑ̃d par 'dɔ̃.

san mə va 'pɑ.
sa mɛ te 'gal.
i nja pɑd 'kwa.
in va pɑ 'bjɛ̃.
sɛ tɑ̃ tɑ̃ 'dy.
i lɑ̃ na 'lɛːr.
la sa lɛ 'plɛn.
ɛ la bɔn 'min.
i lɛ trwɑ 'zœːr.
i lɛ mi 'di.
i lɛ mi 'nɥi.
sɛ ti ny 'til.
bjɛ̃ nɑ̃ tɑ̃ 'dy.
sas pu rɛ 'bjɛ̃.
in vjɛ̃ drɔ̃ 'ply.
i lɛ dɑ̃l 'trɛ̃.
i fo ja 'le.
san sə vwa 'pɑ.
i nɑ̃ fo 'pɑ.

63. Assertions with 5 syllables[1]:

```
    __ _  _  _
   _____
  __            \
  _____
```

sɛ tɛ̃ te rɛ 'sɑ̃.
ɔ̃n vu za tɑ̃ 'ply.

[1] See Chap. IV. for a slightly different intonation of some of these sentences.

i lɛ mi di 'vɛ̃.

nun le vu lɔ̃ 'pa.

nu nɑ̃ sa vɔ̃ 'rjɛ̃.

nun le zɛ mɔ̃ 'pa.

ʒən le ze pa 'vy.

in va pa trɛ 'bjɛ̃.

ʒe tru ve mɔ̃ 'li:vr.

ʒən se pa skə 'sɛ.

in fo pa lɥi 'di:r.

in vø ply rəv 'ni:r.

ɛl se bjɛ̃l frɑ̃ 'sɛ.

ʒna lɛ pa trɛ 'bjɛ̃.

il la aʃ te 'jɛ:r.

ʒə rɑ̃ tra pa'ri.

ɛ li a pɑ̃ 'se.

vun mɑ̃ nɥi je 'pa.

ɔ̃n pø ply ɑ̃ 'tre.

la vwa ty rɛ 'la.

nu za lɔ̃ le 'vwa:r.

i vjɛ̃ drɔ̃ sə 'swa:r.

nu zi rɔ̃ də 'mɛ̃.

ʒɛm mjø npa ja 'le.

ʒə sɥi rɑ̃ tre 'ta:r.

vu zɛt bjɛ̃ ʒɑ̃ 'ti:j.

ʒe a vu par 'le.

ʒə pɑ̃ si a 'le.

64. Assertions with 6 syllables[1] :

nun le za vjɔ̃ pa   'vy.

i   lɛ mi di mwɛ̃ 'vɛ̃.

i   lɛ ty nœ red 'mi.

i lɛ dɑ̃ le za 'fɛ:r.

i lɛ sɛ̃ kœr mwɛ̃l 'ka:r.

in mɑ̃ ʃo pa bo 'ku.

nu na vɔ̃ pa kɔ̃ 'pri.

nu le vwa jɔ̃ su 'vɑ̃.

im fo kɛk ʃoz kɔm 'sa.

nu zɑ̃ na vɔ̃ bo 'ku.

i la swa sɑ̃t sɛ̃ 'kɑ̃.

ʒə rɑ̃ trə re bjɛ̃ 'to.

ʒən tjɛ̃ pa al sa 'vwa:r.

sɛ tɔ̃̃ nom də ʒe 'ni.

sɛ tɔ̃̃ nom ko mil 'fo.

im di ki nɑ̃ na 'pa.

ʃkɔ̃ prɑ̃ bjɛ̃ skə vu 'dit.

yn de por tɛ fɛr 'me.

sas pas tu ʒur kom 'sa.

nu som par ti ply 'ta:r.

nu nu prom nɔ̃ dɑ̃l 'park.

tul mɔ̃ dɛ to ky 'pe.

ʒə le vy tu ta 'lœ:r.

ʒvø bjɛ̃ vu ze ku 'te.

---

[1] See Chap. IV for a slightly different intonation of some of these.   Also § 143 for the "breaking" and §§ 202–4 for the division of many of these groups.

65. Assertions with 7 syllables[1]:

nu le za võ kɔ mã 'de.
ɛl na pɑ vu ly ʃã 'te.
i nu zɛ̃ te rɛs bo 'ku.

i ja vɛ dy mɔ̃d par 'tu.
in vœl pɑ sã nɔ ky 'pe.
in fo pɑ lɥi ã vu 'lwaːr.
tu de pã də skɔ̃ pre 'fɛːr.
ɛl sra kɔ̃ tãt də vu 'vwaːr.
ʒe vu ly vu za vɛr 'tiːr.
vu pu ve kɔ̃ te syr 'mwa.
vu le vɛ re a prɛd 'mɛ̃.

ʒə le fi ni a sɛ 'tœːr.
ʒə lɥi e di kãʒ le 'vy.
ɔ̃s prɔ mɛn kã ti fɛ 'bo.
ʒə kɔ̃ prã bjɛ̃ skə vu 'dit.
i vo mjø nu zã pɑ 'se.
sɛ tɔ̃̃ gar sɔ̃ trɛ sã 'sibl.
ɔ̃ di rɛ ki va plœ 'vwaːr.
i la fɛ bo jɛr ma 'tɛ̃.

66. Assertions with 8 and 9 syllables.[1]

It is possible to pronounce these many syllabled sentences with the simple tune indicated here only in very rapid connected speech, which is their natural setting.[2] In this isolated form, many of them sound unnatural and unconvincing. In pronouncing them, the range of intonation may be considerably narrowed and some of the non-final syllables pronounced quickly on a monotone. In slow speech, certain modifications would be introduced into the intonation, which would give prominence to other words besides the final one. (See footnote 1.)

nu nã na vɔ̃ pɑ le mwa 'jɛ̃.

[1] See Chap. IV for a slightly different intonation of all these. Also § 143 for the "breaking" and §§ 202–4 for the division of these groups.

[2] This applies to all sentences of many syllables treated as simple intonation groups. (For definition of a simple intonation groups see § 112.)

i la vu ly nu fɛr par 'le.
i ja bjɛ̃ lɔ̃ tɑ̃ gʒən vu ze 'vy.
ʒə lɥi e te le fɔ ne sma tɛ̃.
ʒə vu drɛ ɛ tra pa ri sə 'swaːr.
ʒe tɛ vny vu dmɑ̃ de œ̃ kɔ̃ 'sɛːj.
i lɛ ta ri ve ɑ̃ mɛm tɑ̃k 'mwa.
i ljɛ rɛs te yn sə mɛ nɑ̃ 'tjɛːr.
nun la vɔ̃ pɑ vy dy prə mje 'ku.
i lɛ rɛs te la pɑ̃ dɑ̃ di 'zɑ̃.
i li ɛ rɛs te pɑ̃ dɑ̃ trɑ̃ 'tɑ̃.
vu le rɑ̃ kɔ̃ trə re sɛ ti 'vɛːr.

67. Assertions with a varying number of syllables, with expressions of a parenthetical nature added[1]:

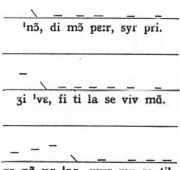

'nɔ̃, di mɔ̃ pɛːr, syr pri.

ʒi 've, fi ti la se viv mɑ̃.

ʒə nɑ̃ vø 'pɑ, myr my ra til.

'wi, dil ʒœ nɔm.
ʒə ne 'rjɛ̃, re pɔ̃ di mɔ̃ pɛːr, sɛʃ mɑ̃.
ʒə vø 'bjɛ̃, mə di til.
mɛr si 'bjɛ̃, ma dam.
nun sa vɔ̃ 'pɑ, a fir ma til.
nu ni rɔ̃ 'pɑ, de kla ra tɛl.
i vjɛ̃ 'dra, mə di til.
sɛ ti ny 'til, lɥi re pɔ̃ diːʒ.
ʒe y dla 'ʃɑ̃ːs, re pɔ̃ di ʒaːk, trɛ sɛ̃ sɛr mɑ̃.

[1] For the intonation of long appended expressions see Chap. XXVI.

ʒən sɥi pɑ kɔ̃ ˈtɑ̃, ma vɛ til di bjɛ̃ su vɑ̃.

ɛl nə vjɛ̃ dra ˈpɑ, re pɔ̃ di tɛl.

sa srɛ tɛ̃ pɔ ˈsibl, re pɔ̃ diːʒ.

ʒə vur mɛr ˈsi, mə di mɔ̃ nu vɛ la mi.

sɛ tɑ̃ tɑ̃ ˈdy, de kla ra mɔ̃ pɛːr.

sɛ tœ̃ po ˈvrɔm, fi mɔ̃ nɔ̃ːkl.

ʒə ˈpaːr di ti lɑ̃s lə vɑ̃.

ʒə kɔ̃ ˈprɑ̃, di ti lo bu dœ̃ mɔ mɑ̃.

CHAPTER IV

ANOTHER FORM OF THE RISING-FALLING INTONATION

68. In pronouncing the following sentences,[1] already given with the intonation

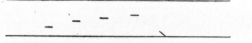

the student is asked to place the highest pitch on the syllable marked ⁻ [2] instead of on the penultimate syllable. E.g.

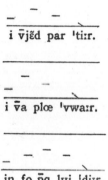

i v̄jĕd par 'tiːr.

i v̄a plœ 'vwaːr.

in fo p̄a lüi 'diːr.

69. This will have the effect of bringing the word pronounced with the highest pitch into greater prominence than it would have with the intonation

---

[1] Only a few examples are taken from §§ 62, 63, 64, and all from §§ 65, 66.

[2] This mark is used throughout the book to show which syllable of an *unemphatic* Rising-Falling group has the highest pitch when this is not borne by the penultimate syllable. In all orthographic examples and texts the mark is placed *before* the syllable concerned and not above.

but not into prominence great enough to justify the term emphatic.
The syllable having the highest pitch need not be pronounced with
more than normal stress.

70. Examples of sentences with the Rising-Falling intonation
in which the highest pitch is not on the penultimate syllable:

i v̄jɛ̃d par 'tiːr.
i v̄a   plœ 'vwaːr.

ɔ̃ v̄jɛ̃d məl 'diːr.	i lɛ mi d̄i mwɛ̃ 'vɛ̃.
i f̄ɛ dy 'vã.	i lɛ sɛ̃ k̄œːr mwɛ̃l 'kaːr.
i l̄a mɔ̃ 'liːvr.	in mã fo p̄a bo 'ku.
i l̄ɛ ma 'lad.	nu le vwa j̄ɔ̃ su 'vã.
i l̄ɛ trwa 'zœːr.	im fo kɛk ʃ̄oːz kɔm 'sa.
i l̄ɛ dãl 'trɛ̃.	nu zã na v̄ɔ̃ œ̃ 'pø.
i f̄o ja 'le.	ʒə rã trə r̄e bjɛ̃ 'to.
ʒvud m̄ãːd par 'dɔ̃.	sas pas tu ʒ̄uːr kɔm 'sa.
in va p̄a trɛ 'bjɛ̃.	nu sɔm par t̄i ply 'taːr.
ʒən se p̄a skə 'sɛ.	nu nu prom n̄jɔ̃ dãl 'park.
in fo p̄a lɥi 'diːr.	ɛl na pa vu l̄y ʃã 'te.
in vø p̄ly rəv 'niːr.	i nu zɛ̃ te r̄ɛs bo 'ku.
ɔ̃n pø p̄ly ã 'tre.	i ja vɛ dy m̄ɔ̃ːd par 'tu.
nu za l̄ɔ̃ le 'vwaːr.	vu pu ve kɔ̃ t̄e syr 'mwa.
i vjɛ̃ d̄rɔ̃ sə 'swaːr.	ʒe e te ɔ ky p̄e sma 'tɛ̃.
nu zi r̄ɔ̃ də 'mɛ̃.	ʒə lɥi e te le fɔ n̄e sma 'tɛ̃.
ɛl sɛ b̄jɛ̃l frã 'sɛ.	ʒdwa ɛ tra pa r̄i sə 'swaːr.
ʒna lɛ p̄a trɛ 'bjɛ̃.	

For the intonation of the examples which follow, see also § 143
for the "breaking" and §§ 202-4 for the division of these groups:

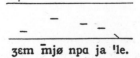

ʒɛm m̄jø npa ja 'le.

ʒən tjɛ̃ p̄a al sa 'vwaːr.

sɛ tœ̃ n̄ɔm də ʒe 'ni.

sɛ tœ̃ n̄ɔm kɔ mil 'fo.

ʃkɔ̃ prã b̄jɛ̃ skə vu 'dit.

yn de p̄ɔr tɛ fɛr 'me.

ʒə le v̄y tu ta 'lœːr.

vu le vɛ r̄e a prɛd 'mɛ̃.

i la fɛ b̄o jɛr ma 'tɛ̃.

nu le za v̄ɔ̃ kɔ mã 'de.

ɛl sra kɔ̃ t̄ãːt də vu 'vwaːr.

ʒə le fi n̄i a sɛ 'tœːr.

ʒə lɥi e d̄i kãʒ le 'vy.

ʒə kɔ̃ prã b̄jɛ̃ skə vu 'dit.

sɛ tœ̃ gar s̄ɔ̃ trɛ sã 'sibl.

ɛl sə sɔ̃ ku ʃ̄e a se 'taːr.

i va vu par l̄e tu ta 'lœːr.

nu nã na vɔ̃ p̄a le mwa 'jɛ̃.

ʒe tɛ vny vu dmã d̄e œ̃ kɔ̃ 'sɛːj.

i fə zɛ tyn ʃa l̄œːr a kɑ 'blãːt.

vu le rã kɔ̃ trə r̄e sɛ ti 'vɛːr.

i l̄ɛ dã le za 'fɛːr.

im d̄i ki nã na 'pɑ.

in vœl p̄a sã nɔ ky 'pe.

in fo pa lɥi ã vu 'lwaːr.

tu de p̄ã də skɔ̃ pre 'fɛːr.

ʒe vu l̄y vu za vɛr 'tiːr.

ɔ̃s prɔ m̄ɛn kã ti fɛ 'bo.

i vo m̄jø nu zã pɑ 'se.

ʒən mə poz p̄a dpa rɛj kɛs 'tjɔ̃.

tu le ʒ̄ã nsɔ̃ pɑ kɔm 'sa.

i lɛ ta l̄e ʒys ka la 'pɔrt.

ʒe œ̃ kɔ̃ s̄ɛːj a vu dmã 'de.

vu za le v̄waːr kɔm sɛ fa 'sil.

i la vu l̄y nu fɛr par 'le.

i ja bjɛ̃ lɔ̃ t̄ɑ̃ gʒən vu ze 'vy.

i lɛ ta ri v̄e ɑ̃ mɛm tɑ̃k 'mwa.

nun la vɔ̃ pɑ v̄y dy prə mje 'ku.

i li ɛ rɛs t̄e pɑ̃ dɑ̃ di 'zɑ̃.

ɔ̃ di r̄ɛ ki va plœ 'vwaːr.

tul m̄ɔ̃ː dɛ tɔ ky 'pe.

i ʒu o tɛ n̄is tu le di 'mɑ̃ːʃ.

nu za lɔ̃ ɑ̃ nɑ̃ glə t̄ɛːr trwɑ fwa pa 'rɑ̃.

i pɑs lœr va k̄ɑ̃ːs a la kɑ̃ 'paɲ.

lə vwa ja ʒɑ̃ no tɔ mɔ b̄i lɛ ta gre 'aːbl.

ʒe de l̄ɛ tra mɛ tra la 'pɔst.

i li ɛ rɛs t̄e yn sə mɛ nɑ̃ 'tjɛːr.

nu nɑ̃ nɔ rɔ̃ p̄ɑ a vɑ̃d mɛ̃ ma 'tɛ̃.

nul vwa j̄ɔ̃ trwɑ fwa par sə 'mɛn.

CHAPTER V

THE FALLING INTONATION IN FRENCH

1. DESCRIPTION AND USE.

71. The Rising-Falling intonation, the outline of which is

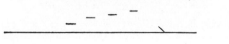

is not the typical one for questions beginning with a specific interrogative word, nor for commands, though it may be used for
these types of sentences. (See Chap. VI, §§ 80-85.) Notice that
it does not give a high pitch to the first important word, i.e. in the
question, to the specific interrogative word, which puts the hearer
at once into focus for a question; in the command to the verb,
which expresses the idea of command. The typical French tune
for questions of this type and for commands and requests is nearly
the same as the Falling intonation in English. Its outline is

72. The Falling intonation may also be used for questions
which may be answered by saying "Yes" or "No," but it is not
the typical intonation for such questions. (See Chap. VIII,
§ 103(b).)

73. The main differences between the English and French
Falling intonations are:

(a) In French the Falling intonation often begins at a higher
pitch than the English one, though this higher starting
point is not essential.

33

(*b*) The musical intervals between the pitch of the non-final stressed syllables in English are greater than those between pairs of successive non-final syllables in French.

(*c*) There is a bigger musical interval in French between the pitch of the last two syllables because the final syllable does not fall from so great a height.   It is sometimes low and level.   These differences are illustrated in the following outlines :

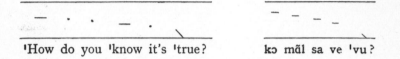

'How do you 'know it's 'true?   kɔ mãl sa ve 'vu ?

2. EXAMPLES OF THE FALLING INTONATION IN FRENCH.

74. Specific Interrogative Sentences :

a   kwa pã se 'vu ?[1]
kɔ mãl sa ve 'vu ?

ki ɛ 'la ?   də kwa par lə 'tɔ̃ ?
kə dit 'vu ?   a kwa tra vaj 'til ?
u a lɔ̃ 'nu ?   kɛs kə vu za ve 'la ?
ki dmã de 'vu ?   ʃe ki ɛ tɛ la 'le ?
kɛl rut dwaʒ 'sɥiːvr ?   də kwa sa ʒi 'til ?
də ki par le 'vu ?   kɔ mã sas fɛ 'til ?
kɛ lœ ra ve 'vu ?   kã dwav til par 'tiːr ?

[1] In questions where the specific interrogative word is preceded by a preposition, the preposition may have a lower pitch than the interrogative word. E.g.

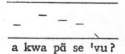

a kwa pã se 'vu ?

ki de zi re vu 'vwaːr?

kɛ lɔm ni bys dwaʒ 'prãːdr?

kɔ̃ bjẽd liːvr a ve 'vu?

la kɛl pre fe re 'vu?

kə vu le vu kəʒ 'fas?

kɛs kə vu za le 'fɛːr?

kɛl ku lœr pre fe re 'vu?

a ki vu le vu par'le?

kɛs kə sɛ ksɛ tis 'twaːr?

u ɛt vu a le jɛr 'swaːr?

kə kɔ̃ te vu fɛr də 'mɛ̃?

kə vu le vu gʒə vu 'diːz?

dã kɛl di rɛk sjɔ̃ a le 'vu?

a ki a le vu le dɔ 'ne?

a vɛk ki kɔ̃ te vur və 'niːr?

ki ɛs ki vu za did rã 'tre?

kɛs kɛl pãs də sɛ ta fɛr 'la?

pur kwa dit vu de ʃoz pa 'rɛːj?

pur kwa lɥi a ve vu ze 'kri?

kɔ mã vu le vu gʒə fas 'sa?

ki ɛs ki sɛ tɔ ky ped 'sa?

kɔ mã di tɔ̃ sa ã ʃrã 'sɛ?

ki vu za di ki fa lɛ fɛr 'sa?

kɔ mã sa pɛl lə prə mje mwa dla 'ne?

kɛs kə vu za ve vy la smɛn dɛr 'njɛːr?

pur kwan vø ti pa nu dir ski sɛ pa 'se?

kɔ mã sfɛ ti gvun swa je pa zã kɔr par 'ti?

pur kwa na ve vu pa vã dy sɛt me 'zɔ̃?

pur kwa na til pa vu ly nu dɔ ne də rã ɛɲ 'mã?

75. Specific Interrogative Sentences with parenthetical expressions added[1]:

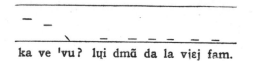

ka ve 'vu? lɥi dmã da la vjɛj fam.

kɛs ki 'ja?   kɛs tjɔn la ba rɔn.

ki sla pø ti 'lɛːtr?   sə dmã dɛ ʒaːk.

kɛs kə sla si ɲi 'fi?   myr my ra til, kɔ̃ tra rje.

u va 'ty?   lɥi dmã da ti la vɛ kãk sje te.

a kir sã blə 'tɛl?   də mã da ti la si mɔ̃.

[1] For the intonation of the *long* appended expressions given here, see also Chap. XXVI.

ka ve ˈvu, mɔ̃ ʃɛ rɑ̃ fɑ̃? mə di tɛl, ɑ̃ ma pɛr sə vɑ̃.

ka le vu ˈfɛːr? mə dmɑ̃ da til, a kɛl kə zœr də la.

kɔ mɑ̃ va vɔt fa ˈmiːj? lɥi dmɑ̃ dɛːʒ.

kɔ mɑ̃ sa pɛl sɛ ˈtɔm? də mɑ̃ da tɛl, a vɛ kœ̃ muv mɑ̃ brysk
     də la tɛːt.

kɛs ˈdɔ̃ːk? re pe ta mɔ̃ pɛːr, ki a vɛ tœ̃ pø pɑ li.

76. Commands.

vjɛ̃ a vɛk ˈmwa.
prə ne sɛt ˈplas.
u vre vo ˈliːvr.

ni va ˈpɑ.

rɛst trɑ̃ ˈkil.

fɛ ted ˈvwaːr.

vat prɔm ˈne.

nəl fɛt ˈpɑ.

a le vu ˈzɑ̃.

nɛ̃ sis te ˈpɑ.

tə ne vu ˈdrwa.

ni a le ˈpɑ.

mɛ lə syr la ˈtabl.

nə lœr də mɑ̃d ˈrjɛ̃.

ni va pɑ sɑ̃ ˈmwa.

fɛ zɑ̃ skə ty ˈvø.

lɛs lə de ʒœ ˈne.

va ʃɛr ʃe tɔ̃ ˈliːvr.

rɑ̃ ʒe vo za ˈfɛːr.

fɛt lə kɔ mil ˈfo.

rɛs te a vɛk ˈmwa.

e ku te mwa ˈbjɛ̃.

nə lɥi fɛt pɑ ˈpœːr.

swa je ply se ˈrjø.

fɛt lɥi fɛr sed ˈvwaːr.

nəl de rɑ̃ ʒe ˈpɑ.

a sɛ je vu ˈdɔ̃ːk.

na le pɑ a vɛ ˈkɛl.

nə lɥi ɑ̃ par le ˈpɑ.

də mɑ̃d lɥi u i ˈva.

pri je lə dmɔ̃ ˈte.

dit lə dɔ̃k tut ˈsɥit.

nə lɥi dit pɑ skə ˈsɛ.

nə vu zɑ̃ nɔ ky pe ˈpɑ.

dɔ ne mwa ski ja dɑ̃ vɔt ˈsak.

rə mɛ te le liː vra lœr ˈplas.

e ku te ski la a vu ˈdiːr.

dit mwa pur kwa vu zi ɛt za ˈle.

nə lɥi ra kɔ̃ te rjɛ̃ dsɛ ta fɛr ˈla.

nə lɥi di pɑ skə ty a dɑ̃ ta ˈpɔʃ.

nə lɥi mɔ̃ tre pɑ skəʒ vu ze dɔ ˈne.

də mɑ̃ de lɥi œ̃ pø si la lɛ̃ tɑ̃ sjɔ̃d par tir sə ˈswaːr.

77. Commands with parenthetical expressions added.[1]

fɛt skõ vu kɔ ˈmãːd, ɔr dɔ na til sɛʃ mã.

dɔ ne mwa ski ja dã vɔt ˈsak, mə di til dœ̃ tõ ki nad mɛ tɛ pɑd re plik·
nə lɥi ra kõ te rjɛ̃ dsɛ ta fɛr ˈla, mə rə kɔ mã da til.
rə mɛ te le liː vra lœr ˈplas, ɔr dɔ na tɛl.
ra kõ te nu pur kwa vu za ve fɛ ˈsa, nu di til dœ̃ tõ trɛ du.
nəˈlɥi mõ tre pɑ skəʒ vu ze dɔ ˈne, mə di tɛl kõ fi dã sjɛl mã.

78. Requests.

The typical intonation for requests differs little from the typical tune for commands.

If the request is of a formal nature, the addition of such expressions as *donc, je vous prie, monsieur, madame,* along with a kindly voice, are sufficient to produce the right effect without any modification of the intonation.

In very informal requests the range of intonation is generally wider. But even in these the effect is produced more by the kind of voice, the gesture and the facial expression which accompany the words than by intonation. The addition of such expressions as *mon ami, ma chère, ma petite,* also helps to give the impression of a request. In fact, expressions of this kind would never be added after true commands and at the same time retain their literal meaning.

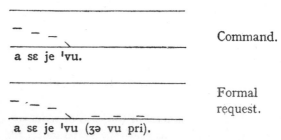

a sɛ je ˈvu.   Command.

a sɛ je ˈvu (ʒə vu pri).   Formal request.

---

[1] For the intonation of long appended expressions see Chap. XXVI.

a sɛ je 'vu, mɔ̃ ʃɛːr.

Informal
request.

vjɛ̃ a vɛk 'nu.

Command.

vjɛ̃ a vɛk 'nu, ma ptit.

Request.

rɛs te a vɛk 'mwa.

Command.

rɛs te a vɛk 'mwa (mɔ̃ ʃɛːr).

Request.

va ʃɛr ʃe tɔ̃ 'liːvr.

Command.

va ʃɛr ʃe tɔ̃ 'liːvr (mi ɲɔ̃).

Request.

It is not possible, in the case of requests, to use the Rising-Falling intonation of the statement; for that, as we shall see, adds a certain strength to the command. (See § 84.)

79. The Falling intonation for "Yes" and "No" questions.

"Yes" and "No" questions, normally asked with the Rising intonation (see Chap. VIII, § 103(b)), sometimes have the Falling intonation which introduces an element of command not perhaps so strong as when the Rising-Falling intonation is used (see Chap. VI, §§ 86, 87):

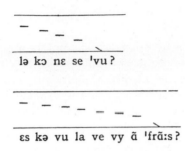

lə kɔ nɛ se 'vu ?

ɛs kə vu la ve vy ã 'frã:s ?

The same use of the Falling intonation is made in English :

'Have you 'read "'Jane 'Eyre" means

"Tell me if you've read 'Jane Eyre'."

CHAPTER VI

OTHER USES OF THE RISING-FALLING INTONATION

1. THE RISING-FALLING INTONATION FOR SPECIFIC INTERROGA-
TIVE SENTENCES.

80. Most of the questions of § 74 may be asked with the Rising-
Falling intonation of an assertion. With this "tune" the question
is no longer felt to be merely a question. It assumes at the same
time something of the nature of a command. Thus, *Où allez-vous?*
with the intonation

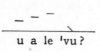

means *Dites-moi où vous allez*:

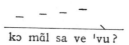

Comment le savez-vous? with the intonation

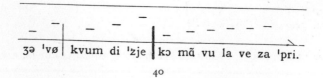

means *Je veux que vous me disiez comment vous l'avez appris*:

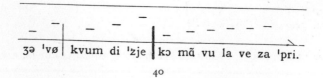

81. The words expressing the command: *Dites-moi, Je vous commande, Je veux que vous me disiez, J'exige, J'insiste pour qu'on me dise, Je veux savoir*, etc., are not stated, but the intonation of the words expressing the interrogation is the same as would be used if the command element were actually stated in words.

82. Thus, a question with the intonation of an assertion may be regarded as performing two functions. The interrogative element is weakened at the expense of the command element which is introduced. That is why many of the examples which immediately follow may strike the reader as unnatural, or even rude, especially as they are lifted out of their context.

83. Examples:

a kwa pã se 'vu?
kɔ mãl sa ve 'vu?

ki ɛ 'la?
kə dit 'vu?
u a lɔ̃ 'nu?
ki dmã de 'vu?
kɛl rut dwaʒ 'sɥiːvr?
də ki parle 'vu?
kɛ lœ ra ve 'vu?
də kwa par lə 'tɔ̃?
a kwa tra vaj 'til?
də kwa sa ʒi 'til?
kɔ mã sas fɛ 'til?
kã dwav til par 'tiːr?
ki de zi re vu 'vwaːr?
kɛ lɔm ni bys dwaʒ 'prãːdr?
kɔ̃ bjɛ̃d liː vra ve 'vu?
la kɛl pre fe re 'vu?

kə vu le vu kəʒ 'fas?
kɛs kə vu za le 'fɛːr?
a ki vu le vu par 'le?
kə vu le vu gʒə vu 'diːz?
kɛs kə vu za ve 'la?
ʃe ki ɛ tɛ la 'le?
ki ɛs ki sɛ tɔ ky ped 'sa?
u ɛt vu a le jɛr 'swaːr?
kə kɔ̃ te vu fɛr də 'mɛ̃?
a ki a le vu le dɔ 'ne?
a vɛk ki kɔ̃ te vur və 'niːr?
pur kwa lɥi a ve vu ze 'kri?
kɛs kɛl pãs də sɛ ta fɛr 'la?
pur kwa na til pa vu ly nu
    dɔ ne de rã sɛɲ 'mã?

In most of the above examples the highest pitch could be given to a syllable other than the penultimate, without increasing the stress of this syllable[1] :

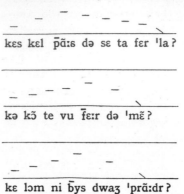

kɛs kɛl p̄ɑ̄:s də sɛ ta fɛr 'la?

kə kɔ̃ te vu f̄ɛ:r də 'mɛ̃?

kɛ lɔm ni b̄ys dwaʒ 'prɑ̄:dr?

2. THE RISING-FALLING INTONATION FOR COMMANDS.

84. Here most of the commands of § 76 are given with the Rising-Falling intonation of an assertion. The gradual working up to the highest pitch, instead of starting with it and immediately falling away from it, suggests self-control and quiet power, and for this reason a command given quietly and firmly with the Rising-Falling intonation, and a special kind of voice, carries with it more weight than the same command given in the same circumstances with the Falling intonation.

N'y va pas with this intonation

ni va 'pɑ.

gives the same impression as *Je te dis de ne pas y aller, Je t'ordonne de ne pas y aller:*

ʒə tə 'di | dən pɑ zi a 'le.

<hr />

[1] See also Chap. IV for the use of this different form of the Rising-Falling ntonation in the case of assertions.

If the command is given in a tone of great severity the Falling intonation seems to produce much the same effect as the Rising-Falling.

85. Examples:

```
  __  __         __
              \
  vjɛ̃ a  vɛk 'mwa.
  prə ne sɛt 'plas.
  ʃɛr ʃe vo 'liːvr.
```

ni va 'pa.

rɛst trɑ̃ 'kil.

fc tɛd 'vwaɪl.

vat prɔm 'ne.

nəl fɛt 'pa.

a le vu 'zɑ̃.

tə ne vu 'drwa.

ni a le 'pa.

mɛ lə syr la 'tabl.

nə lœr də mɑ̃d 'rjɛ̃.

ni va pa sɑ̃ 'mwa.

fɛ zɑ̃ skə ty 'vø.

va ʃɛr ʃe tɔ̃ 'liːvr.

rɑ̃ ʒe vo za 'fɛːr.

fɛt lə kɔ mil 'fo.

rɛste a vɛk 'mwa.

e ku te mwa 'bjɛ̃.

nə lɥi fɛt pa 'pœːr.

swa je ply se 'rjø.

tɛt lɥi fɛr sed 'vwaːr.

nəl de rɑ̃ ʒe 'pa.

na le pa a vɛ 'kɛl.

nə lɥi ɑ̃ par le 'pa.

də mɑ̃d lɥi u i 'va.

nə lɥi dit pa skə 'sɛ.

nə vu zɑ̃ nɔ ky pe 'pa.

dɔ ne mwa ski ja dɑ̃ vɔt 'sak.

rə mɛ te le li vra lœr 'plas.

e ku te ski la a vu 'diːr.

dit mwa pur kwa vu zi ɛt za 'le.

nə lɥi ra kɔ̃ te rjɛ̃d sɛ ta fɛr 'la.

nə lɥi di pa skə ty a dɑ̃ ta 'pɔʃ.

nə lɥi mɔ̃ tre pa skəʒ vu ze dɔ 'ne.

In many of the above examples the highest pitch could be given to a syllable other than the penultimate, without increasing the stress of this syllable[1]:

```
  _____
  __  __  __   __   __
  _____
                        \
  rə mɛ te le līː vra lœr 'plas.
```

[1] See also Chap. IV and § 83 for the use of this other form of the Rising-Falling intonation in the case of assertions and questions respectively.

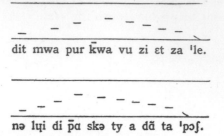

dit mwa pur k̄wa vu zi ɛt za ˈle.

nə lɥi di p̄ɑ skə ty a dɑ̃ ta ˈpɔʃ.

3. THE RISING FALLING INTONATION FOR "YES" AND "NO" QUESTIONS.

86.   The typical intonation for questions which can be answered by "Yes" or "No" is the Rising intonation. (See Chap. VIII, § 103(*b*).) But "Yes" and "No" questions may sometimes have the Rising-Falling intonation of an assertion. This introduces an element of authority. The questioned person feels rather as if he is under cross examination and is compelled to give an answer:

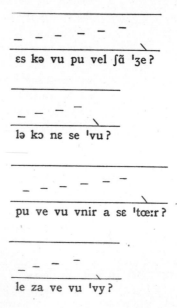

ɛs kə vu pu vel ʃɑ̃ ˈʒe?

lə kɔ nɛ se ˈvu?

pu ve vu vnir a sɛ ˈtœ:r?

le za ve vu ˈvy?

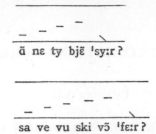

ã nɛ ty bjɛ̃ 'syːr ?

sa ve vu ski võ 'fɛːr ?

87. In some cases a question of this type with the Rising-Falling intonation does not expect an answer. E.g. *Savez-vous ce qu'ils vont faire?* with this intonation

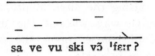

sa ve vu ski võ 'fɛːr ?

may mean : *Vous n'en avez aucune idée, n'est-ce pas? Eh bien, moi, je vais vous le dire.*

E

B. RISING INTONATIONS (Simplest Forms)

CHAPTER VII

THE FALLING-RISING INTONATION IN ENGLISH

88. The following are examples of statements which are not of so definite and final a type as those given in Chapter II. They suggest that the speaker leaves unspoken some idea which he manages, nevertheless, to convey to his hearer. He does this by the simple device of raising the pitch finally, thus expressing his meaning in an effective way without the use of words. The implication depends, of course, upon the context. Suggested implications are given in brackets.

There's 'no need to 'look so 'worried about it.

(It's not at all serious.)

It 'won't give me 'much 'trouble.

(So you needn't hesitate to accept my help.)

You 'needn't get ex'cited.   (Everything's going on quite all right.)

I 'think she'll 'manage it.   (But I'm not quite sure.)

46

'Good'bye!   (I hope to see you again soon.)

It 'won't 'bite you.   (You may go quite near.)

You 'needn't look so 'shocked.

(What I'm doing isn't very dreadful.)

89. Such statements are extremely common in English. They are found, of course, in conversation, where there is a give and take of ideas. The hearer may infer many things from them, e.g. that the speaker is in doubt, that he wants to warn, threaten, encourage, invite discussion, show deference, politeness, suggest a contrast, arouse interest, etc., etc. In all cases there is a lack of finality.

90. Some people use statements with implications much less than others. The thoroughly capable person who knows his own mind and allows nothing to interfere with the attainment of his object generally prefers to use the Falling intonation when it would be possible to use the Falling-Rising. Similarly, dogmatic people have little use for statements with an implication. The last thing they want to do is to suggest the existence of any other point of view than their own. They express their own opinion, which they regard as final, and the Falling intonation informs the other person very effectively that the "last word" has been said.

91. On the other hand, those who realise that the other person may have a point of view worth considering leave the door open by using the Rising intonation. They invite discussion. Sometimes the frequent use of statements with the Rising intonation suggests that the speaker is suffering from a sense of his own inferiority and is constantly feeling out for the approval of his

hearers or expecting their condemnation. Sometimes it suggests that the speaker is too ashamed or polite or cowardly or merciful to state the implication in words.

92.   In emphasis the implication is more strongly suggested than in unemphatic speech. (See § 315.)

1.   ANALYSIS OF FALLING-RISING INTONATION IN ENGLISH.

93.   Notice that, until the last stressed syllable is reached, the intonation is the same as that used for definite, conclusive statements. (See § 31.) The pitch of the last stressed syllable is generally level and low, the rise essential for the implication being spread over the unstressed syllables which follow. If there are no unstressed syllables, as in the last example given in § 88, the last stressed syllable carries the pitch upwards.[1]

94.   This is the tune that an English speaker must try to avoid in cases where the rising intonation is used in unemphatic French. (See §§ 101-3.)

95.   All expressions of small significance like *he said, he explained, he added, he suggested, you know, I think, I understand*, etc., occurring after statements of this kind, have the rising intonation of final unstressed syllables, even if some of the words are stressed.[2]   The pitch of words expressing the names of persons addressed also rises.   E.g.

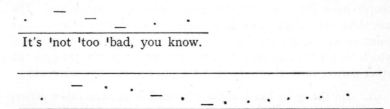

It's 'not 'too 'bad, you know.

There's 'no need to 'look so 'worried about it, Mrs. Smith.

---

[1] This appears to be the *typical* Falling-Rising intonation.   Sometimes the first important word is low in pitch and the rise made from that point.

[2] This applies also to such expressions when appended to questions having the Falling-Rising intonation and to requests.

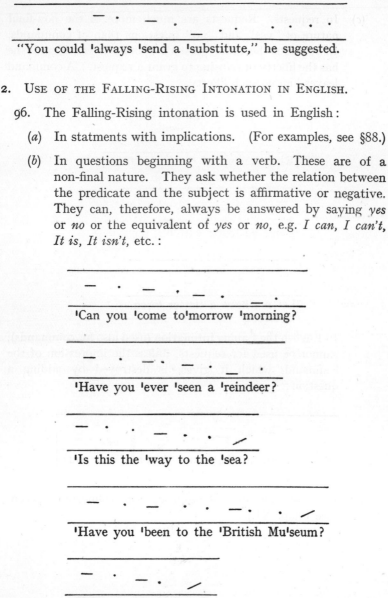

"You could 'always 'send a 'substitute," he suggested.

2. USE OF THE FALLING-RISING INTONATION IN ENGLISH.

96. The Falling-Rising intonation is used in English:

(a) In statments with implications. (For examples, see §88.)

(b) In questions beginning with a verb. These are of a non-final nature. They ask whether the relation between the predicate and the subject is affirmative or negative. They can, therefore, always be answered by saying *yes* or *no* or the equivalent of *yes* or *no*, e.g. *I can, I can't, It is, It isn't*, etc.:

'Can you 'come to'morrow 'morning?

'Have you 'ever 'seen a 'reindeer?

'Is this the 'way to the 'sea?

'Have you 'been to the 'British Mu'seum?

'Will you 'do it 'now?

(c) In requests. Requests are much more of the non-final nature of "yes" and "no" questions than of commands. In requests the other person's opinion is considered : he has the liberty of refusing to grant a request.   A command leaves him no such liberty.

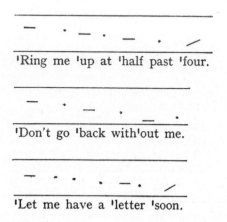

'Ring me 'up at 'half past 'four.

'Don't go 'back with'out me.

'Let me have a 'letter 'soon.

In English the Falling intonation (used also for commands), cannot be used for requests, unless the impression of the command, which it gives, is destroyed by adding a question :

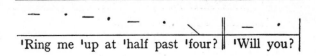

'Ring me 'up at 'half past 'four? ‖ 'Will you?

(d) In most non-final sense-groups in connected speech. (See Chap. XI.)

Chapter VIII

THE RISING INTONATION IN FRENCH

97.   In French, as in English, a rising[1] intonation is used for statements when a speaker wants to imply something without actually stating the implication in words. But the average Frenchman is not given to repressing his feelings; and in many cases he is not content to suggest the implication by intonation alone : he prefers to make sure that he is understood by stating it in words immediately afterwards.

98.   The following are examples of statements with implications. (Suggested implications are given in brackets.)

mɛ sɛ trɛ ʒɔ 'li.
(Pourquoi n'en voulez-vous pas?)

i la bo ku dar 'ʒɑ̃.
(Il est naturel qu'il en dépense beaucoup.)

ʒe bjɛ̃l 'tɑ̃.
(Pourquoi me pressez-vous?)

sɛ di fi 'sil.
(Mais nous y arriverons.)

---

[1] Falling-Rising in English.

51

_ _ _ _ _ —

san vu de rãʒ 'pɑ.
(Pourquoi n'êtes-vous pas content?)

_ _ _ _ —

i lɛ syr la 'tabl.
(Vous n'avez pas bien regardé.)

1. ANALYSIS OF RISING INTONATION IN FRENCH.

99. The intonation is like the ascending part of the Rising-Falling intonation, the part which suggests that there is more to follow. (See also § 103(*b*).) Note the *level* pitch of the last syllable.

100. Unimportant expressions of the type *dit-on, ajouta-t-il, monsieur, madame, mon cher, vous savez, il me semble,* etc., appended to statements[1] of this kind have a rising intonation as in English. It is convenient to regard the intonation of such short appended expressions as forming part of the preceding intonation group:

i fə zɛ 'bo, a ʒu ta til.

san vu de rãʒ 'pɑ, di til sɛʃ mã.

i lɛ kɔ̃ 'tã, vu sa ve.

[1] The same applies to such expressions appended to *questions* which have the Rising intonation.

2. THE FALLING-RISING INTONATION OF ENGLISH AND THE RISING INTONATION OF FRENCH COMPARED.

101. It is important to notice the different ways in which the rise is made in the English and French tunes. In English the pitch generally descends gradually before the final rise :

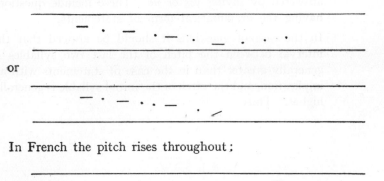

or

In French the pitch rises throughout :

102. Thus, an English learner, who rightly stresses the final syllable of each unemphatic French sentence, is tempted to use the English Falling-Rising intonation and wrong vowel length in the unemphatic sentences given in § 98, and to say :

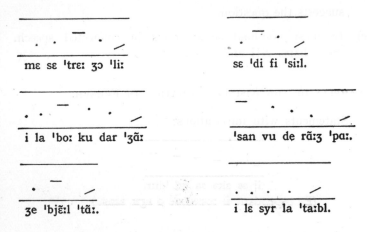

mɛ sɛ 'trɛ: ʒɔ 'li:

sɛ 'di fi 'si:l.

i la 'bo: ku dar 'ʒɑ̃:

'san vu de rɑ̃:ʒ 'pɑ:.

ʒe 'bjɛ̃:l 'tɑ̃:.

i lɛ syr la 'ta:bl.

3. USE OF THE RISING INTONATION IN FRENCH.

  103. The Rising intonation is used in French :

  (a) For statements with an implication.

  (b) It is the typical intonation for questions which can be answered by saying *yes* or *no*. These include questions having the grammatical form of statements.

  In the case of questions it should be noticed that the interval between the pitch of the last two syllables is generally greater than in the case of statements with an implication, and the pitch of the initial syllable is generally higher. Thus

i lɛ kɔ̃ 'tã.

  suggests the statement with an implication such as *Pourquoi lui offrir autre chose?*

i lɛ kɔ̃ 'tã.

  suggests the question.

  (c) In most non-final sense-groups in connected speech. (See Chaps. XII and XIII.)

4. EXAMPLES OF THE RISING INTONATION IN FRENCH.

  104. Statements with implications:

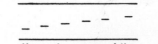

il sɛ skə sa vø 'diːr.
(Et cependant il continue d'agir ainsi.)

ɛ le tɛ syr la ˈtabl.
    (Pourquoi ne l'avez-vous pas prise?)

la pɔr te tɛ tu ˈvɛrt.
    (Et il n'est pas entré.)

nu lə lɥi a vɔ̃ ˈdi.
    (Et il l'a fait quand même.)

il le za de ʒa ˈvy.
    (Pourquoi a-t-il l'air si étonné?)

ⁱl fɔ̃ skil ˈpœːv.
    (Il ne faut pas vous plaindre.)

vul sa ve ˈbjɛ̃.
    (Pourquoi poser toutes ces questions?)

i li ɛ dɔ ʒa a ˈle.
    (Il n'aura pas de surprise.)

nun le kɔ nɛ sɔ̃ ˈpɑ.
    (Nous ne pouvons pas leur confier ça.)

il ni vɔ̃ ʒa ˈmɛ.
    (Pourquoi y sont-ils allés aujourd'hui?)

vu sa ve bjɛ̃ knu rɑ̃ trɔ̃ tu ʒur a sɛ ˈtœːr.
    (Le dîner devrait être prêt.)

nu vu za vɔ̃ a tɑ̃ ˈdy.
    (Votre retard ne s'expliquait pas.)

i fə zɛ trɛ ˈbo.
    (Nous sommes étonnés qu'ils ne soient pas venus.)

i nu srɛ trɛ za gre a blə di a ˈle.
    (Mais nous n'avons pas été invités.)

se ta blo nsɔ̃ pɑ trɛ ʒɔ ˈli.
    (Mais c'est tout ce que nous pouvons nous offrir pour le moment.)

nu ni rɔ̃ ˈpɑ.
    (Puisque c'est impossible.)

ʒi re la ne prɔ ˈʃɛn.
    (Puisque je ne peux pas y aller cette année.)

i lɛ ʒɑ̃ ˈti.
    (Tu peux le toucher. Il ne te fera pas mal.)

i nɛ pɑ me ˈʃɑ̃.
   (Il ne te mordra pas.)

ɛ lɛ pur tɑ̃ bjɛ̃ ʒɔ ˈli.
   (Et cependant, ils n'en veulent pas.)

ɛ la ve ky ɑ̃ frɑ̃s tut sa ˈvi.
   (Et pourtant elle ne parle pas comme une Française.)

105.   Questions which can be answered by saying "Yes" or "No":

ɛs kə vu ʃɛr ʃe kɛl ˈkœ̃?
pu ve vu vni ra sɛ ˈtœːr?
ɛs kə vu pu vel ʃɑ̃ ˈʒe?

nɛs pɑ ˈvrɛ?
ɛs kɛ lɛ ˈla?
lə kɔ nɛ se ˈvu?
ɑ̃ nɛ ty bjɛ̃ ˈsyːr?
ja til de za ni ˈmo?
ɛs kə vu vu le kɛk ˈʃoːz?
vu le vum dir kɛ lœ ri ˈlɛ?
ɛs kə vu la ve vy ɑ̃ ˈfrɑ̃ːs?
ɛs ki lɛ ta le kɛk fwa ʃe ˈvu?
ɛ ty kɔ̃ tɑ̃d tɔ̃ na prɛ mi ˈdi?
ɛs kə vu za ve kɔ̃ fjɑ̃ sɑ̃ ˈlɥi?
nə sa ve vu pɑ ki lɛ par ˈti?
ɛs kə sɛt pɛr sɔ na e te a rɛ ˈte?
ɛs kɔ̃ pu ra tru ve kɛk ʃo za mɑ̃ ˈʒe?

fo til le mɔ̃ ˈtre? di tɛ la mi vwa.[1]

ɛs kɛl tra ˈvaːj? məd mɑ̃ da sɔ̃ pɛːr.
ɛ ty kɔ̃ ˈtɑ̃? lɥi diːʒ.
mə pɛr mɛ te vu dvu za kɔ̃ pa ˈɲe? lɥi diʒ tiᵢmid mɑ̃.

---

[1] For the intonation of long appended expressions see Chap. XXVI.

106. Questions having the grammatical form of statements:

———————————
          —

—   —   —

pɛr sɔn nɛv 'ny?
vu zɛt kɔ̃ 'tɑ̃?
ɔ̃ pø ɑ̃ 'tre?

sɛ 'vrɛ?	ɛl ni va 'pɑ?
sɛ 'sa?	vu na ve pɑd 'lɛtr?
sa 'va?	vun mɑ̃ vu le 'pɑ?
sa vu 'plɛ?	vu za ver mar 'ke?
vu tru 've?	san vu de rɑ̃ʒ 'pɑ?
sɛ kɔ 'prɪ?	i nja pɑ ot 'ʃoːz?
snɛ pɑ 'vrɛ?	sɛ tɛ̃ te rɛ 'sɑ̃?
vu zɛt 'prɛ?	vu na ve pɑ sɔ 'mɛːj?
san va 'pɑ?	vu la kɔ nɛ se trɛ 'bjɛ̃?
ty nɛ pɑ 'libr?	vu za ve tu tɑ̃ tɑ̃ 'dy?
in rə gard 'pɑ?	sa vu frɛ vrɛ mɑ̃ plɛ 'ziːr?
i va fɛr 'bo?	vu za ve tru ve tu ski vu fa 'lɛ?
i nɑ̃ vø 'pɑ?	

———   —   —   —

— — — — —

vu par te də 'mɛ̃? mə dmɑ̃ da til.

i nja rjɛ̃d nu 'vo? də mɑ̃ da ʒɑːk.
ʒə pøm rə ti 're? də mɑ̃ da til.
vu la ve 'vy? fəzɛ la po vrə vjɛːj.
il le zɔ̃ rɑ̃ kɔ̃ 'tre? fi ti la vɛ kɛ̃ te rɛ.
i sɔ̃ ta ri 've? se kri a til.
vu le za ve 'vy? kɛs tjɔ na tɛl.

"Yes" and "No" questions with a Falling-Rising intonation.

107. In "Yes" and "No" questions the rise may be preceded by

a fall which puts the rise into greater relief. A question with

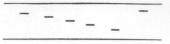

even if no extra stress is used, may be regarded as a slightly emphatic form of a question with

One no longer feels it to be a question, pure and simple. It seems to contain also a greater element of curiosity, surprise. The pitch of the initial and final syllables may vary considerably in height and convey different impressions. In emphasis it is high, and a strong impression of curiosity, surprise, authority, irony, etc., is conveyed. (See § 295.)

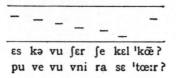

εs kə vu ʃεr ʃe kεl 'kœ̃ ?
pu ve vu vni ra sε 'tœːr ?

108. Beware of using English rhythm and the English Falling-Rising intonation in these examples. English learners are tempted to say :

'puː ve vu 'vniː ra sε 'tœːr ?

with the pitch of the final syllable *gliding* up from a lower level than that of the penultimate. In French the pitch *leaps* from the penultimate to a level high final syllable.

109. Examples of "Yes" and "No" questions with Falling-Rising intonation :

εs kε lε 'la ?
lə kɔ nε se 'vu ?

ã nɛ ty bjɛ̃ 'syːr ?

ja til de za ni 'mo ?

la ve vu fɛ pur 'mwa ?

ɛs kə vu vu le kɛk 'ʃoːz ?

ɛs kə vu la ve vy ã 'frãːs ?

ɛs ki lɛ ta le kɛk fwa ʃe 'vu ?

ɛ ty kɔ̃ tãd tɔ̃ na prɛ mi 'di ?

ɛs kə vu za ve kɔ̃ fjã sã 'lɥi ?

ɛs kə pɛr sɔn na e te a rɛ 'te ?

ɛs kɔ̃ pu ra a vwar kɛk ʃo za mã 'ʒe ?

sa ve vu ski vɔ̃ 'fɛːr ?

lə kɔ nɛ se vu də pɥi lɔ̃ 'tã ?

lɥi a ve vu rã dy sɔ̃ pa ra 'plɥi ?

lœ ra ve vu di knu dvɔ̃ rã tre lœ̃ 'di ?

vɔ̃ til su vã a le trã 'ʒe ?

a ve vu a pri li ta ljɛ̃ dãl pe 'i ?

110. Examples of questions having the grammatical form of statements with Falling-Rising intonation :

pɛr sɔn nɛv 'ny ?
vu zɛt kɔ̃ 'tã ?
ɔ̃ pø ã 'tre ?

sa vu 'plɛ ?

sɛ kɔ̃ 'pri ?

snɛ pa 'vrɛ ?

vu zɛt 'prɛ ?

san va 'pa ?

in rə gard 'pa ?

i va fɛr 'bo ?

i nã vø 'pa ?

ɛl ni va 'pa ?

vu na ve pad 'lɛtr ?

vun mã vu le 'pa ?

vu za ver mar 'ke ?

san vu de rãʒ 'pa ?

i nja pa ot 'ʃoːz ?

sɛ tɛ̃ te rɛ 'sã ?

vu na ve pa sɔ 'mɛːj ?

vu la kɔ nɛ se trɛ 'bjɛ̃ ?

sa vu frɛ vrɛ mã plɛ 'ziːr ?

vu za ve tru ve tu ski vu fa 'lɛ ?

C. BROKEN INTONATION GROUPS

Chapter IX

BROKEN INTONATION GROUPS IN ENGLISH

111. The English tonal patterns we have described,

(1) the Falling intonation suggesting finality :

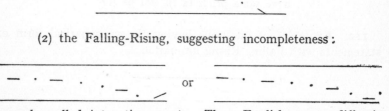

(2) the Falling-Rising, suggesting incompleteness :

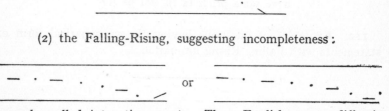

or

may be called *intonation groups*. These English groups differ in their final direction.

112. In pronouncing sentences (such as all those previously given) which contain no more than may be easily grasped in one effort by the hearer, the intonation curve is a simple one. It is broken by no indentations; i.e. there is no sudden change in its direction followed by a sudden return to the original direction. E.g.

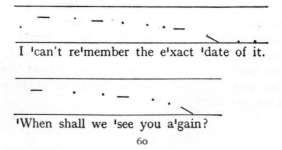

I 'can't re'member the e'xact 'date of it.

'When shall we 'see you a'gain?

'Send them 'off by the 'two 'train.

It 'won't take 'much of my 'time.

I 'think I can 'do it to'morrow.

Such an intonation may be said to constitute a *simple intonation group*.

113.   In a sentence containing matter of such length or importance or difficulty that a number of mental efforts are necessary both to express and to grasp it, the intonation seldom consists of an unbroken curve, i.e. it is seldom simple.   In his effort to express himself clearly the speaker instinctively modifies the intonation, sometimes by raising the pitch slightly at an important place or places, continuing the descent immediately after each rise.[1]   The effect is to give extra prominence to the words containing the raised syllables, and the hearer is thus helped in his effort to grasp the meaning of the sentence.

114.   Take, for example, an assertion: *They 'live in that 'large 'house on the 'other 'side of the 'bridge.*   This might be pronounced with the intonation of a simple group:

They 'live in that 'large 'house on the 'other 'side of the 'bridge.

But an intonation of this kind, with a continuous descent from the first prominent syllable, such as is used for short statements of a

[1] See also §§ 146–149, and Chap. XI.

F

simple nature, is hardly possible here except in the course of very rapid speech.

115.   The intonation may also be

They 'live in that 'large 'house on the ↑other 'side of the 'bridge.

In this case the pitch is raised slightly on the first syllable of *other* and the descent continued from this point.   This brings the position of the house into more prominence than it would have if the intonation consisted of a continuous descent without this "break."

116.   ↑ marks the rise in pitch and replaces the usual stress mark.

117.   The intonation group may be said to be *"broken,"*[1] by this sudden change and return to the original direction.

118.   A "broken" intonation group is normally pronounced with a single breath.

119.   The intonation group of the above statement may be "broken" at two points :

They 'live in that ↑large 'house on the ↑other 'side of the 'bridge.

The pitch is raised on both *large* and *other* and gives the ideas of the size and position of the house more prominence than they would have in a long unbroken descent.

120.   The position of a break in English is determined by the division into sense-groups : it is made as soon as possible after the completion of a sense-group, i.e. on the appropriate syllable of the first important word which follows.   The above sentence may be divided into three grammatical groups :

    (*a*)   They 'live
    (*b*)   in that 'large 'house
    (*c*)   on the 'other 'side of the 'bridge.

---

[1] "Broken" is not a very satisfactory term.

The first break is made by raising the pitch of the first important word occurring in the second group, i.e. of *large*. The second break is made by raising the pitch of the first important word occurring in the third group, i.e. of *other*.[1]

121. The raising of the pitch of any word draws more than ordinary attention to the idea expressed by that word, and is, for this reason, a step in the direction of emphasis. At the same time, in the case of long sentences, it prevents the pitch of the voice from reaching its lowest level before the completion of the intonation group. The outline of the intonation group is

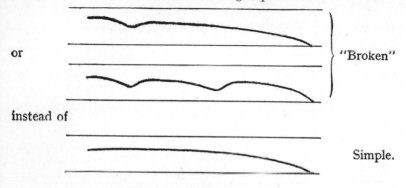

or   "Broken"

instead of

                                                               Simple.

122. Other examples of "broken" groups which could also be pronounced as simple intonation groups:

You're the 'first 'person I've 'met who ↑hasn't 'noticed it be'fore.

I 'feel it would be 'wiser if we ↑told him 'how it 'all 'happened.

You can 'tell me 'all the 'details when you ↑come on 'Thursday.[2]

[1] See § 150(c) and (d) for division of this group.
[2] See § 152 for division of these groups.

Chapter X

BROKEN INTONATION GROUPS IN FRENCH

123. The French tonal patterns we have described,

(1) the Rising-Falling intonation, suggesting finality:

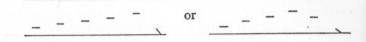

(2) the Falling intonation, also suggesting finality:

(3) the Rising intonation, suggesting incompleteness:

may be called *simple* intonation groups.

124. These intonation groups may be "broken" for the same reason that English intonation groups are "broken." (See § 113.) The way in which the break is made in the different types of intonation group occurring in French is described in the following paragraphs.

1. BREAK IN A RISING-FALLING INTONATION GROUP.

125. Take, as an example, *Elle sera contente de vous voir*, which has two sense-groups, (1) *Elle sera contente*, (2) *de vous voir*.

§ 126. The intonation group of this sentence may be simple, as in all the examples given in Sections A and B:

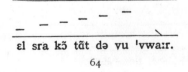

ɛl sra kɔ̃ tɑ̃t də vu ˈvwaːr.

It may also be broken :

ɛl sra kɔ̃ tãːt ↓də vu 'vwaːr.

127. We have noticed that a break in an intonation group has the effect of adding prominence to some word. In unemphatic French the important words occur finally in sense-groups ; and it is the prominence of these final words in non-final sense-groups which is affected by breaks.

128. The position of the break depends on the trend of the intonation. If the intonation is rising, the break is made by a slight *lowering* of the pitch (indicated by ↓), generally immediately *after* a sense-group.[1] This lowering increases the prominence of the syllable preceding the break by leaving it on a pitch higher than that of the syllable on either side of it.

129. In the above example the pitch is lowered very slightly on the syllable *de* after *contente* which terminates the sense-group *Elle sera contente* ; and the rise is at once continued from this point until the penultimate syllable is reached. The lowering of the pitch of *de* gives more prominence to the idea of *contente* than it would have in an unbroken ascent, and at the same time breaks the monotony of a fairly long ascent. The outline is

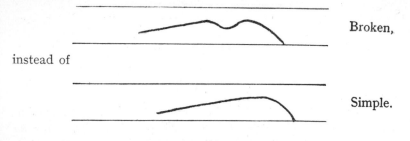

Broken,

instead of

Simple.

130. The subject matter assumes greater importance still if the intonation is divided definitely into two groups by means of a

[1] For an exception to the position of the break in the intonation of an assertion, see § 133. See also Appendix 2.

greater musical interval between the pitch of *con-* and *-tente*, and by a still greater lowering of the pitch of *de*.[1]

131.   It will be remembered that the Rising-Falling intonation has another form : the highest pitch may be on a syllable other than the penultimate, with the result that the word bearing it (marked ⁻), receives greater prominence. (See §§ 68, 69.) Thus, *Elle sera contente de vous voir* may be pronounced as a simple intonation group with its highest pitch on *-tente* instead of on *vous* :

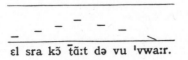

εl sra kɔ̃ t̄ɑ̃:t də vu 'vwa:r.

132.   This intonation group may also be broken by lowering the pitch of *de* and then by immediately changing the direction again until the penultimate is reached :

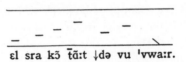

εl sra kɔ̃ t̄ɑ̃:t ↓də vu 'vwa:r.

Notice that in this case the break occurs after the highest pitch of the group has been reached, and not before, as in

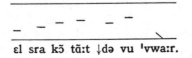

εl sra kɔ̃ tɑ̃:t ↓də vu 'vwa:r.

133.   When a non-final sense-group in an assertion ends with a syllable containing the sound ə, this syllable does not count as final so far as the intonation is concerned, and the break occurs immediately before it.   Take, for example, *Je vais le mettre dans ma chambre*, which may be divided into two sense-groups : *Je vais le mettre*, and *dans ma chambre*. It is the constant syllable *met-* which is made prominent by the lowering of pitch which immediately

---

[1] See §§ 162(c), 163.

follows it, and not the unstable[1] syllable *-tre*, which, from the point
of view of meaning, is the final syllable of its sense-group:

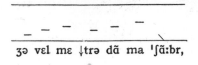

or, with more prominence given to *mettre*:

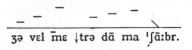

134. In rapid speech, the sound ə and the consonant sound
preceding it may be dropped altogether:

2. BREAK IN A FALLING INTONATION GROUP.

135. A break may also occur in a falling intonation group:

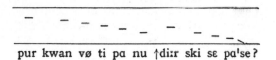

In this case, the trend of the intonation being downwards, the
break is effected by *raising* the pitch of the final syllable of the
sense-group *Pourquoi ne veut-il pas nous dire*. (The break is
marked ↑.) The descent is then continued.

136. A break in a Falling intonation group never occurs *after*
the last syllable of a sense-group. In order that the important,
i.e. the final word of the non-final sense-group may be made more
prominent, the break must be made by raising its pitch, or, in the

[1] See §§ 134, 138, 141.

case of a word of more than one syllable, by raising the pitch of its final syllable. In this latter case the break occurs within the word :

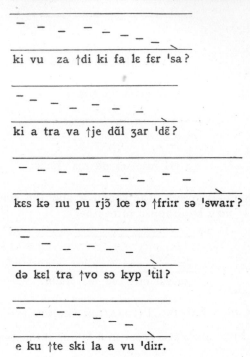

ki vu za ↑di ki fa lɛ fɛr 'sa?

ki a tra va ↑je dã̃l ʒar 'dɛ̃?

kɛs kə nu pu rjɔ̃ lœ rɔ ↑friːr sə 'swaːr?

də kɛl tra ↑vo sɔ kyp 'til?

e ku ↑te ski la a vu 'diːr.

137. When a non-final sense-group of a sentence pronounced with the Falling intonation ends with the sound ə the pitch of the penultimate syllable is raised instead of the final :

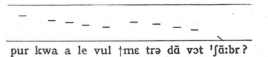

pur kwa a le vul ↑mɛ trə dã vɔt 'ʃãːbr?

138. In rapid speech the sound ə and the preceding consonant may be dropped altogether :

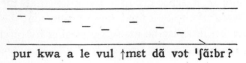

pur kwa a le vul ↑mɛt dã vɔt 'ʃãːbr?

3. Break in a Rising Intonation Group.

139.   A break may also be made in a Rising intonation group. This is generally done by lowering the pitch after the final syllable of a sense-group[1] and continuing the ascent as is done in the rising part of the Rising-Falling intonation group:

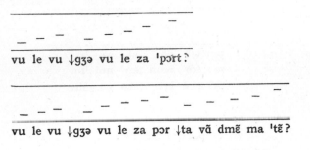

vu le vu ↓gʒə vu le za ˈpɔrt?

vu le vu ↓gʒə vu le za pɔr ↓ta vã dmɛ̃ ma ˈtɛ̃?

140.   If the final syllable of the sense-group ends with the sound ə the break immediately precedes this final syllable:

vu za lel mɛ ↓trə dã ma ˈʃã:br?

141.   In rapid speech the sound ə and the consonant preceding it may be dropped altogether:

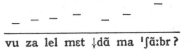

vu za lel mɛt ↓dã ma ˈʃã:br?

142.   Thus in all cases of breaks in French, the final syllable of a sense-group (unless it ends in ə) may be made prominent, either by lowering the pitch immediately after it, thus *leaving* it relatively high (as in the rising part of an intonation group),[2] or by raising its pitch, thus *making* it relatively high (as in the falling part of an intonation group).

[1] See also § 140 and Appendix 2.   [2] See also Appendix 2

4. EXAMPLES OF BROKEN INTONATION GROUPS IN FRENCH.

143. Assertions.

(i) In which the break occurs before the highest pitch of the group is reached :

```
ʒən tjɛ̃  pɑ  ↓al  sa  'vwaːr.
sɛ   tœ̃  nɔm ↓kɔ  mil 'fo.
ʃkɔ̃ prɑ̃ bjɛ̃ ↓skə vu  'dit.
```

ʒə le vy ↓tu ta 'lœːr.
yn de pɔr ↓tɛ fɛr 'me.
nu le za võ ↓kɔ mɑ̃ 'de.
ɛl sra kɔ̃ tɑ̃ːt ↓də vu 'vwaːr.
ʒə le fi ni ↓a sɛ 'tœːr.
ʒə lɥi e di ↓kɑ̃ ʒle 'vy.
sɛ tœ̃ nɑ̃ fɑ̃ ↓trɛ sɑ̃ 'sibl.
ɛl sə sɔ̃ ku ʃe ↓a se 'taːr.
il va vu par le ↓tu ta 'lœːr.
nu nɑ̃ na võ pɑ ↓le mwa 'jɛ̃.
ʒe de lɛ ↓tra mɛ tra la 'pɔst.
lə fak tœːr ↓nɛ pɑ zɑ̃ kɔr pɑ 'se.
i li ɛ rɛs te ↓yn sə mɛ nɑ̃ 'tjɛːr.
tul mɔ̃ː ↓dɛ tɔ ky 'pe.
ʒvø bjɛ̃ ↓vu ze ku 'te.
ɔ̃ di rɛ ↓ki va plœ 'vwaːr.
ʒe tɛ vny vu dmɑ̃ de ↓œ̃ kɔ̃ 'sɛːj.
i lɛ ↓dɑ̃ le za 'fɛːr.
im di ↓ki nɑ̃ na 'pɑ.
in vœl pɑ ↓sɑ̃ nɔ ky 'pe.
in fo pɑ ↓lɥi ɑ̃ vu 'lwaːr.
tu de pɑ̃ ↓də skɔ̃ pre 'fɛːr.
ʒə vu lɛ ↓vu za vɛr 'tiːr.
ʒən mə poz pɑd ↓pa rɛj kɛs 'tjɔ̃.
tu le zɑ̃ fɑ̃ ↓nsɔ̃ pɑ kɔm 'sa.

i lɛ ta le ↓ʒys ka la 'pɔrt.

vu vwa je bjɛ̃ ↓gʒən le pɑ 'fɛt.

ʒe œ̃ kɔ̃ sɛː↓ja vu dmɑ̃ 'de.

vu za le vwaːr ↓kɔm sɛ fa 'sil.

i la vu ly ↓nu fɛr par 'le.

i ja bjɛ̃ lɔ̃ tɑ̃ ↓gʒən vu ze 'vy.

i lɛ ta ri ve ↓ɑ̃ mɛm tɑ̃k 'mwa.

nun la vɔ̃ pɑ vy ↓dy prə mje 'ku.

i lɛ rɛs te la ↓pɑ̃ dɑ̃ di 'zɑ̃.

il fo le prɑ̃ː ↓drə pɑ̃ dɑ̃ le va 'kɑ̃ːs.

nu vu lɔ̃ le rɑ̃ː↓drə də mɛ̃ ma 'tɛ̃.

il vu drɛ le rə vɑ̃ː↓drə sɛ ta 'ne.

nu nu zɛ fɔr srɔ̃ dle kɔ nɛː↓trə sɛ ti 'vɛːr.

ɛl vjɛn ku ↓drə tu le ʒø 'di.

il nə fo pɑ krɛ̃ː ↓drə se za ni mo 'la.

se plɑ̃t nə pœv krwɑː ↓trə kə dɑ̃ zœ̃ tɛ rɛ̃ 'sɛk.

ɔ̃ va rə pɛ̃ː↓drə tut le me 'zɔ̃.

il fɔ drɛ re zu ↓drə se kɛs tjɔ̃ 'la.

il fo le sɥiː ↓vrə dɑ̃ lœ re vɔ ly 'sjɔ̃.

(ii) In which the breaks occurs *after* the highest pitch of the group has been reached. The syllable pronounced with the highest pitch is marked ‾.

ʒən tjɛ̃ p̄ɑ ↓al sa 'vwaːr.

sɛ tœ̃ n̄ɔm ↓kɔ mil 'fo.

ʃkɔ̃ prɑ̃ b̄jɛ̃ ↓skə vu 'dit.

ʒə le v̄y ↓tu ta 'lœːr.

yn de p̄ɔr ↓tɛ fɛr 'me.

nu le za v̄ɔ̃ ↓kɔ mɑ̃ 'de.

ɛl sra kɔ̃ t̄ɑ̃ːt ↓də vu 'vwaːr.

ʒə le fi n̄i ↓a sɛ 'tœːr.

ʒə lɥi e d̄i ↓kɑ̃ ʒle 'vy.

sɛ tœ̃ nɑ̃ f̄ɑ̃ ↓trɛ sɑ̃ 'sibl.

ɛl sə sɔ̃ ku ʃe ↓a se 'taːr.

il va nu par ˉie ↓tu ta ꞌlœːr.
nu nã na vɔ̃ p̄a ↓le mwa ꞌjɛ̃.
ʒe tɛ vny vu dmã ˉde ↓œ̃ kɔ̃ ꞌsɛːj.

i ˉiɛ ↲dã le za ꞌfɛːr.

im ˉdi ↓ki nã na ꞌpa.
in vœl p̄a ↓sã nɔ ky ꞌpe.
in fo p̄a ↓lɥi ã vu ꞌlwaːr.
tu de p̄ã ↓də skɔ̃ pre ꞌfɛːr.
ʒə vu ˉiɛ ↓vu za vɛr ꞌtiːr.
i vo ˉmjø ↓nu zã pa ꞌse.

There is no need to repeat all the examples given in § 143. In all of them the highest pitch may be given to the syllable immediately preceding the break, instead of to the penultimate.

144. Specific Interrogative Sentences, Commands.

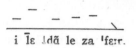

dã kɛl di rɛk ↑sjɔ̃ a le ꞌvu?
kɔ mã vu le ↑vu gʒə fas ꞌsa?
  ra kɔ̃ te ↑nu skə vu za ve ꞌvy.

pur kwa dit ↑vu de ʃoz pa ꞌrɛːj?
kɔ mã di tɔ̃ ↑sa ã frã ꞌsɛ?
kɛs kə vu za ve ↑fɛ dpɥi tã ꞌto?
ki vu za ↑di ki fa lɛ fɛr ꞌsa?
kɛs kə vu za ve ↑vy la smɛn dɛr ꞌnjɛːr?
kɔ mã sa pɛl lə prə mje ↑mwa dla ꞌne?
pur kwa nɛt vu pa a le le ↑vwaː rã rã ꞌtrã?
u krwa je ↑vu kil swa par ꞌti?
kə vu zɔ̃ til ↑di a vãd par ꞌtiːr?

ki vu za kõ sɛ ↑je dle 'prãːdr?

dã kɛl ma ɡa ↑zɛ̃ le za ve vu aʃ 'te?

kã kõ te ↑vu ja 'le?

dã kɛl ↑pjɛs fo til le 'mɛtr?

kã vu le ↑vu knu sɔr 'tjõ?

u kõ te vu le rã kõ ↑tre pã dã vɔt prɔ ʃɛ̃ vwa 'jaːʒ?

pu ve vu nu dir pur ↑kwa in sõ pɑv 'ny?

u le zã fã pɑ srõ til lœr va ↑kãːs sɛ te 'te?

kɔ mã sfɛ ↑ti ɡvun swa je pɑ zã kɔr par 'ti?

pur kwa na ve vu pɑ vã ↑dy sɛt me 'zõ?

pur kwa na til pɑ vu ly nu dɔ ↑ne de rã sɛɲ 'mã?

u də vrõ nu le ↑mɛ trã rã 'trã?

pur kwa vœl til ↑pɛ̃ː drə sef 'nɛːtr?

pur kwan vœl tɛl pɑ ↑ku drə mɛ̃t 'nã?

pur kwan vœl til pɑ le ↑vãː drãs mɔ 'mã?

kɔ mã pu võ nu re ↑zu drə sɛt kɛs 'tjõ?

kɔ mã dvõ nu nu zi ↑prãː drə pur fɛr 'sa?

kɛs kə nu pu rjõ ↑prãː drə ʃel flœ 'rist?

kɛl kur də võ nu ↑sɥiː vrə lə mɛr krə 'di?

dit mwa pur ↑kwa vu zi ɛt za 'le.

e ku ↑te ski la a vu 'diːr.

dɔ ne ↑mwa ski ja dã vɔt 'sak.

rə mɛ te le ↑liː vra lœr 'plas.

145. Questions which may be answered by "Yes" or "No."

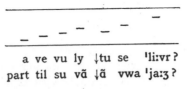

a ve vu ly ↓tu se 'liːvr?

part til su vã ↓ã vwa 'jaːʒ?

ɛ mə rje vu sɔr tiːr ↓sɛ ta prɛ mi 'di?

ã nɔ re vu bə zwɛ̃ ↓a vã dmɛ̃ 'swaːr?

kɔ nɛ se vu kɛl kœ̃ ↓ki i rɛ a vɔt 'plas?

lœ re kri ve vu ↓re ɡy ljɛr 'mã?

rsə ve vu su vã ↓dlœr nu 'vɛl?

sɔ kyp tɛl su vã ↓dʒar di 'naːʒ?

va tɛl su vã ↓a le trã 'ʒe?

ɛ me vu vwa ja ʒe ↓pã dã li 'vɛːr?

a ve vu tru ve sɛt me zɔ̃ ↓a vɔt 'gu?

kɔ̃ te vu le vwaː ↓ra vã vɔt de 'paːr?

vu le vu gʒə vu le za pɔr ↓ta vã dmɛ̃ ma 'tɛ̃?

ɛs kə vu kɔ̃ te fɛr sə vwa jaːʒ ↓sɛ ta 'ne?

pu rje vu pɑ se ʃe mwa ↓dãl ku rã dla smɛn prɔ 'ʃɛn?

vu le vu ↓gʒə vu le za pɔr ↓ta vã dmɛ̃ ma 'tɛ̃?

ɛs kə vu kɔ̃ te ↓fɛr sə vwa jaːʒ ↓sɛ ta 'ne?

pu rje vu pɑ se ʃe mwa ↓dãl ku rã ↓dla smɛn prɔ 'ʃɛn?

kɔ nɛ se vu kɛl kœ̃ ↓ki i rɛ ↓a vɔt 'plas?

vu le vu ↓knu za ljɔ̃ le vwaːr ↓pã dã le va kãs də 'paːk?

lœ ra ve vu di pur kwa ↓nu ni sɔm pɑ za le ↓jɛr 'swaːr?

sa ve vu pur kwa ↓i nja pɑ yd re y njɔ̃ ↓la smɛn dɛr 'njɛːr?

kɔ nɛ se vu kɛl kœ̃ ↓ki pu rɛ nu dɔ ne ↓se rã sɛɲ mã 'la?

ɛ mə rje vu ↓fɛr sə vwa jaʒ la ↓ã no tɔ mɔ 'bil?

a ve vu zyl tã ↓dvi zi te ↓le prɛ̃ si po mɔ ny 'mã?

a ve vu ly ↓kɛl kə ʃoz dɛ̃ te rɛ sã ↓də pɥi nɔt dɛr njɛr rã 'kɔ̃ːtr?

kɔ nɛ se vu œ̃ ʒœ nɔm ↓a ki ɔ̃ pu rɛ kɔ̃ fje ↓stra vaj 'la?

mɔ tɔ ri ze vu ↓ar və niːr ↓vu ra kɔ̃ te 'sa?

pu rje vum rə sə vwaː ↓rœ̃ ʒur kɛl kɔ̃ːk ↓də sɛt sə 'mɛn?

pu rje vu ↓pɑ se ʃe mwa ↓dãl ku rã ↓dla smɛn prɔ 'ʃɛn?

vu le vu ↓knu nu zɔ ky pjɔ̃ ↓dsɛ ta fɛr la ↓i me djat 'mã?

sa ve vu pur kwa ↓il nɔ̃ pɑ vu ly ↓nu za kɔ̃ pɑ ɲe ↓o te 'aːtr?

vu dri je vum mɔ̃ tre ↓kɔ mã i fo si prãː ↓drə pur fɛr 'sa?

vu le vu nu diːr ↓kɛl rut nu dvɔ̃ prãː ↓drə pu ra le ʃe 'vu?

sa ve vu pur kwa ↓in vœl pɑ vãː ↓drə lœr me 'zɔ̃?

a le vu lœr fɛr kɔ nɛː ↓trə la de si zjɔ̃ ↓kə vjɛn də prãː ↓drə lœr pa'rã?

ɛs yn ʃoːz ↓kə nu dvɔ̃ krɛ̃ː ↓drə pur le zã 'fã?

də vɔ̃ nu nu re zu ↓dran le prãː ↓drə kə la smɛn prɔ 'ʃɛn?

fo dra til vu fɛr sɥiː ↓vrə vɔt kɔ rɛs pɔ̃ dãːs ↓pã dã vɔ trap 'sãːs?

pu vɔ̃ nu fɛr rə pɛ̃ː ↓drə la me zɔ̃ ↓sɛ te 'te?

D. DIVIDED INTONATION GROUPS

146. A sentence may contain matter of such importance or length that a slight change in pitch which has the effect of simply "breaking" the intonation group is not strong enough to give the desired prominence to its different ideas.

147. The ideas of a sentence are brought out with greater prominence if the intonation group is divided into a number of intonation groups, the number varying according to the amount and nature of the subject matter of the sentence.

148. If the subject matter is important or difficult, the tendency is to express it rather slowly, and to use a greater number of intonation groups than if it is simple or conversational, making small demands on the hearer's power of attention.

149. The same sentence, under different conditions, may often be treated from the point of view of intonation as a simple group, a broken group, or a divided group, consisting of two or more groups, according to the prominence which the speaker gives to its different sense-groups.

CHAPTER XI

DIVIDED INTONATION GROUPS IN ENGLISH

150. Study again the example *They 'live in that 'large 'house on the 'other 'side of the 'bridge.* The intonation may vary according to the importance which the speaker attaches to its different ideas; but in all cases it has the downward trend characteristic of an English assertion.

(*a*) As a simple group the intonation of the important syllables descends gradually with a distinct fall within the last syllable :[1]

Simple Intonation Group.

They 'live in that 'large 'house on the 'other 'side of the 'bridge.

(*b*) As a broken group the pitch of *other* and *large* may be lifted out of the regular descent, these words thereby becoming more prominent :

Broken Intonation Group.

They 'live in that ↑large 'house on the ↑other 'side of the 'bridge.

(*c*) As a divided group the pitch of *house* is lowered, thus increasing the musical interval between it and that of the stressed words on either side of it, i.e. of *large* and *other*. The result of this lowering is to make evident two "peaks" divided by a low "valley."

This valley can, of course, occur only where the grammatical structure of the statement allows it, i.e. at the end of a sense-group. Its effect is to bring into greater

[1] See, however, § 114.

prominence the meaning of the sense-groups it divides. A pause may be made between the groups, but is not necessary (unless physiologically) in a sentence so simple in meaning as this:

Divided Intonation Group.

Non-final Group.   Final Group.

They 'live in that 'large 'house | on the 'other 'side of the 'bridge.

or   Divided Intonation Group.

Broken non-final Group.   Final Group.

They 'live in that ↑large 'house | on the 'other 'side of the 'bridge.

This changing of the pitch of *house* divides the whole intonation group, then, into two, the first rising, the second falling. The rising tone on *house* suggests that more is to follow and that there is a close connection between the ideas of the two parts.

Notice that although the first intonation group is a rising one, the general trend of the two related groups is down: the highest pitch of the non-final group is higher than the highest pitch of the final group. Thus the intonation of the assertion as a whole may be described as a falling one.

(*d*) Non-final Group.   Final Group.

They 'live in that 'large 'house‖ on the 'other 'side of the 'bridge.

Here the non-final intonation group falls. This fall destroys the close connection between the ideas of the two parts. It suggests that the position of the house was added as an afterthought. The subject matter does not justify a division after *live* or after *side*.

Again notice that the highest pitch of the non-final group is higher than the highest pitch of the final group.

151. *The dog stole a piece of meat and ran off with it to his kennel.*

(*a*) Simple Intonation Group :

The 'dog 'stole a 'piece of 'meat and 'ran 'off with it to his 'kennel.

This long unbroken descent is possible only in very rapid speech, such as might be used in a quick preliminary reading of the story to get the gist of it before giving the final reading. In telling the story to a child one would certainly divide the group as in (*d*) and (*f*), to bring out its ideas more vividly.

(*b*) Broken Group :

The 'dog 'stole a 'piece of 'meat and ↑ran 'off with it to his 'kennel.

This also is possible only in quick speech.

(*c*) Divided into two intonation groups, the first rising :

The 'dog 'stole a 'piece of 'meat | and 'ran 'off with it to his 'kennel.‖

(*d*) Divided into three intonation groups, the first and second rising :

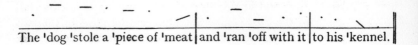

The 'dog 'stole a 'piece of 'meat | and 'ran 'off with it | to his 'kennel.‖

(e)   Divided into two intonation groups, the first falling:

The 'dog 'stole a 'piece of 'meat ‖ and 'ran 'off with it to his 'kennel. ‖

(f)   Divided into three intonation groups, the first falling, the second rising:

The 'dog 'stole a 'piece of 'meat ‖ and 'ran 'off with it │ to his 'kennel. ‖

152.   Other examples of divided groups which could also be pronounced as broken or simple intonation groups (see § 122):

You're the 'first 'person I've 'met │ who 'hasn't 'noticed it at 'once. ‖

I 'feel it would be 'wiser │ if we 'told him 'how it 'all 'happened. ‖

You can 'tell me 'all the 'details │ when you 'come on 'Thursday. ‖

153.   In all the examples given it will be noticed that the general trend of the intonation of the related groups is down.   The non-final groups generally rise.   Sometimes they fall.

154.   In some statements it is impossible, or at any rate unusual, for non-final intonation groups to fall,[1] e.g.

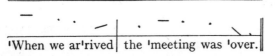

'When we ar'rived │ the 'meeting was 'over. ‖

[1] Some speakers who have a slow, deliberate and rather authoritative way of talking almost invariably use a falling intonation in non-final groups.   But this is exceptional.

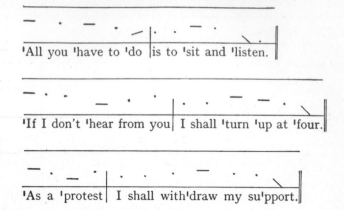

155. In all such statements the first sense-group is not complete in meaning, and this lack of finality is expressed by a rising intonation.

156. The falling of the English Falling intonation may thus take place in a continuous descent from the first stressed syllable, as in a simple intonation group; there may be small irregularities due to a slight raising followed by a lowering of the pitch at certain important places as in a broken intonation group; or there may be irregularities so great as to give rise to a number of intonation groups. The more the speaker throws his sense-groups into relief the greater the number of intonation groups he uses.

157. A non-final sense-group generally has a rising intonation if its meaning is incomplete. In some cases it is complete grammatically, but a rising intonation expresses a very close logical connection between it and the following sense-group.

158. At the end of each intonation group a pause may be made unless it would prevent the expression of a necessary closeness of meaning between groups. Pauses are often made when there is no need to make them for the purpose of renewing the breath supply; many mark still further the division into groups.

159. Try to read the following connected passage slowly, with the intonation recorded here. Then read it at a suitable speed.

Is the intonation given here the intonation you would use?   Some
readers will probably make slight differences.   E.g. they may
prefer to pronounce *doors* with a rising intonation instead of a
falling one ; they may emphasise *everything*.   The intonation shown
here was given by nine out of the twelve English people who were
asked to read the passage.   Two readers pronounced *doors* with a
rising intonation.   One of these made no division after *names*.   The
remaining reader's intonation was so monotonous that nothing
stood out clearly.

A falling intonation group is closed by ‖ ; a rising group by | .

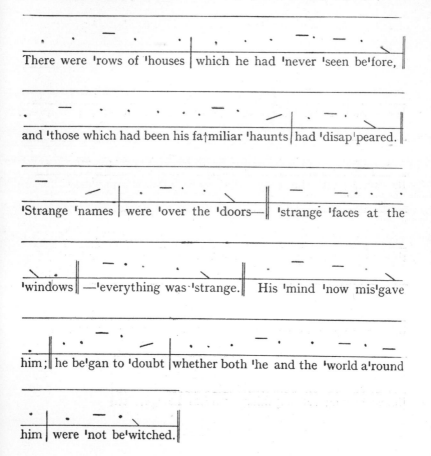

160. Notice that when a number of related groups (enclosed by ‖) occur, the highest notes of these groups tend to form a descending scale. E.g. in the last three groups of the above passage, the pitch of -*gan* is higher than that of *he* in the next group; and that of *he* is higher than that of *not* in the final group. Thus the Falling intonation runs through these closely connected groups:

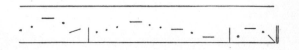

161. Study the intonation of the following passage pronounced without emphasis:

We're 'all of us 'selfish. ‖ But 'most of us make an 'effort to con'ceal

the fact. ‖ 'With the re'sult | that we're 'always being 'asked to 'do

things ‖ and 'having to in'vent e↑laborate ex'cuses | for 'not 'doing

them. ‖ And 'that makes us ↑very un'popular. ‖ For 'everyone

↑hates 'asking for anything ‖ un'less he 'gets it. ‖

CHAPTER XII

DIVIDED INTONATION GROUPS IN FRENCH

1. DIVISION IN A RISING-FALLING INTONATION GROUP.

162. The intonation of *Elle sera contente de vous voir* may be :

(a) Simple :

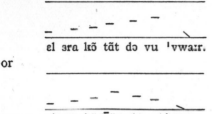

εl ɜra kɔ̃ tɑ̃t dɔ vu ˈvwaːr.

or

εl sra kɔ̃ tɑ̃ːt də vu ˈvwaːr.

(b) Broken.

    i. The break occurring before the highest pitch is reached :

εl sra kɔ̃ tɑ̃ːt ↓də vu ˈvwaːr.

    ii. The break occurring after the highest pitch is reached :

εl sra kɔ̃ tɑ̃ːt ↓də vu ˈvwaːr.

(c) Divided :

    < - Rising - >   <-Falling->
    Non-final Group.   Final Group.

εl sra kɔ̃ ˈtɑ̃ːt | də vu ˈvwaːr.

163. The musical interval between *con-* and *-tente* is greater than in (*a*) or (*b*), thus bringing *contente* into greater prominence. The pitch on *de* is lower than in (*a*) or (*b*). The large musical interval thus created between *-tente* and *de* and the stress placed on *-tente* give the effect of group-division, each group making prominent a particular idea, the ascending group the idea of pleasure, the descending group the cause of the pleasure. The outline is

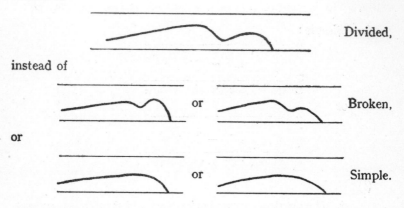 Divided,

instead of

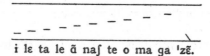 Broken,

or

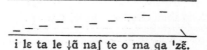 Simple.

164. The intonation of *Il est allé en acheter au magasin* may be :

(*a*) Simple :

i lɛ ta le ã naʃ te o ma ga 'zɛ̃.

Such an intonation is possible only in very quick speech. The importance of *allé* and *acheter* is not very clearly expressed in the gradual ascent.

(*b*) Broken :

i lɛ ta le ↓ã naʃ te o ma ga 'zɛ̃.

In this, the sense-group *il est allé* stands out slightly more

than in (*a*) owing to the break in the ascending scale of
steps which occurs after the syllable -*lé*.

(*c*) Broken (2 breaks) :

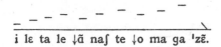

i lɛ ta le ↓ã naʃ te ↓o ma ga 'zɛ̃.

Here *en acheter* has greater prominence than in (*a*) or (*b*).

(*d*)   Divided into two groups, the first broken :

<--- Rising - - ->   <-Falling->
Non-final Group.   Final Group.

i lɛ ta le ↓ã naʃ 'te │ o ma ga 'zɛ̃. ‖

The size of the musical interval between -*ter* and *au*
divides the intonation group into two. The stress on
-*ter* is another dividing factor. The syllable -*ter* has the
highest pitch in the sentence. It terminates the ascending
group.

(*e*) Divided into three groups .

<- - - - - - Rising - - - -> <- -Falling- ->
Non-final   Non-final   Final
Group.   Group.   Group.

i lɛ ta 'le │ ã naʃ 'te │ o ma ga 'zɛ̃. ‖

The idea of *acheter* still stands out with the most prominence and still terminates the rising part of the intonation
of the whole statement. The pitch of the syllables
preceding -*ter* rises irregularly to this level. It is the
musical interval between the first two groups which gives

more prominence to *il est allé* than it has in (*d*). The pitch of the syllables following *acheter* also rises, before the final fall takes place; but the rise is not carried to so high a pitch as in the preceding group.

165. It is important to notice that the pitch does not rise to the same height in each related group, unless, as in enumerations or in the reading of passages of a dull, lifeless character, monotony is aimed at. A Frenchman would not say

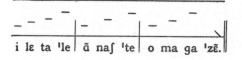

i lɛ ta 'le | ɑ̃ naʃ 'te | o ma ga 'zɛ̃.

with each group beginning on the same pitch and rising to the same height.

166. When a non-final sense-group ends with the sound ə the division occurs before the last syllable.[1] E.g. in *Je vais le mettre dans ma chambre* the division (like the break) is made before the completion of the sense-group *Je vais le mettre* :

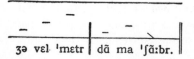

ʒə vɛl 'mɛ | trə dɑ̃ ma 'ʃɑ̃:br.

In cases of this kind sense-groups and intonation groups do not coincide, and no pause may be made between them. Grammatically -*tre* belongs to the sense-group *Je vais le mettre*. Tonetically it belongs to the group following. If a pause is made after the first sense-group the sound ə is omitted :

ʒə vɛl 'mɛtr | dɑ̃ ma 'ʃɑ̃:br.

[1] In cases of this kind the tendency is to "break" rather than "divide."

167. Notice that, in English, the last stressed syllable in each non-final group generally has the lowest pitch of the group. In French, the last stressed syllable in each non-final group has the highest pitch of its group.

2. DIVISION IN A FALLING INTONATION GROUP.

168. A Falling intonation group in French generally has no greater irregularity than a break (or breaks). If a specific interrogative question or a command is asked with an intonation consisting of two groups the intonation is as follows:

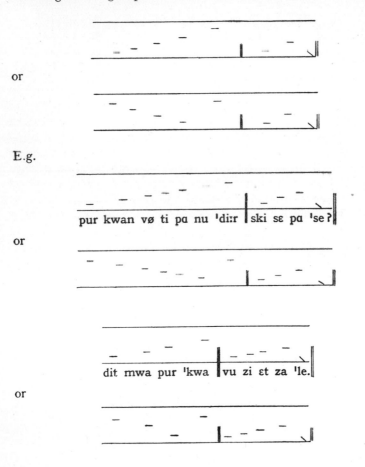

or

E.g.

pur kwan vø ti pɑ nu 'diːr ski sɛ pɑ 'se ?

or

or

dit mwa pur 'kwa vu zi ɛt za 'le.

or

3. DIVISION IN A RISING INTONATION GROUP.

169. Compare the following intonation with that of the same examples given in § 139 with breaks:

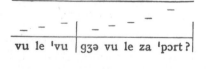

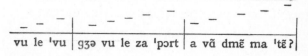

E. INTONATION OF LONG EXAMPLES WITH THREE OR MORE INTONATION GROUPS (French).

170. We have seen that the intonation of some short sentences may consist of a simple, broken, or divided group. There are the three ways, according to the importance the speaker attaches to the ideas they express. Many sentences cannot be pronounced as one intonation group, even in rapid speech, mainly because of their length. The study of the intonation of a number of such sentences will show, however, that it exhibits the general characteristics of that of the short statement which can be pronounced as one intonation group: it always rises to a certain point and descends from that point. The sense-groups in the rising part introduce some idea or ideas and leave us in a state of expectation; there is nothing final about them. The sense-groups in the descending part all contribute towards giving us some impression of completeness regarding the ideas presented in the ascending part.

171. The position of the point of highest pitch in a given example sometimes varies.

CHAPTER XIII

ANALYSIS OF THE INTONATION OF SENTENCES WITH THREE OR MORE INTONATION GROUPS

172. The intonation of a number of examples requiring three or more intonation groups is now analysed in some detail.

Example (*a*) *Il tenait à la main une lettre tout ouverte qu'il venait à la minute même de recevoir de Paris.*

173. The intonation of the whole sentence rises irregularly to a certain point and falls irregularly away from it, these irregularities occurring where the sense permits, and giving rise to a number of intonation groups, in this case corresponding to the following grammatical divisions:

(1) Il tenait à la main
(2) une lettre tout ouverte
(3) qu'il venait à la minute même
(4) de recevoir
(5) de Paris.

174. Most French people would give the highest pitch to *-verte,* the ascending groups introducing *la lettre ouverte.* The ascent is not made continuously up to *-verte,* but in such a way that *il tenait à la main* receives some prominence en route. It receives this because of the big musical interval made between *main* and *une,* and because of the stress which is placed on *main*:

il tə nɛ ta la ˈmɛ̃ | yn lɛ trə tu tu ˈvɛrt

175. In spite of the division after *main* the impression given is that the intonation from the beginning is working up to the point of highest pitch.

89

If the musical interval between *main* and *une* were not so great, the effect of a break would be given.   (It is possible in quick speech to pronounce this part of the sentence with a break after *main* instead of a division.)

176.   The pitch descends from *ouverte* in such a way that the ideas in 3, 4 and 5 are brought clearly to our notice :

< - - - - - - - - - - - - Falling - - - - - - - - - - - - - >

kil və nɛ ta la mi nyt 'mɛːm | də rə sə 'vwaːr | də pa'ri.

177.   The pitch of *qu'il* is low, creating an interval between *-verte* and *qu'il* great enough to make a division.   The intonation rises from *qu'il* to the end of the sense-group in which it occurs, i.e. to *même*, which is lower than *-verte*.   Then again comes a considerable drop in pitch to *de*, the first syllable of the next sense-group.   Again the intonation rises, but not to such a height as in the preceding group.   Again there is a fall in pitch to the *de* of the final group, followed by a slight rise and final fall.

178.   Thus the descent from the point of highest pitch is made in such a way that the intonation of the final syllables of the non-final groups forms a descending scale, the final syllable of the last group carrying the pitch to a low point suggesting finality.

179.   It is important to notice here that when, as in the example given above, the falling away from the point of highest pitch is long (see § 176) the interval between the final syllable and the preceding one is of necessity *small*.   In cases of this kind English learners should avoid raising the pitch of the penultimate syllable. E.g. in the above context they should avoid saying

də pa 'ri.

180.   In the groups preceding the point of highest pitch the initial (as well as the final) syllables of each group may form an

ascending scale.   In the groups following the point of highest pitch,
the initial (as well as the final) syllables of each group may form a
descending scale, though the intonation of each group rises.   This
difference in the height of the pitch of initial syllables is not made in
very slow, deliberate speech, especially when a pause is made between
each group.   In these circumstances the initial syllables all begin
at about the same low pitch.

181.   The outline of the intonation of the whole sentence can
be seen more clearly in the following:

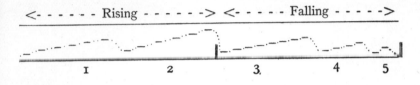

<- - - - - - - Rising - - - - - - -> <- - - - - - Falling - - - - ->

| 1 | 2 | 3. | 4 | 5 |

182.   The groups in the rising part work up to the point of
highest pitch, the groups in the falling part fall away from it.   It is
the final syllables of the five grammatical divisions which carry the
Rising-Falling intonation of the complete sentence.   The rising
steps leading to these final syllables do not destroy the impression
of the Rising-Falling intonation of the whole sentence:

< - - - - - - - Rising - - - - - - - >

il tə nɛ ta la 'mɛ̃ | yn lɛ trə tu tu 'vɛrt

<- - - - - - - - - - - Falling - - - - - - - - - - - - >

kil və nɛ ta la mi nyt 'mɛːm | də rə sə 'vwaːr | də pa'ri.

Example (b) *Il vient d'apprendre que son père a acheté une
maison à la campagne.*

183.   The highest pitch could be on the final syllable of *apprendre*,
the sense-group *il vient d'apprendre* arousing our curiosity as to

the news. The sense-groups which follow state the news. The intonation of these could fall in several ways according to the importance given by the speaker to *père* and *acheter*. The following variations are possible:

184.

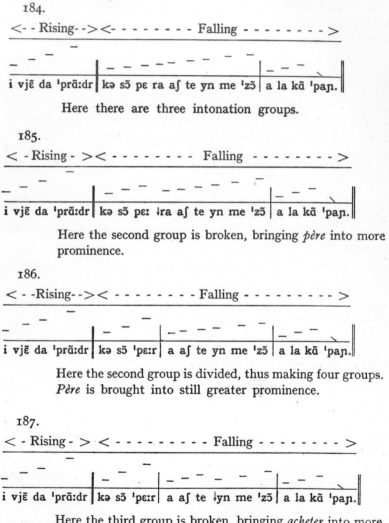

Here there are three intonation groups.

185.

Here the second group is broken, bringing *père* into more prominence.

186.

Here the second group is divided, thus making four groups. *Père* is brought into still greater prominence.

187.

Here the third group is broken, bringing *acheter* into more prominence.

188.

<- -Rising- -> < - - - - - - - - Falling - - - - - - - - >

i vjɛ̃ da 'prɑ̃:dr | kə sɔ̃ 'pɛ:r | a aʃ'te | yn me 'zɔ̃ | a la kɑ̃ 'paɲ.

Here the third group is divided, bringing *acheter* into still greater prominence and making five groups. The simple nature of the subject matter does not justify this division into five intonation groups, but it is possible in very slow speech.

189. It is possible also to make *Il vient d'apprendre* less important by giving the highest pitch to *maison*:

< - - - - - - - - - Rising - - - - - - - - - > <- Falling ->

i vjɛ̃ da 'prɑ̃:dr | kə sɔ̃ pɛ: ↓ra aʃ te yn me 'zɔ̃ | a la kɑ̃ 'paɲ.

or

< - - - - - - - - - - Rising - - - - - - - - > <- Falling ->

i vjɛ̃ da 'prɑ̃:dr | kə sɔ̃ 'pɛ:r | a aʃ te yn me 'zɔ̃ | a la kɑ̃ 'paɲ.

190. It is also possible to give the highest pitch to *père*:

<- - - - - Rising - - - -> < - - - - - Falling - - - - - - >

i vjɛ̃ da 'prɑ̃:dr | kə sɔ̃ 'pɛ:r | a aʃ te ↓yn me 'zɔ̃ | a la kɑ̃ 'paɲ.

Example (c) *Un jour, je quittai la ville de bonne heure et m'en allai seul, au hasard, me promener sur les grandes routes.*

191. Here, many speakers would include one short sense-group, *un jour*, in the ascending part. This introduces the occasion

H

and arouses our curiosity as to what happened on that occasion ; the sense-groups in the descending part give the experiences of that particular day. Other speakers might rise up to *heure*, so that the early hour of leaving the town is included in the introduction, and does not therefore give such a strong impression that it forms part of the recital of the day's experiences.

192.   The intonation of the ascending part may thus be :

$$< \text{Rising} >$$

$$-$$

$$-$$

œ̃ 'ʒuːr,

or

$$< \text{- - - - - - - - Rising - - - - - - - >}$$

$$-$$

$$- \quad - \quad - \quad - \quad - \quad - \quad -$$

œ̃ 'ʒuːr, | ʒə ki te la vil də bɔ 'nœːr

or

$$< \text{- - - - - - - - Rising - - - - - - - >}$$

$$-$$

$$- \quad - \quad - \quad - \quad -$$

œ̃ 'ʒuːr, | ʒə ki te la vil ↓də bɔ 'nœːr

193.   The pitch of the descending groups falls in such a way that *de bonne heure, m'en allai seul, au hasard, me promener, sur les grandes routes*, all stand out because of the stress of *heure, seul, -sard, -ner, routes* and the size of the musical interval between each of these syllables and the following one:

$$< \text{- - - - - - - - -Falling- - - - - - - - - - -}$$

$$-$$

$$- \quad - \quad - \quad - \quad - \quad - \quad - \quad -$$

ʒə ki te la vil də bɔ 'nœːr | e mã na le 'sœl,

$$\text{- - - - - - - - - Falling - - - - - - - - - - >}$$

$$- \quad - \quad \quad - \quad \quad - \quad -$$

o a 'zaːr, | mə prɔm 'ne | syr le grãd 'rut.

194. The intonation of the whole sentence could be this:

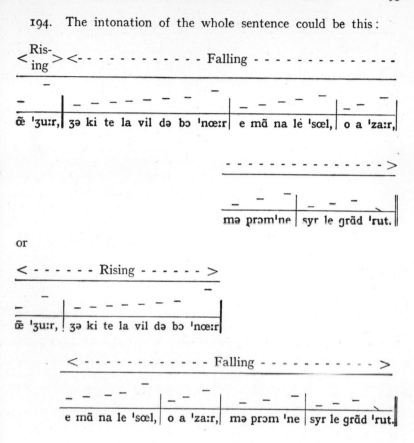

or

195. In each case there may be a slight lowering of pitch after *ville*. It is also possible to give a separate intonation group to *seul*, pronouncing it with the pitch of the final syllable of the preceding sense-group.

> Example (*d*) *Il habitait une maison isolée sur la limite d'un village, mais aussi près que possible des champs.*

196. Here, *village* demands the highest pitch. It seems impossible to give it to any other word.

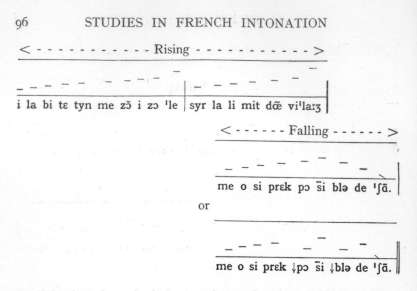

A slight lowering of pitch may be made after *habitait, maison, limite, près.*

197. The above examples illustrate the fact that unemphatic assertions in French have a Rising-Falling intonation, the rising and falling often running through a series of related groups. They show also that in the case of any one assertion the method of rising and falling is by no means fixed for all speakers, not even for the same speaker in different circumstances, but admits of a large number of variations depending mainly on the importance the speaker gives to his different ideas, and on the hearer's power of sustained attention.

198. The effectiveness of a speaker in expressing his own ideas or in interpreting those of others, depends, to a very great degree, on his ability to make full use of intonation.

199. In reading, a "break" or a "division" in a certain place often makes all the difference between a right and a wrong interpretation, between sense and nonsense.

RHYTHM IN FRENCH.

200. Rhythm in French is caused mainly by the occurrence of stressed syllables at fairly regular intervals of time. These stressed

syllables are, as we have seen, the final syllables of important sense-groups. In order that the time intervals between the stresses shall be more or less the same, the sense-groups which contain few syllables are pronounced more slowly than those which contain many; and for this reason their ideas are more closely brought to our notice than those of the many-syllabled groups.

201. This regularity in the occurrence of the stresses of a sentence, even of a sentence of great length, does not result in the monotony which is associated with the repetition of numbers or of lists of things. Monotony is avoided by raising the pitch to a different height in each intonation group, and, to a lesser degree, by giving a different pitch to the initial syllables of each group. The variation in the number of syllables in each group also militates against monotony, the difference in time being made up in extra speed in the case of many-syllabled groups, and in a decrease of speed or in added length or pauses in the case of the groups containing few syllables.

CHAPTER XIV

SENTENCES WITH TWO OR MORE INTONATION GROUPS
(WITHOUT BREAKS)

Assertions.

202. Two syllables in second group:

<Rising> <Falling>

nu zi ˈrɔ̃ | də ˈmɛ̃.
i zi ˈvɔ̃ | su ˈvɑ̃. ‖

ɛ la fi ˈni | sa ˈlɛtr. ‖
ʒə le ze ˈvy | di ˈmɑ̃ːʃ. ‖
nu ni rɔ̃ ˈpɑ | sə ˈswaːr. ‖
nun sa vɔ̃ ˈpɑ | skə ˈsɛ. ‖
nu la vɔ̃ ˈvy | ʃe ˈzɛl. ‖
ɛl sɔr ti ˈrɔ̃ | ply ˈtaːr. ‖
nu vwa ja ˈʒɔ̃ | ɑ̃z ˈgɔ̃ːd. ‖
in vœl pɑv ˈniːr | mɛ̃t ˈnɑ̃. ‖
ʒən kɔ̃ prɑ̃ ˈpɑ | ski ˈdi. ‖
in ʒu pɑ su ˈvɑ̃ | ɑ̃ ˈsɑ̃ːbl. ‖
i fo tja ˈle | tut ˈsɥit. ‖
lə ʒar ˈdɛ̃ | ɛ ˈgrɑ̃. ‖
le zɑ̃ ˈfɑ̃ | sa ˈmyːz. ‖
sə ta ˈblo | mə ˈplɛ. ‖
nu nɛ mɔ̃ ˈpɑ | le ˈvwaːr. ‖
ʒə lɥi e te le fɔ ˈnc | sma ˈtɛ̃. ‖
nu nɑ̃ vu lɔ̃ ˈpɑ | bo ˈku. ‖
ɛl le ˈtruːv | ʒɔ ˈli. ‖

i fɔ dra i a 'le | bjɛ̃ 'to. ‖
nu zi a 'lɔ̃ | lʒø 'di. ‖
nɔ trə 'kuːr | ɛ 'ptit. ‖
i lɛ sɛ̃ 'kœːr | mwɛ̃l 'kaːr. ‖
nu nu prɔm 'nɔ̃ | dɑ̃l 'park. ‖
i nu zɛ̃ te 'rɛs | bo 'ku. ‖
i ja vɛ dy 'mɔ̃ːd | par 'tu. ‖
ʒe e te ɔ ky 'pe | sma 'tɛ̃. ‖

203.   Three syllables in second group:

<- - Rising - > < - - Falling - - >

‾	‾		‾	‾	＼	‖
ʒən	tjɛ̃	'pɑ	al	sa	'vwaːr.	‖
sɛ	tɛ̃	'nɔm	kɔ	mil	'fo.	‖
ʃkɔ̃	prɑ̃	'bjɛ̃	skə	vu	'dit.	‖

ʒə le 'vy | tu ta 'lœːr. ‖
yn de 'pɔrt | ɛ fɛr 'me. ‖
nu lɛ za 'vɔ̃ | kɔ mɑ̃ 'dɛ. ‖
ɛl sra kɔ̃ 'tɑ̃ːt | də vu 'vwaːr. ‖
ʒə le fi 'ni | a sɛ 'tœːr. ‖
ʒə lɥi e 'di | kɑ̃ ʒle 'vy. ‖
sɛ tɛ̃ gar 'sɔ̃ | trɛ sɑ̃ 'sibl. ‖
ɛl sə sɔ̃ ku 'ʃe | a se 'taːr. ‖
il va nu par 'le | tu ta 'lœːr. ‖
nu nɑ̃ na vɔ̃ 'pɑ | le mwa 'jɛ̃. ‖
ʒe tɛ vny vu dmɑ̃ 'de | ɛ̃ kɔ̃ 'sɛːj. ‖
ʒɛm 'mjø | npɑ ja 'le. ‖
i na vɛ pɑ 'ply | də pɥi si 'mwa. ‖
la tɑ̃ pe ra ty ra ʃɑ̃ 'ʒe | su dɛn 'mɑ̃. ‖
sɛ ty nis twar di fi 'sil | a kɔ̃ 'prɑ̃ːdr. ‖
ɔ̃ sɑ̃ de ʒa li 'vɛːr | ki a 'riːv. ‖
il fɔ drɛ le 'prɑ̃ː | drə tut 'sɥit. ‖
(or) il fɔ drɛ le 'prɑ̃ːd (r) | tut 'sɥit. ‖
ɛl zɛm rɛ le 'ku | drə mɛ̃t 'nɑ̃. ‖
(or) ɛl zɛm rɛ le 'kud (r) | mɛ̃t 'nɑ̃. ‖

204. Four syllables in second group :

$< -$ - Rising - - $> < -$ - - - Falling - - - $>$

in	vœl	ˈpɑ	sɑ̃	nɔ	ky	ˈpe.
in	fo	ˈpɑ	lɥi	ɑ̃	vu	ˈlwaːr. ‖
tu	de	ˈpɑ̃	də	skɔ̃	pre	ˈfɛːr. ‖
nu	də vrɔ̃ re	ˈzu	drə	sɛt	kɛs	ˈtjɔ̃. ‖
(or)	nu də vrɔ̃ re	ˈzud (r)		sɛt	kɛs	ˈtjɔ̃. ‖

ʒe vu ˈly ‖ vu za vɛr ˈtiːr. ‖
i vo ˈmjø ‖ nu zɑ̃ pɑ ˈse. ‖
i ˈlɛ ‖ dɑ̃ le za ˈfɛːr. ‖
im ˈdi ‖ ki nɑ̃ na ˈpɑ. ‖
ʒən mə poz ˈpɑ ‖ dpa rɛj kɛs ˈtjɔ̃. ‖
tu le ˈʒɑ̃ ‖ nsɔ̃ pɑ kɔm ˈsa. ‖
i lɛ ta ˈle ‖ ʒys ka la ˈpɔrt. ‖
ʒe de kɔ̃ ˈsɛːj ‖ a vu dmɑ̃ ˈde. ‖
vu za le ˈvwaːr ‖ kɔm sɛ fa ˈsil. ‖
i la vu ˈly ‖ nu fɛr par ˈle. ‖
i lja bjɛ̃ lɔ̃ ˈtɑ̃ ‖ gʒən vu ze ˈvy. ‖
i lɛ ta ri ˈve ‖ ɑ̃ mɛm tɑ̃k ˈmwa. ‖
nun la vɔ̃ pɑ ˈvy ‖ dy prə mje ˈku. ‖
i lɛ rɛs te ˈla ‖ pɑ̃ dɑ̃ di ˈzɑ̃. ‖
tul ˈmɔ̃ːd ‖ ɛ tɔ ky ˈpe. ‖
ʒvø ˈbjɛ̃ ‖ vu ze ku ˈte. ‖
ɔ̃ di ˈrɛ ‖ ki va plœ ˈvwaːr. ‖
i ʒu o tɛ ˈnis ‖ tu le di ˈmɑ̃ːʃ. ‖
nu zi a ˈlɔ̃ ‖ trwɑ fwa pa ˈrɑ̃. ‖
ɛl nə kɔ nɛ ˈpɑ ‖ sɛ tɑ̃ drwɑ ˈla. ‖
lə vɑ̃ su ˈflɛ ‖ a vɛk vjɔ ˈlɑ̃ːs. ‖
nu sɔm mɔ̃ ˈte ‖ ʒys ko sɔ ˈmɛ. ‖
il pas lœr va ˈkɑ̃ːs ‖ a la kɑ̃ ˈpaɲ. ‖
lə vwa ja ʒɑ̃ no tɔ mɔ ˈbil ‖ ɛ ta gre ˈaːbl. ‖
il nə fo pɑ ˈzɛː ‖ trə trɔ prɛ ˈse. ‖
(or) i n fo pɑ ˈɛt ‖ trɔ prɛ ˈse. ‖

205.   Five syllables in second group :

<---Rising ---> <---- Falling ---->

```
  _    _    _    _
                _
 _                   _    _    _
                               _
─────────────────┃──────────────────────╢
nu nã nɔ rɔ̃ 'pɑ ┃ a vã dmɛ̃ ma 'tɛ̃. ╢
```

i li ε rεs 'te | yn sə mε nã 'tjεːr. ‖
lə pe 'i | ε ku vεr də 'pɛ̃. ‖
ʒe de 'lεtr | a mε tra la 'pɔst. ‖
nul vwa 'jɔ̃ | trwɑ fwa par sə 'mεn. ‖
nu ni rɔ̃ 'pɑ | a vã vɔt rə 'tuːr. ‖
i la fε 'ʃo | pã dã kεl kə 'mwɑ. ‖
lɑ mɔ̃ 'taɲ | e tε ta se 'oːt. ‖
ɔ̃ sã de 'ʒa | li vεr ki a 'riːv. ‖
nu zi rɔ̃ 'prɑ̃ː | drə də lœr nu 'vεl. ‖
(or)   nu zi rɔ̃ 'prɑ̃ːd (r) | də lœr nu 'vεl. ‖
nu vu dri jɔ̃ zã 'tɑ̃ː | drə sεt kɔ̃ fe 'rɑ̃ːs. ‖
(or)   nu vu dri jɔ̃ zã 'tɑ̃ːd (r) | sεt kɔ̃ fe 'rɑ̃ːs. ‖
vu də ve zã kɔ̃ 'prɑ̃ː | drə tu le de 'taɾj. ‖
(or)   vu də ve zã kɔ̃ 'prɑ̃ːd (ɾ) | tu le de 'taɾj. ‖
se plãt nə pœv pɑ 'viː | vrə dã sə pe 'i. ‖
(or)   se plãt nə pœv pɑ 'viːv (r) | dã s pe 'i. ‖

206.   Six syllables in second group :

<-- Rising -- > <---- Falling ---->

```
  _    _    _
            _                   _
 _              ┃ _    _    _        _
                ┃                        ＼
─────────────────┃──────────────────────╢
sε ty nis 'twaːr ┃ di fi si la kɔ̃ 'prɑ̃ːdr.╢
```

il nə sav pɑ pur 'kwa | ɔ̃ le za kɔ̃ vɔ 'ke. ‖
la tã pe ra 'tyːr | a ʃã ʒe su dεn 'mã. ‖
lə fak 'tœːr | nε pɑ zã kɔr pɑ 'se. ‖
il vu drεl kɔ 'nε | trə lə ply vit pɔ 'sibl. ‖
(or)   il vu drεl kɔ 'nεːt (r) | lə ply vit pɔ'sibl. ‖

207. Examples with three groups. A heavy upright line is used after the group which rises to the highest pitch :

<Rising> <- - - - - - - - - Falling - - - - - - - - - >

i la fɛ ˈʃo │ pã dã le dø dɛr njɛr sə ˈmɛn │ dy mwɑ ˈdu. ‖

nu nɛ mɔ̃ pɑ bo ˈku │ a le ã nɛs ˈpaɲ │ pã dã le ˈte. ‖
no ʒœn ˈʒã │ pre fɛ ra le ã ˈsɥis │ pã dã li ˈvɛːr. ‖
le stɑ sjɔ̃ di ˈvɛːr │ sɔ̃ fre kã ˈte │ par le ze trã ˈʒe. ‖
la prɔk si mi te dy ˈpark │ ɛ ty na trak ˈsjɔ̃ │ ɛ̃ kɔ̃ tɛs ˈtaːbl. ‖
nu za vɔ̃ zy dy bo ˈtã │ pã dã la prə mjɛr parˈti │ dno va ˈkãːs. ‖

Questions.

208. Beginning with a specific interrogative word :

<- - Rising - - -> <Falling>

kə kɔ̃ te vu ˈfɛːr │ də ˈmɛ̃ ? ‖

(or)

u va ˈtɔ̃ │ le ˈmɛtr ? ‖
kɛ lɔm ni ˈbys │ dwaʒ ˈprãːdr ? ‖
kə vu le ˈvu │ kəʒ ˈfas ? ‖
kɛl ˈrut │ dwaʒ ˈsɥiːvr ? ‖
u ɛt vu a ˈle │ jɛr ˈswaːr ? ‖
ki vu za ˈdi │ drã ˈtre ? ‖
fo til sã nɔ ky ˈpe │ tut ˈsɥit ? ‖

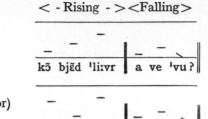

< - Rising - > <Falling>

kɔ̃ bjɛ̃d 'liːvr | a ve 'vu ?

(or)

kɔ 'mɑ̃ | lsa ve 'vu ? ‖
'ki | dmɑ̃ de 'vu ? ‖
də 'ki | par le 'vu ? ‖
kɛ 'lœːr | a ve 'vu ? ‖
də 'kwa | par lə 'tɔ̃ ? ‖
a 'kwa | tra vaj 'til ? ‖
də 'kwa | sa ʒi 'til ? ‖
kɔ 'mɑ̃ | slas fɛ 'til ? ‖
kɛs kə 'sɛ | kɛs tis 'twaːr ? ‖
dɑ̃ kɛl di rɛk 'sjɔ̃ | a le 'vu ? ‖
kɔ mɑ̃ vu le 'vu | gʒə fas 'sa ? ‖
kɔ mɑ̃ di tɔ̃ 'sa | ũ lĩũ 'sɛ ? ‖
kɛs kə vu za ve 'fɛ | də pɥi tɑ̃ 'to ? ‖
pur kwa na ve vu pa vɑ̃ 'dy | sɛt me 'zɔ̃ ? ‖

<- Rising -> <- - Falling - ->

kɛl ku 'lœːr | pre fe re 'vu ?

(or)

pur kwa dit 'vu | de ʃoz pa 'rɛːj ? ‖
kɛs kə vu za ve 'vy | la smɛn dɛr 'njɛːr ? ‖
pur kwan vø ti pa nu 'diːr | ski sɛ pa 'se ? ‖
ʃe 'ki | ɛ tɛ la 'le ? ‖
də kwa sa ʒi 'til | dɑ̃ sɛ tis 'twaːr ? ‖
'kɑ̃ | dwav til par 'tiːr ? ‖

pur kwa na til pɑ vu ly nu dɔ ˈne ┃ de rɑ̃ sɛɲ ˈmɑ̃ ? ‖
u vu le ˈvu ┃ knu le mɛ ˈtjɔ̃ ? ‖
kɔ mɑ̃ vu le ˈvu ┃ knu fa sjɔ̃ ˈsa ? ‖

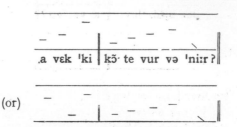

(or)

ki vu za ˈdi ┃ ki fa lɛ fɛr ˈsa ? ‖
kɛs kɛl ˈpɑ̃ːs ┃ də sɛ ta fɛr ˈla ? ‖
pur ˈkwa ┃ nɑ̃ vu le vu ˈpɑ ? ‖
u pas til ʒe ne ral ˈmɑ̃ ┃ la sɛ zɔ̃ de ˈte ? ‖
kə kɔ̃t til ˈfɛːr ┃ pɑ̃ dɑ̃ lœr va ˈkɑ̃ːs ? ‖
kɛ lɛ la ku ˈlœːr ┃ kə vu pre fe ˈre ? ‖
a ˈki ┃ a le vu le dɔ ˈne ? ‖
pur ˈkwa ┃ lɥi a ve vu ze ˈkri ? ‖
ˈki ┃ sɛ tɔ ky ped ˈsa ? ‖
kɔ mɑ̃ sa ˈpɛl ┃ lə prə mje mwɑ dla ˈne ? ‖
kɔ mɑ̃ sfɛ ˈtil ┃ kə vun swa je pɑ zɑ̃ kɔr par ˈti ? ‖

209.   Capable of being answered by "Yes" or "No.":

< - - - - Rising - - - - >

kɔ nɛ se ˈvu ┃ sɛ tis ˈtwaːr ?

sa ve ˈvu │ skil zɑ̃ ˈpɑ̃ːs ? │
le za ve vu de ˈʒa │ rɑ̃ kɔ̃ ˈtre ? │
le rɑ̃ kɔ̃ tre ˈvu │ kɛl kə ˈfwa ? │
a til bə zwɛ̃ dy rɑ̃ sɛɲ ˈmɑ̃ │ o ʒur ˈdɥi ? │
sa ve ˈvu │ skil sɔ̃ dəv ˈny ? │
sa ve vu pur ˈkwa │ in sɔ̃ pɑ zɑ̃ kɔr rɑ̃ ˈtre ? │

< - - - - - - - - - - - Rising - - - - - - - - - - - >

| kɔ nɛ se vu kɛl ˈkõ̃ | ki pu rɛ ˈfɛːr | sə tra vaj ˈla? |

sa ve vu pur ˈkwa | il nõ pɑ vu lyv ˈniːr | sɛ ta ˈne? |
le za ve vu ˈvy | dpɥi vɔt rə ˈtuːr | di ta ˈli? |
sõ til kõ ˈtɑ̃ | dlœr vwa ˈjaːʒ | ɑ̃ nɔ ˈrjɑ̃? |
pu võ nu ɛs pe ˈre | le vwa ra ri ˈve | sɛ ta ˈne? |
le vɛ rõ ˈnu | a vɑ̃ lœr de ˈpaːr | pur la me ˈrik? |
õ til prɔ fi ˈte | dlœr se ˈʒuːr | a le trɑ̃ ˈʒe? |
ɛs ki lɛ sa tis ˈfɛ | dla re sɛp sjõ ki la ˈy | dɑ̃ le pe i dy ˈnɔɪr? |

210. Alternative questions:

The intonation of alternative questions may consist of a Rising
group (or Falling-Rising), followed by a Rising-Falling group.[1]

< - - - - - Rising - - - - - >< - Falling- - >

| a le vu a le gliz ka tɔ ˈlik | u prɔ tɛs ˈtɑ̃ːt? |

(or)

vu le vu de gɑ ˈto | u de tar ˈtin? ||
i re vu o bɔr də la ˈmɛːr | u dɑ̃ le ˈzalp? ||
vœl tɛl de ˈroːz | u de zœ ˈjɛ? ||
ɔ re vu õ̃ ˈʃjɛ̃ | u õ̃ ˈʃa? ||
ɛ mə rje vu a vwa ry nɔ ˈrɑ̃ːʒ | u yn ˈpɔm? ||

[1] It may also consist of a simple group, with the highest pitch on the final
syllable of the first question:

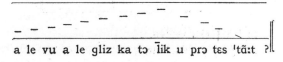

a le vu a le gliz ka tɔ l̄ik u prɔ tɛs ˈtɑ̃ːt ?

bwav til dy ˈvɛ̃ ┃ u dy ˈsiːdr? ‖
prɑ̃ drɔ̃ til de pɔm də tɛr ˈfrit ┃ u dla py ˈre? ‖
mɑ̃ʒ til lœr sa la da vɛk la ˈvjɑ̃ːd ┃ u se pa re ˈmɑ̃? ‖
bwav til lœr te a vɛk dy ˈlɛ ┃ u a vɛk dy si ˈtrɔ̃? ‖
vɔ̃ til ʒwe o tɛ nis mɛ̃t ˈnɑ̃ ┃ u ply ˈtaːr? ‖

211.   Commands.

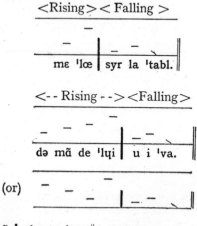

<Rising> <Falling>

ni va ˈpɑ ┃ sɑ̃ ˈmwa.

(or)

va ʃɛr ˈʃe ┃ tɔ̃ ˈliːvr. ‖
fɛt lɥi ˈfɛːr ┃ sed ˈvwaːr. ‖
nə lɥi dit ˈpɑ ┃ skə ˈsɛ. ‖
dɔn lə ˈlɥi ┃ tut ˈsɥit. ‖
va le ˈvwaːr ┃ bjɛ̃ ˈto. ‖
a pɔr te ˈlɛ ┃ sə ˈswaːr. ‖

<Rising> < Falling >

mɛ ˈlœ ┃ syr la ˈtabl.

<-- Rising --> <Falling>

də mɑ̃ de ˈlɥi ┃ u i ˈva.

(or)

fɛ ˈzɑ̃ ┃ skə ty ˈvø. ‖
rɑ̃ ˈʒe ┃ vo za ˈfɛːr. ‖

di 'mwa ❘ u i 'lɛ. ‖
fɛt 'lœ ❘ kɔ mil 'fo. ‖
va le 'vwaːr ❘ dɛ tõr 'tuːr. ‖
na le 'pɑ ❘ a vɛ 'kɛl. ‖
ni va 'pɑ ❘ a vã sə 'swaːr. ‖
də mãd 'lɥi ❘ u i 'va. ‖
rə mɛ te le 'liːvr ❘ a lœr 'plas. ‖
dɔ ne 'lœːr ❘ skil də 'mãːd. ‖

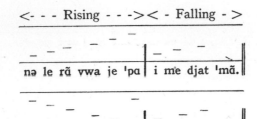

<- - - Rising - - ->< - Falling - >

nə le rã vwa je 'pɑ │ i me djat 'mã.

(or)

mɛ te de 'flœːr ❘ dã tut le 'pjɛs. ‖
fi ni tõ tra 'vaɪj ❘ a vãd sɔr 'tiːr. ‖
fɛrm laf 'nɛɪtr ❘ a vãd par 'tiːr. ‖
fɛ 'lœ ❘ kɔm ty vu 'dra. ‖
nə lɥi ra kõ te 'rjɛ̃ ❘ dsɛ ta fɛr 'la. ‖
kɔ mã de 'lɛ ❘ a vã sə 'swaːr. ‖

< - Rising - > <- - - Falling - ->

di a mã 'mã │ skə ty ã na 'fɛ.

(or)

ra kõ te 'nu ❘ skə vu za ve 'vy. ‖
a tã 'de ❘ knu swa jõ rã 'tre. ‖
nə lœr dit 'pɑ ❘ knu nã vu lõ 'pɑ. ‖
dɔ ne 'mwa ❘ ski ja dã vɔt 'sak. ‖

e ku ˈte | ski la a vu ˈdiːr. ‖
dit mwa pur ˈkwa | vu zi ɛt za ˈle. ‖
nə lɥi mɔ̃ tre ˈpɑ | skəʒ vu ze dɔ ˈne. ‖
a pɔr te le ˈliːvr | ki sɔ̃ syr la ˈtabl. ‖
nu bli je pɑd lœ re ˈkriːr | pɑ̃ dɑ̃ vɔ trap ˈsɑ̃ːs. ‖
nə lɥi di ˈpɑ | skə ty a dɑ̃ ta ˈpɔʃ. ‖
də mɑ̃ de lɥi œ̃ ˈpø | si la lɛ̃ tɑ̃ sjɔ̃d par ˈtiːr. ‖
nə le rɑ̃ vwa je ˈpɑ | a vɑ̃ dnu le za vwar mɔ̃ ˈtre. ‖

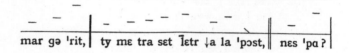

ni a le ˈpɑ | a vɑ̃ da vwar də mɑ̃ ˈde | si ɔ̃ pø vur sə   ˈvwaːr.‖

or

fɛt vɔt re kla mɑ ˈsjɔ̃ | a vɑ̃ la fɛr mə ˈtyːr | dy by ˈro. ‖
nə le lœr rɑ̃ de ˈpɑ | a vɑ̃ dsa ˈvwaːr | skə nu zɑ̃ pɑ̃ ˈsɔ̃. ‖
a le ˈzi | si vu vu ˈle | lœr fɛr ple ˈziːr. ‖
nə prə ne pɑd de si ˈzjɔ̃ | a vɑ̃ dnu za vwar kɔ my ni ˈke | lœr re ˈpɔ̃ːs.‖
nə vɑ̃ de la me ˈzɔ̃ | kə lɔrs kə vu sre ˈsyːr | də pu vwa raʃ te sɛl ˈsi. ‖
de po ze vɔ trə ˈplɛ̃ːt | a vɑ̃l kɔ mɑ̃s ˈmɑ̃ | dy mwɑ prɔ ˈʃɛ̃. ‖
nə par te a vɛk la vwa ˈtyːr | kə lɔrs kɛ lɔ ra e te swa ɲøːz ˈmɑ̃ | re pa ˈre. ‖
vœ je vu zɑ̃ nɔ ky ˈpe | a vɑ̃ nɔ trə rə ˈtuːr | ɑ̃ nɑ̃ glə ˈtɛːr. ‖
fi ni se skə vu ˈfɛt | a vɑ̃ dɑ̃ trə ˈprɑ̃ːd (r) | skɔ̃ vjɛ̃ dvu kɔ mɑ̃ ˈde. ‖

Commands having the grammatical form of statements.

212. In giving orders to servants, the Future instead of the Imperative, is often used. Such orders still demand obedience, but, unless pronounced with a very authoritative voice, give the impression that the speaker is not so much imposing her will on the servant as attempting to make the servant's wishes coincide with her own. This impression is further strengthened when the name of the servant is prefixed, and *n'est-ce pas* added :

mar gə ˈrit, | ty mɛ tra sɛt lɛtr ↓a la ˈpɔst, ‖ nɛs ˈpɑ ?

or

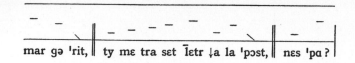

mar gə 'rit, ‖ ty mε tra sεt lɛtr ↓a la 'pɔst, ‖ nɛs 'pɑ?

This form is also often used, as in English, to confirm an order already given, or to remind one of a wish already expressed.

213. Examples of Commands having the grammatical form of Statements:

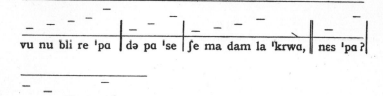

vu nu bli re 'pɑ | də pɑ 'se | ʃe ma dam la 'krwɑ, ‖ nɛs 'pɑ?

or

vu nu bli re 'pɑ | etc.

vun re põdre 'pɑ | ʒi ɔ̃ 'sɔn. ‖
vu ni re 'pɑ | a vɑ̃ nɔt de 'paːr. ‖
ty nɑ̃ di ra 'rjɛ̃ | a vɑ̃ nɔ tra ri 've. ‖
vu lœr di 're | knu rɑ̃ trə rɔ̃ sə 'swaːr. ‖
vu pre par rel di 'ne | pur sε 'tœːr. ‖
vu pas 're | ʃel tɛ̃ ty 'rje. ‖
vu zi re prɑ̃d le gɑ 'to | ʃe dy 'bwɑ. ‖
ty fra ted 'vwaːr | a vɑ̃d sɔr 'tiːr. ‖
ty i ra 'vwaːr | si ɔ̃ na bzwɛ̃d 'twa. ‖
vu dmɑ̃ dre o flœ 'rist | dɑ̃ vwa je le 'roːz. ‖

CHAPTER XV

SENTENCES WITH TWO OR MORE INTONATION GROUPS
(WITH BREAKS)

Examples :

214.   Assertions.

< - - - - - Rising - - - - - > < - - Falling - ->

‾   ‾   ‾   ‾   ‾   ‾

sɛ tœ̃ nɑ̃ drwɑ ↓trɛ fre kɑ̃ ˈte | par le ze trɑ̃ ˈʒe.‖

nu le za vɔ̃ rɑ̃ kɔ̃ tre ↓la ne dɛr ˈnjɛːr | o mwɑd ʒɥi ˈjɛ. ‖
in tjɛn pɑ ar və niːr ↓sɛ ta ne ˈsi | ɑ̃ nɑ̃ glə ˈtɛːr. ‖
i vɔ drɛ mjø ↓sɑ̃ nɔ ky ˈpe | a vɑ̃ le ˈte. ‖
nu pre fe rɔ̃ ↓a le le ˈvwaːr | sɛt sə ˈmɛn. ‖
nu zɛs pe rɔ̃ bjɛ̃ ↓a le o te ˈɑːt | sɛt sə ˈmɛn. ‖
nu nɛ mɔ̃ pɑ bo ku ↓vwa ja ˈʒe | pɑ̃ dɑ̃ li ˈvɛːr. ‖
nu le za vɔ̃ vy ↓lo trə ˈswaːr | o kɔ̃ ˈsɛːr. ‖
sɛ tar tik ↓vjɛ̃d pa ˈrɛt | dɑ̃l ʒur ˈnal. ‖
lə pɛr mi ↓sra de li ˈvre | sə mwɑ ˈsi. ‖

< - - - - - - - - Rising - - - - - - -> < - Falling - ->

‾   ‾   ‾   ‾   ‾   ‾   ‾

nun sa vɔ̃ pɑ zɑ̃ kɔːr ↓si nu zi rɔ̃ ↓sɛ ta ˈne | u la ne prɔ ˈʃɛn.‖

se pa rɑ̃ ↓lɥi ɔ̃ pɛr mi ↓drɛs te ɑ̃ ˈfrɑ̃ːs | pɑ̃ dɑ̃ kɛl kə ˈmwɑ. ‖
i ˈsrɛ pre fe raːbl ↓də rə mɛt sə vwa jaːʒ ↓ɑ̃ na me ˈrik | ʒys ka la ne
    prɔ ˈʃɛn. ‖
le mar ʃɑ̃ diːz ↓sə rɔ̃ li vre ↓a dɔ mi ˈsil | kɔ̃ trə rɑ̃ bur sə ˈmɑ̃. ‖
nu nu zɛs ta lɔ̃ ↓ʒe ne ral mɑ̃ ↓a la kɑ̃ ˈpaɲ | pɑ̃ dɑ̃ le ˈte. ‖
nu frɔ̃ se za ʃa ↓kɑ̃ nu rɑ̃ trə rɔ̃ ↓a pa'ri | ɑ̃ nɔk ˈtɔbr. ‖

< - - - - - - - Rising - - - - - - - > < - Falling ->

la mɑ̃ dje ↓e lɔ li ˈvje | pus trɛ ˈbjɛ̃ | dɑ̃s pe i ˈla.

la kyl tyːr ↓də la ˈviɲ | ɛ la sœl rə ˈsurs | de za bi ˈtɑ̃. ‖
la pɛːʃ ↓e la ˈʃas | sɔ̃ le sœl zɔ ky pɑ ˈsjɔ̃ | de zɛ̃ di ˈʒɛn. ‖
le zɑ̃ fɑ̃ ↓sɔ̃ ta le ɑ̃ va ˈkɑ̃ːs | o bɔr də la ˈmɛːr | pɑ̃ dɑ̃l mwɑd ʒɥi ˈjɛ.‖
nu le za võ rɑ̃ kɔ̃ tre ↓la ne dɛr ˈnjɛːr | pɑ̃ dɑ̃ lo ˈtɔn | ɑ̃ na me ˈrik.‖

<- - - - - - Rising - - - - - - > < - - - - Falling - - - - >

nu zi rɔ̃ pɑ se li vɛːr ↓ɑ̃ nɛs ˈpaɲ | si no za ˈfɛːr | mar ʃə ˈbjɛ̃. ‖

nu za vjɔ̃ zɛs pe re ↓pu vwar par ˈtiːr | a vɑ̃ la ˈfɛ̃ | de va ˈkɑ̃ːs.‖
i vɔ dre mjø ↓fɛr ˈsa | pɑ̃ dɑ̃ la prə mjɛr parˈti | dy tri ˈmɛstr. ‖
le zɑ̃ fɑ̃ ↓sɔ̃ par ˈti | də pɥi la dɛr njɛr sə ˈmɛn | də sɛp ˈtɑ̃ːbr. ‖

< - - - - - - Rising - - - - - - > < - - - - Falling - - - ->

ʒɛs pɛr bjɛ̃ ↓pɑ se yn swa re ↓a vɛ ˈkø |a vɑ̃d par ˈtiːr| pur la me ˈrik. ‖

il zɔ̃ tɑ̃ trə pri ↓œ̃ tra vaːj ↓ɛ̃ te rɛ ˈsɑ̃ | syr la ˈlɑ̃ːg | de zɛ̃ di ˈʒɛn. ‖
i lja vɛ ↓də vjø myr rɥi ne ↓tɔ̃ bɑ̃ tɑ̃ ˈpudr | e sɛr vɑ̃d rə ˈtrɛt | o le ˈzaːr. ‖
la lɛt ↓kə nu za tɑ̃ djɔ̃ ↓də pɥi si lɔ̃ ˈtɑ̃ | vjɛ̃ tɑ̃ ˈfɛ̃ | da ri ˈve. ‖
nu zɛ mə rjɔ̃ ↓fɛ rœ̃ vwa jaːʒ ↓ɑ̃ nal ʒe ˈri | a vɑ̃ la ˈfɛ̃ | dla ne prɔ ˈʃɛn.‖
le tra vo ↓ki ɔ̃ te te ɑ̃ trə pri ↓i lja dø ˈzɑ̃ | nə sɔ̃ pɑ zɑ̃ ˈkɔːr | tɛr mi ˈne.‖

215. Longer examples:

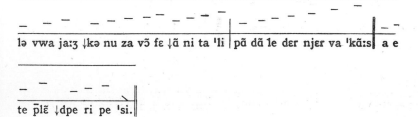

lə vwa jaːʒ ↓kə nu za võ fɛ ↓ɑ̃ ni ta ˈli |pɑ̃ dɑ̃ le dɛr njɛr va ˈkɑ̃ːs| a e

te p̄lɛ̃ ↓dpe ri pe ˈsi.‖

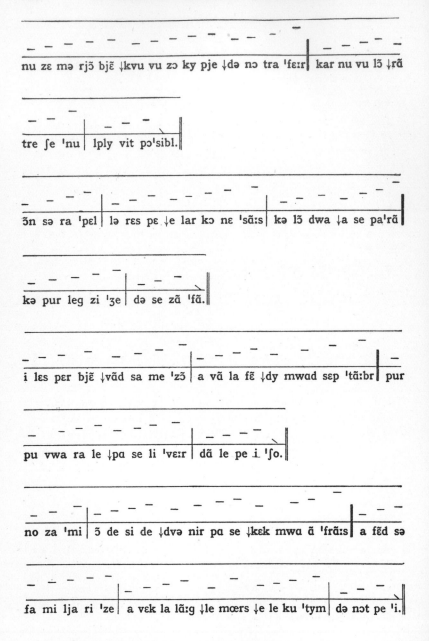

nu zɛ mə rjɔ̃ bjɛ̃ ↓kvu vu zɔ ky pje ↓də nɔ tra ¹fɛːr║ kar nu vu lɔ̃ ↓rɑ̃

tre ʃe ¹nu │ lply vit pɔ¹sibl.║

ɔ̃n sə ra ¹pɛl │ lə rɛs pɛ ↓e lar kɔ nɛ ¹sɑ̃ːs │ kə lɔ̃ dwa ↓a se pa¹rɑ̃

kə pur leg zi ¹ʒe │ də se zɑ̃ ¹fɑ̃.║

i lɛs pɛr bjɛ̃ ↓vɑ̃d sa me ¹zɔ̃ │ a vɑ̃ la fɛ̃ ↓dy mwad sɛp ¹tɑ̃ːbr║ pur

pu vwa ra le ↓pɑ se li ¹vɛːr │ dɑ̃ le pe i ¹ʃo.║

no za ¹mi │ ɔ̃ de si de ↓dvə nir pɑ se ↓kɛk mwa ɑ̃ ¹frɑ̃ːs║ a fɛ̃d sə

fa mi lja ri ¹ze │ a vɛk la lɑ̃ːg ↓le mœrs ↓e le ku ¹tym │ də nɔt pe ¹i.║

tə ny o ku rã ↓də vɔ trap sã:s ↓par vɔ trə ʃɛf ↓də by 'ro,| e ɛ̃ kjɛ

↓pur vɔt sã 'te | ʒe ã vwa je si ʃwal ↓met sɛ̃ ↓dy mi nis 'tɛ:r| prã

drə ʃe 'vu | dvo nu 'vɛl.

Questions.

216. Beginning with an interrogative word.

< - - - - - - - Rising - - - - - - - >   <Falling>

pur kwa a til bə zwɛ̃ ↓dy rã sɛɲ 'mã | o ʒur 'dɥi?

u vø til ↓kə nu pɑ sjɔ̃ no va 'kɑ:s | sɛ ta 'ne? ||
kɛl sɔ̃ le zu vra:ʒ ↓ɛ̃ te rɛ 'sã | də la 'ne? ||
u le zã fã ↓sɔ̃ ti la 'le | jɛr ma 'tɛ̃? ||
də kwa sa ʒi til ↓dã lis 'twa:r | kɛl vɔ̃ 'li:r? ||
kɛl sɔ̃ le pe i ↓kə vu kɔ nɛ 'se | ã nœ 'rɔp? ||

kə pã se vu ↓dyn prɔm 'nad | kə nu fə 'rjɔ̃ | ã no tɔ mɔ 'bil?

u vu le vu ↓knu le mɛ 'tjɔ̃ | ã na tã dã ↓kvu zã prə 'nje | la rɛs
   pɔ̃ sa bi li 'te? ||
kə fɔ̃ til ↓ʒe ne ral mã ↓də lœr 'ʃjɛ̃ | kã til 'part | ã va 'kɑ:s? ||
pur kwa ɛt vu za le ↓ã nɛs paɲ ↓la ne dɛr 'njɛ:r | o ljø da le ↓ã ni
   ta 'li | kɔm vu za ve la bi'tyd | dəl 'fɛ:r? ||

217.   Capable of being answered by "Yes" or "No."

< - - - - - - - - Rising - - - - - - - - >

a ve vu lɛ̃ tã sjɔ̃ ↓di a 'le | pã dã le 'te ?|

vu le vu ↓knu zi mɛ 'tjɔ̃ | œ̃ ry bã 'ruːʒ ? |
pu rɔ̃ nu gar niːr ↓sə ʃa po 'la | a vɛ kœ̃ ry bã 'vɛir ? |
i re vu fɛir ↓tut se vi zit 'la | a vã vɔt de 'pair ? |
krwɑ je vu ↓ksə vwa jaiʒ ↓swa tɛ̃ te rɛ 'sã | ã ni 'vɛir ? |

<- - - - - - - - - - - Rising - - - - - - - - - - - ->

sa ve vu ↓skil sɔ̃ dəv 'ny | də pɥi lœr rə 'tuir| da me 'rik ?|

nə pu rje vu pɑ ↓za le le 'vwair | a vã la 'fɛ̃ | dsɛ ta ne 'si ? |
sa ve vu ↓si vu pu re a le o te 'ait | pã dã la dɛr njɛr sə 'mɛn |
    də nɔ 'vãibr ? |
kɔ nɛ se vu kɛl kœ̃ ↓ki vu drɛ bjɛ̃ ↓sɔ ky ped 'sa | pã dã vɔt se
    'ʒuir | ã nos tra 'li ? |
pu rje vu ↓nu zɛ de ↓a fi nir sə tra 'vair | a vã la 'fɛ̃ | dy mwad
    sɛp 'tãibr ? |
krwɑ je vu ↓kil swa pɔ 'sibl | dã trə 'prãid | sə tra vaj 'la ? |

218.   Commands.

< - - - - Rising - - - - > < - Falling - >

nə lɛ se pɑ rã tre ↓sə 'ʃjɛ̃| dã la me 'zɔ̃.‖

mɔ̃ tre nu ↓ski jad ply zɛ̃ te rɛ 'sã | dã la 'vil. ‖
rã de mwa ↓sə 'liivr | a vã dmɛ̃ ma 'tɛ̃. ‖
nu bli je pɑ ↓da le pɔr te le 'lɛtr | a la 'pɔst. ‖

nu bli je pɑ ↓dfɛr no kɔ mi 'sjɔ̃ | a vɑ̃ mi 'di. ‖
a le nu ʃɛr ʃe ↓de bi 'jɛ | pur sə 'swaːr. ‖
fɛt nu vwaːr ↓skə vu za 've | dɑ̃ sɛt ʒɔ li 'bwat. ‖
a le vwaːr ↓o kwɛ̃d la 'ry | si ɔ̃ le za pɛr 'swa. ‖
de sɑ̃ de ↓no ba 'gaːʒ | i me djat 'mɑ̃. ‖

< - - - - Rising - - - -> < - - - - - - - Falling - - - - - - ->

də mɑ̃ de lɥi ↓ski lɑ̃ 'pɑːs | a vɑ̃d prɑ̃ dryn de si 'zjɔ̃ | de fi ni 'tiːv.‖

nə vu zɔ ky pe pɑ ↓dsɛ ta fɛr 'la | a vɑ̃ da vwar rə 'sy | dno nu 'vɛl. ‖
a le vwaːr ↓si le kɔ 'li | ɔ̃ te te li 'vre | jɛ ra prɛ mi 'di. |
dit lœːr ↓kə ʒɛm rɛ le 'vwaːr | a vɑ̃ lœr de 'paːr | pur lir 'lɑ̃ːd. ‖

< - - - - Rising - - - -> < - - - - - - - Falling - - - - - - ->

a le nu ʃɛr ʃe ↓de bi 'jɛ | pur lar pre zɑ̃ ta ˉsjɔ̃d ↓də mɛ̃ 'swaːr.‖

mɔ̃ tre nu ↓de li vrɛ̃ te rɛ 'sɑ̃ | pur de zɑ̃ ˉfɑ̃d ↓sɛ̃ ka si 'zɑ̃. ‖
mɔ̃ tre nu ↓de mɑ̃ 'to | pur yn ʃi jɛt ↓də ɥi 'tɑ̃. ‖
ɑ̃ pɔr te ↓tu se vjø 'mœbl | ʃe zɔ̃ɛ mar ˉʃɑ̃ ↓dɑ̃ ti ki 'te. ‖
a pɔr te nu ↓ɔ̃ɛ ʃwad ta 'pi | a vɑ̃l kɔ mɑ̃s ˉmɑ̃ ↓dla smɛn prɔ 'ʃɛn. ‖
de sɑ̃ de ↓no ba 'gaːʒ | i me djat ˉmɑ̃ ↓a prɛl de ʒœ 'ne. ‖

< - - - - - - - - - - - - - - - Rising - - - - - - - - - - - - - >

a le vwaːr ↓si la twa 'lɛt | kə ma da ↓ma kɔ mɑ̃ de ↓lo trə 'ʒuːr‖

< - - - - Falling - - - >

.sra li ˉvre ↓a vɑ̃ di 'mɑ̃ːʃ. ‖

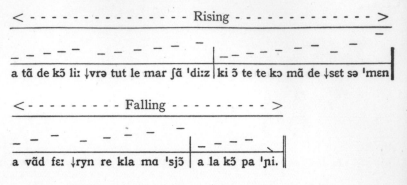

< - - - - - - - - - - - - - - Rising - - - - - - - - - - - - - >

a tã de kɔ̃ liː ↓vrə tut le mar ʃã 'diːz │ ki ɔ̃ te te kɔ mã de ↓sɛt sə 'mɛn

< - - - - - - - - - Falling - - - - - - - - - >

a vãd fɛː ↓ryn re kla mɑ 'sjɔ̃ │ a la kɔ̃ pa 'ɲi. ‖

219. Commands having the grammatical form of statements.

< - Rising - >< - - - Falling - - >

vu zi re 'vwaːr │ si ma d̄a ↓mɛ rã 'tre. ‖

vu di re a la fam də 'ʃãːbr │ dəv n̄iːr ↓mə par 'le. ‖
vu pre vjẽ drel ʃo 'fœːr │ kə nu la tã d̄rɔ̃ ↓a dø 'zœːr. ‖
vu pre par rel de ʒœ 'ne │ pu ry n̄œːr ↓mwẽ vẽt 'sẽːk. ‖
vu vjẽ dre nu rã kɔ̃ tre ↓a la 'gɑːr │ o t̄rẽ ↓dy nœr ka 'rãːt. ‖

Chapter XVI

INTONATION OF UNEMPHATIC CONNECTED TEXTS

Intonation Group-marks.

220. The following group-marks have already been used with little explanation. They are here given together, and their use explained :

No. 1 is placed at the end of all forms of the Rising-Falling and of the Falling intonation groups. The student should know from the type of sentence whether the Rising-Falling or the Falling intonation is to be used.

No. 2 marks the end of all Rising intonation groups other than those non-final groups (see under No. 3 below) which rise to the highest pitch in a Rising-Falling group.

No. 3 marks the end of a non-final intonation group terminating at the highest point to which the intonation rises. I.e. it separates the groups (or group) with a rising trend from the groups (or group) with a falling trend.

221. The use of the above marks, and also of ¯,[1] ↓,[2] and ↑,[3] which have already been explained, will help the student in his reading of the connected texts which follow, especially of those under § 224, where no pitch-notation is given.

222. We have seen that in a *sentence* which has a series of intonation groups there is a strong tendency to rise to a certain pitch and fall away from it, so that the intonation of each group

[1] See § 68 and footnote.   [2] See § 128.   [3] See § 135.

rises to a different height.   Refer, for example, to the first sentence
in Text No. 6, under § 223, which has this intonation :

The same tendency to avoid striking the same top note is noticeable
also in a *paragraph* where a *number* of series of intonation groups
occurs.   The speaker generally works up the intonation to a climax
and then falls away from it, so that the top note of each *series* of
groups is different.   Refer again to Text No. 6, and you will see
that there are three *series* of related groups, each series terminated
by the mark ‖.   The highest note of each series is followed by the
mark |.   Each of those highest notes is different, the third one
having the highest pitch :

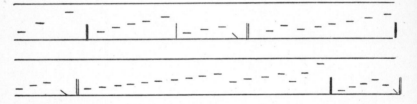

It is difficult to give rules about these relative heights in a paragraph
or to use special marks to indicate them.

223.   TEXTS IN PHONETIC TRANSCRIPTION WITH PITCH NOTATION.

1.

a la fa ˈsɔ̃ │dɔ̃ vu parˈle │ʒə vwa ˈbjɛ̃ │kvu nɛt pɑ kɔ̃ ˈtɑ̃. ‖

2.

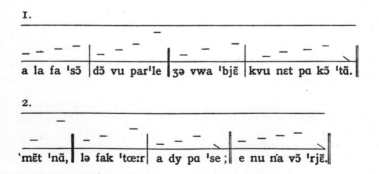

ˈmɛ̃t ˈnɑ̃, ║ lə fak ˈtœːr │ a dy pɑ ˈse ;║ e nu n̈a vɔ̃ ˈrjɛ̃.‖

3.

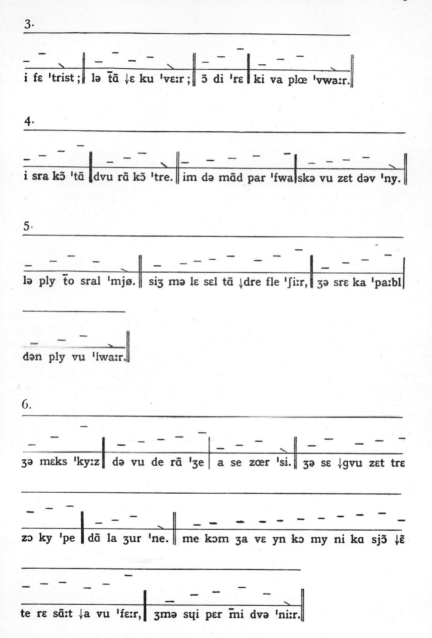

i fɛ 'trist; lə tã ↓ɛ ku 'vɛːr; ɔ̃ di 'rɛ ki va plœ 'vwaːr.

4.

i sra kɔ̃ 'tã dvu rã kɔ̃ 'tre. im də mãd par 'fwa skə vu zɛt dəv 'ny.

5.

lə ply to sral 'mjø. siʒ mə lɛ sɛl tã ↓dre fle 'ʃiːr, ʒə srɛ ka 'paːbl

dən ply vu 'lwaːr.

6.

ʒə mɛks 'kyːz də vu de rã 'ʒe a se zœr 'si. ʒə sɛ ↓gvu zɛt trɛ

zɔ ky 'pe dã la ʒur 'ne. me kɔm ʒa vɛ yn kɔ my ni ka sjɔ̃ ↓ɛ̃

te rɛ sã:t ↓a vu 'fɛːr, ʒmə sɥi pɛr mi dvə 'niːr.

7.

—kɛ lɛl prɔ gram pur sɛ ta prɛ mi 'di? də mã da ʃar la sa sœːr,

ã de ʒœ 'nã.

—e 'bjɛ̃, ↓re põ di te lɛn, | nu dvõ ↓a le fɛr vi 'zit | a a 'ni. ‖ ɛl kit

pa 'ri | a prɛd 'mɛ̃ .‖. . i fok vu zi və ɲje o 'si. ‖ ʒe kɔ mã de la

vwa 'tyːr | pur ka t̄rœ red 'mi. ‖ ʒys kə 'la, | vu zɛt 'libr. ‖ —trɛ 'bjɛ̃.‖

Ève Victorieuse (Pierre de Coulevain).
Calmann-Lévy, Editeurs.

8.

ʒmə su 'vjɛ̃ | kõ̃ ma tɛ̃ da vril ↓ud 'mɛ, | mõ pɛːr ↓mə fi mõ te a

vɛk lɥi ↓dã sa vwa 'tyːr | pu ra le ↓a la kã 'paɲ | ʃe ma tãːt plã 'te. ‖

L'Enfant à la Balustrade (René Boylesve).
Calmann-Lévy, Editeurs.

9.

e vi da 'mã | sɛ tɔ 'tɛl | nɛ p̄ɑ ↓zœ̃ pa 'lɛ :‖ le ʃãː ↓brə ni õ rjɛ̃ dɛks

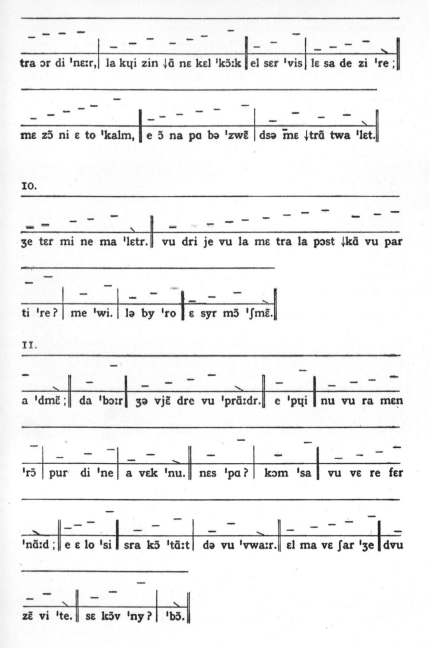

tra ɔr di 'nɛːr, | la kɥi zin ↓ɑ̃ nɛ kɛl 'kɔ̃ːk | el sɛr 'vis | lɛ sa de zi 're ;

mɛ zɔ̃ ni ɛ to 'kalm, | e ɔ̃ na pɑ bə 'zwɛ̃ | dsə m̄ɛ ↓trɑ̃ twa 'lɛt.

10.

ʒe tɛr mi ne ma 'lɛtr. | vu dri je vu la mɛ tra la pɔst ↓kɑ̃ vu par

ti 're? | me 'wi. | lə by 'ro | ɛ syr mɔ̃ 'ʃmɛ̃.

11.

a 'dmɛ̃ ; | da 'bɔːr | ʒə vjɛ̃ dre vu 'prɑ̃ːdr. | e 'pɥi | nu vu ra mɛn

'rɔ̃ | pur di 'ne | a vɛk 'nu. | nɛs 'pɑ ? | kɔm 'sa | vu vɛ re fɛr

'nɑ̃ːd ; | e ɛ lo 'si | sra kɔ̃ 'tɑ̃ːt | də vu 'vwaːr. | ɛl ma vɛ ʃar 'ʒe | dvu

zɛ̃ vi 'te. | sɛ kɔ̃v 'ny ? | 'bɔ̃.

12.

le fur mi ↓nɔ̃ pɑd grə 'nje ‖ u ɛl za mas ↓pɑ̃ dɑ̃ le 'te │ de prɔ vi

'zjɔ̃ │ pur li 'vɛːr. ‖ la fɔ̃ 'tɛn la 'di, ‖ me la fɔ̃ 'tɛn │ sɛ trɔ̃ 'pe. ‖ la

fɔ̃ tɛn ↓a vɛd lɛs pri ↓e dla bɔ nɔ 'mi │ me il nə kɔ nɛ sɛ pɑ dy tu

↓le zak 'tœːr │ kil mɛ t̄ɛ tɑ̃ 'sɛn. ‖ ɔ̃ kɔr 'bo │ nə pø tɑ̃ pɔr t̄e ↓ɔ̃

frɔ 'maːʒ ‖ e œ̃r 'naːr ‖ nə lə lɥi dis py trɛ 'pɑ. ‖ la fɔ̃ tɛn rə 'sɑ̃ːbl,

su sə ra 'pɔːr, │ o tra dyk tœːr ↓ki sav trɛ bjɛ̃ lə la 'tɛ̃, ‖ e ki tra

dɥiːz ↓dɛk sɛ lɑ̃ la 'tɛ̃ │ ɑ̃ mɔ v̄ɛ frɑ̃ 'sɛ.‖

Voyage Autour de Mon Jardin (Alphonse Karr).
Calmann-Lévy, Editeurs.

13.

ɔ̃ sra pə tɛː ↓trə syr 'pri ‖ ka si 'zɑ̃ │ ʒy sy ni de ↓si pø eg ʒak tə dy 'mɔːd. ‖ me zil fo kɔ̃ si de 're │ kə ʒe tɛ za pɛn ↓sɔr tid pa 'ri │ ul

dɔk tœːr no 'zjɛːr, │ mɔ̃ 'pɛːr, │ e tɛ rət 'ny │ tut la 'ne. ‖ ʒa vɛ 'fɛ,

i lɛ 'vrɛ, │ dø zu trwɑ pti vwa 'jaːʒ │ ɑ̃ ʃmɛ̃t 'fɛːr, ‖ me ʒnɑ̃ na vɛ

ti re ↓o kœ̃ prɔ 'fi ‖ o pwɛ̃d v̄y ↓dla ʒe ɔ gra 'fi. ‖ se tɛ tyn s̄jɑ̃ːs

↓tre ne gli 'ʒe ɑ̃s tɑ̃ la. ‖ ɔ̃ se tɔn ra o 'si │ kə ʒys ↓dy mɔ̃d mɔ'ral

yn kɔ̃ sɛp sjɔ̃ ↓si pø kɔ̃ 'fɔrm │ a la re a li te de 'ʃɔːz. ‖

Pierre Nozière (Anatole France).
Calmann-Lévy, Paris.

14.

lə s̄waːr tɔ̃'bɛ : ‖ le pe i 'zɑ̃ │ a vɛr gɑ 'ɲe │ la kɑ̃ 'paɲ. ‖ la plas ↓el

kɑr 'fuːr │ e tɛ 'libr. ‖ də 'lwɛ̃, │ nu za pɛr sə vjɔ̃ 'lɔrm, │ lə ma rɔ 'nje, | el klɔʃ tɔ̃ ↓dla me 'zɔ̃, | od sy dla ba lys 'trad | e de grɑ̃d

'pɔrt | a pat də 'biʃ ; ‖ sla fɔr mɛ ↓œ̃ ʒɔ li de 'kɔːr | das pɛ ɑ̃ 'sjɛ̃ | ki

fɛr mɛ ↓la ry mɔ̃ 'tɑ̃ːt | kɔ myn twal də 'fɔ̃.

L'Enfant à la Balustrade (René Boylesve).
Calmann-Lévy, Paris.

15.

le pal mje ↓na ʒi tɛ ply ↓od sy de ʒar 'dɛ̃ | lœr bɛl zɛ grɛt ↓fre

mi 'sɑ̃ːt | lœr 'palm | ɑ̃ fɛ sod 'saːbr ; ‖ a lœr 'plas, | yn ve ʒe tɑ sjɔ̃

ba ↓se 'grɛːl | se tɑ̃ 'dɛ | lə lɔ̃ dy rɥi 'so ; ‖ e le sœl zar ↓brə ki ʒa

ji sɛ ↓dse vɛr 'dyːr, | o rɑ dy 'sɔl, | se tɛ də mɛ̃ːs ↓pœ pli 'je | ki pa

rɛ sɛ ply ze 'tik | dɑ̃ se vas tə ʃɑ̃ ↓də ly 'mjɛːr. ‖

La Fête Arabe (Jérôme et Jean Tharaud).

224. Texts in Ordinary Orthography. Intonation suggested by marks.

1.

— Combien de personnes à dîner mercre'di, mère? ‖
— Je n'ai pas encore fait le 'compte. ‖ Il y a les Cler'mont. . . . |
— Ça fait 'trois. ‖
— Les Huve'lin. . . . |
— 'Sept. ‖
— Monsieur Com'pard. . . |
— 'Huit. ‖
— Madame de Rovel ↓et Pau'line . . . | ·
— 'Dix. ‖
— C'est 'tout, je crois. ‖
— Et sept ↓que nous sommes ici, | ça fait dix-'sept. ‖ On peut
être 'vingt. ‖ Voulez-vous inviter ↓les Du'pont, mère? |
— Je ne demande pas 'mieux. ‖ Je vais leur é'crire. ‖
— Ce n'est pas la 'peine. ‖ Je vais les voir ↓à Neu'illy |cet après-
mi'di, | et je les invi'terai. ‖

2.

L'année ↓se trouvait ↓gibo'yeuse, | et nous passions ↓la plupart
↓de nos après-mi'di | à la 'chasse ; ‖ ou 'bien | nous faisions ↓dans
ces campagnes 'nues | une promenade ra'pide | sans autre but ↓le
plus sou'vent | que de côto‾yer la 'mer. ‖

Dominique (Eugène Fromentin).

3.

Il considère ↓la composition d'une toi'lette, | le choix des
'nuances, | les proportions d'un ha'bit, | comme une chose ↓très
sé'rieuse | dans la conduite géné'rale | d'un ‾homme ↓de bon 'ton. ‖

Dominique.

4.

Au de'là | commençait la grande 'mer, | frémissante et 'grise |
dont l'extrémi'té | se per'dait | dans les 'brumes. ‖

Dominique.

5.

Le bouleau ↓élance sa tige 'blanche | sati'née | sans 'nœuds | à
une grande hau'teur, | et livre au 'vent | sur des branches ↓d'une

K

extrême fi'nesse, | son feuillage lé'ger | qui ‾trem↓ble au plus léger 'souffle. ‖

Voyage Autour de Mon Jardin (A. Karr).

Calmann-Lévy, Paris.

6.

Pendant long'temps | le tabac a fleu'ri | solitaire ↓et igno'ré | dans quelques ‾coins ↓de l'Amé'rique. ‖ Les sauvages ↓auxquels nous avons donné ↓de l'eau-de-'vie | nous ont donné en échange ↓le ta'bac | dont la fumée ↓les eni'vrait | dans les ‾grandes ↓circons'tances. ‖ C'est par cet aimable échange ↓de poi'sons | qu'ont commencé les rela'tions | entre les deux 'mondes. ‖

Voyage Autour de Mon Jardin (A. Karr).

Calmann-Lévy, Paris.

7.

C'est à ce mo'ment | que j'en'trai. . . . ‖ La petite ↓pousse un 'cri, | le gros livre 'tombe, | les canaris, ↓les mouches ↓se ré'veillent, | la pendule 'sonne, | le vieux ↓se dresse en sursaut, ↓tout effa'ré,[1] | et moi-même, ↓un peu trou'blé, | je m'a'rrête | sur le 'seuil. ‖

Lettres de Mon Moulin (A. Daudet).

8.

Dans le calme ↓et le demi-jour ↓d'une petite 'chambre, | un bon vieux ↓à pommettes 'roses, | ridé ↓jusqu'au bout des 'doigts, | dormait ↓au fond d'un fau'teuil, | la bouche ou'verte, | les ‾mains sur ses ge'noux. ‖

Lettres de Mon Moulin (A. Daudet).

9.

On apercevait ↓une foule de petites lumières ↓qui cligno'taient, | a'llaient, | ve'naient, | s'agitaient ↓à toutes les fe'nêtres, | et ressem'blaient, | sur le fond som↓bre du bâti'ment, | aux étin'celles | courant dans les cen↓dres de pa‾pier brûlé. ‖

Lettres de Mon Moulin (A. Daudet).

10.

L'animal bourgeois ↓par exce'llence | est la four'mi : ‖ 'sèche,| dis'crète, | pru'dente, | ac'tive, | ména'gère, | qui se re'mue, | 'trotte, |

---

[1] The last note of each intonation group between *La petite* . . . and . . . *tout effaré* could be the same, and thus suggest the enumeration of a number of happenings. The heavy upright line is placed only after *effaré* which terminates the last group in the rising part of the whole sentence : *La petite. . . sur le seuil.* (See § 165.)

'range, | a'masse, | et cherche encore ↓sans autre but ↓qu'ama'sser, |
sans autre plai‐sir qu' a'gir ; ‖ d'un esprit 'net, | ferme ↓et pra'tique, |
qui raisonne ↓avec autant de précision ↓qu'il cal'cule, | railleur
↓comme un homme d'a'ffaires, | inci‐sif ↓comme un avo'cat. ‖

La Fontaine et ses Fables (H. Taine).
Librairie Hachette, Éditeur.

11.

Un théâtre an'glais | vient de pren↓dre une initia'tive | qui a
soulevé ↓un vif inté'rêt | parmi les specta'teurs | et les specta'trices |
. . . de Pa'ris. ‖ Cet établisse'ment, | qui vient de renouveler ↓sa
décoration inté'rieure, | offre désormais ↓à sa clien'tèle | des fauteuils
↓dont la cou'leur | n'est ‐plus uni'forme. ‖ Chacun d'eux ↓est
recouvert ↓d'une é'toffe | de ‐teinte ↓diffé'rente, ‖ et lorsqu'on se
pré'sente | au bureau de loca'tion, | on n'a qu'a consulter ↓le plan
multico'lore | affiché ↓près du gui'chet | pour retenir à son 'gré |
un fauteuil 'mauve, | 'vert, | 'gris | ou 'rose. ‖

Tiré de L'Illustration.

12.

Par la 'pluie, | le 'vent, | la 'neige, | la 'grêle, | la cha'leur, | le
'froid, | la tem'pête,[1] | je voyais apparaî↓tre le cu'ré, | sa soutane
retroussée ↓jusqu' aux ge'noux | et son cha‐peau sous le 'bras. ‖
Je ne sais 'si, | de ma 'vie, | je l'en ai ‐vu coi'ffé. ‖ Il avait la manie
de mar'cher | la tête décou'verte, | souriant aux pa'ssants, | aux
oi'seaux, | aux 'arbres, | aux brins 'd'herbe. ‖ Replet et do'du, | il
paraissait rebondir ↓sur la 'terre | qu'il foulait d'un pas a'lerte, | et
à la'quelle | il semblait 'dire ‖ :«Tu es 'bonne, ‖ et je 't'aime!» ‖
Il était content de 'vivre, | content de lui‐'même, | content de
tout le 'monde. ‖ Sa bonne fi'gure, | rose et 'fraîche, | entourée de
cheveux 'blancs, | me rappelait ↓ces roses tar'dives | qui fleurissent
en'core | sous les premières 'neiges. ‖

Mon Oncle et Mon Curé (Jean de la Brète.)
Plon-Nourrit et Cie.

13.

Je reverrai ↓toute ma 'vie | ce long corridor ↓frais et 'calme, | la
muraille ↓peinte en 'rose, | le jardinet ↓qui tremblait au 'fond | à

---

[1] Each intonation group up to this point could rise to the same height.
See § 165.

travers un store ↓de couleur 'claire,[1] | et sur tous les pa'nneaux |
des 'fleurs | et des vio⁻lons fa'nés. ||

Lettres de Mon Moulin (A. Daudet).

14.

J'ai ache'té, | il y a trois 'ans, | un tapis rui'neux | pour le me↓ttre
dans mon cabi⁻net de tra'vail ; || c'est ainsi ↓que j'appelle une
cham↓bre assez bien arran'gée, | où je m'enfer↓me par'fois | pour
ne rien 'faire | et ne pas ⁻ê↓tre interrom'pu. ||

Ce ta'pis | représente des feuillages ↓d'un vert 'sombre | parse⁻més
↓de grandes fleurs 'rouges. ||

'Hier, | mes yeux sont tom'bés | sur mon ta'pis, | et je me suis
aper'çu | que les couleurs ↓en étaient fort pa'ssées, | que le vert
↓en est devenu d'un verdâ↓tre assez 'laid, | et que le rouge ↓est
fa'né | d'une ma⁻nière ↓déplo'rable. ||

Voyage Autour de Mon Jardin (A. Karr).
Calmann-Lévy, Paris.

15.

Ce sont nos en'fants | qui nous rendront la peine ↓et les en'nuis |
que nous avons coû⁻té ↓à nos 'pères. || De 'même, | ne leur demandons
pas ↓la ten'dresse | que nous leur por'tons, || ce n'est pas à nous
↓qu'ils la 'doivent | et qu'ils la ren'dront. || C'est aux en'fants |
qu'ils au⁻ront plus 'tard || et dont ils se plaindront ↓injuste'ment, |
a'lors, | comme nous nous plaignons 'd'eux | et comme nos 'pères |
se sont ⁻plaints de 'nous. ||

Voyage Autour de Mon Jardin (A. Karr).
Calmann-Lévy, Paris.

16.

C'est une petite 'chambre | au cin'quième ; || une de ces
man'sardes | où la pluie tombe 'droite | sur les vitres ↓à tabatière, |
et 'qui | —la nuit venue ↓comme mainte'nant— | semblent se
per↓dre avec les 'toits | dans le 'noir | et dans la ra'fale. || Pour'tant |
la ⁻pièce est 'bonne, || confor'table, || et l'on éprouve ↓en y en'trant |
je ne sais quel sentiment ↓de bien-'être | qu' augmentent encore
↓le bruit du 'vent | et les torrents de 'pluie | ruisse⁻lant ↓aux
gou'ttières. || On se croirait ↓dans un nid bien 'chaud, | tout en
⁻haut ↓d'un grand 'arbre. || Pour le mo'ment, | le nid est 'vide. ||

[1] Each intonation group up to this point could rise to the same height.
See § 165.

Le maître du lo'gis | n'est pas 'là ; ‖ mais on sent ↓qu'il va rentrer
bien'tôt, | et tout ↓chez 'lui[1] | a ⁻l'air de l'a'ttendre. ‖ Sur un bon
feu cou'vert,[2] | une petite marmite ↓bout tranquille'ment | avec
un mur'mure | de satisfac'tion. ‖

Contes du Lundi (A. Daudet).

17.

Malgré le 'vent, | malgré la 'brume, | l'homme ↓suit les 'quais, |
pour a⁻ller ↓à son bu'reau. ‖ Il pourrait ⁻pren↓dre un au↓tre
che'min, ‖ mais la ri'vière | paraît avoir un attrait ↓mystérieux |
pour 'lui. ‖ C'est son plai'sir | de s'en aller ↓le long des para'pets, |
de frôler ↓ces rampes de 'pierre | u'sées | aux ⁻coudes ↓des flâ'neurs. ‖
A cette 'heure, | et par le temps qu'il 'fait, | les flâ⁻neurs sont
'rares. ‖ Pour'tant, | de loin en 'loin, | on rencontre une femme
↓chargée de 'linge | qui se repose ↓contre le para'pet, | ou quelque
pauvre dia↓ble accou'dé, | penché vers 'l'eau | d'un ⁻air d'en'nui. ‖

Chaque 'fois | l'homme se re'tourne, | les regarde ↓curieuse'ment |
et ⁻l'eau ↓après 'eux ; ‖ comme si une pensée in'time | mêlait dans
son es'prit | ces ⁻gens ↓à la ri'vière. ‖

Contes du Lundi (A. Daudet).

---

[1] Better if *tout* were emphasised :

e "tu ʃe 'lɥi.

---

[2] Better if *bon* were emphasised :

sy rɑ̃ "bɔ̃ fø ku 'veːr.

PART II

EMPHATIC INTONATION IN ENGLISH
AND FRENCH

CHAPTER XVII

EMPHASIS OR SPECIAL PROMINENCE: INTENSITY AND CONTRAST

225.   When we emphasise we use various devices, which give very special prominence to certain words or to certain sentences. The kind of device depends on the nature of the special prominence or emphasis which may be of two kinds.

226.   There is the special prominence which amplifies the meaning of words, enabling them to express *to a very great degree* the particular things they imply.   For example, *an enormous improvement* can be said in such a way that the speaker expresses his sense of a very *great degree* of improvement.   The word *blue* may be pronounced so that many degrees of blueness are suggested; *ridiculous* may call up many degrees of absurdity.   A noun like *fog* can be so pronounced that it suggests a very great degree of discomfort; *fire* so that it suggests degrees of horror or comfort.   The meaning of many verbs, e.g. *long, sigh, blaze, run, arrive*, etc., etc., may be intensified if pronounced in a special way.   The effect of words of the type *never, nothing, all, without, full, empty, entirely*, each of which in itself implies the maximum degree of some quality, can be heightened by pronouncing them with a certain kind of emphasis. This emphasis or special prominence by which the meaning of words is intensified may be called *emphasis for intensity.*

227.   Emphasis for intensity is marked ‖ in this book.

228.   Then there is the special prominence a speaker gives to certain words which enables these words to express a *contrast* of some kind, sometimes in the form of an idea which is new or entirely unforeseen, and which therefore forms a contrast to what already exists.[1]   *There's an enormous improvement* may be said with the object, not of showing the great degree of improvement, but of contradicting some such remark as *I see very little improvement* or *There's no improvement at all.*   Or it may be that the speaker is

---

[1] Sometimes it is very difficult to say what the contrast is.

expressing a fact which, judging by his experience, is totally un-
expected. The word *enormous* is then brought into very special
prominence, mainly by the introduction of a change in intonation,
the effect of which is to express a contrast to *very little* or *none at all*.
Such prominence may be called *emphasis for contrast*.

229. Emphasis for contrast is marked thus ".

230. Intensity and contrast concerning degree sometimes
occur in pronouncing the same syllable. The mark " is then used.

231. The two kinds of emphasis and the different ways by which
they are expressed in both English and French will now be dealt
with in detail.

Chapter XVIII

INTENSITY IN ENGLISH

232. The most important thing we do when we show intensity is to increase the amount of energy we use in pronouncing certain words.

233. Increase of effort is manifested in the first place by greater activity in the various parts of the speech mechanism : by greater lung pressure, greater muscular tension, greater jaw movement, the more vigorous working of all the articulating organs; in other words, by *extra stress*, which is not just a question of extra force of exhalation, but of an all-round increase of energy in which even one's fingers and toes may take part. Thus, *There's an enormous improvement*, pronounced with the falling intonation of an ordinary statement, but with extra stress on the appropriate syllable of *enormous*, i.e. on *-nor-*, has the effect of intensifying the meaning of *enormous* :

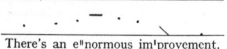

There's an e‖normous im′provement.

This extra stress is the essential thing, but as a rule it does not act alone. With it are present one or more of the following:

234. A widening of the range of intonation, especially when impatience, enthusiasm, admiration, courage, surprise, indignation, triumph, towering rage, in fact, any feelings of an exuberant nature, are present :

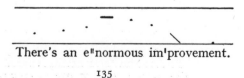

There's an e‖normous im′provement.

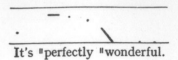

It's "perfectly "wonderful.

235. A variation of the intonation of the intensified word. Often added intensity is given to a word by *gliding* instead of leaping to the high pitch of the intensified syllable from the fairly low level of the pitch of the preceding syllable.   Thus the intonation

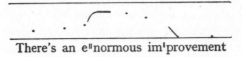

There's an e"normous im'provement

gives a greater degree of intensity to *enormous* than the intonation

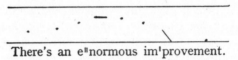

There's an e"normous im'provement.

The use of this rapid upward glide in pronouncing the intensified syllable is extremely common in English.   (It is not recorded in the examples which follow, though it is in most cases present.)

236. A narrowing of the range of intonation, especially when one expresses to a great degree awe, shame, indignation, sarcasm, contempt, secrecy, pity, tenderness, despair, fear, resignation, rage, or any feeling so great that verbal expression is difficult.   The final syllables of the group are often pronounced without voice:

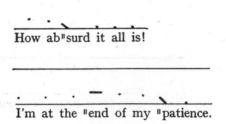

How ab"surd it all is!

I'm at the "end of my "patience.

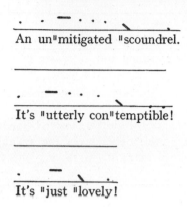

An un"mitigated "scoundrel.

It's "utterly con"temptible!

It's "just "lovely!

237. Addition of length to certain sounds:

It's a "perfect "gem.

(The sounds of *p* and of *er* of *perfect* and all the sounds of *gem* may be lengthened.)

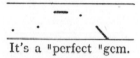

Tre"mendous en'thusiasm.

(The *m* and *n* of *tremendous* may be lengthened.)

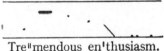

What a "lovely 'garden!

(All the sounds of *love-* may be lengthened.)

238.   Shortening of sounds :

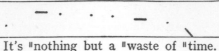

It's "nothing but a "waste of "time.

This, rattled off very quickly, suggests impatience, irritability.

239.   Introduction of the glottal plosive before a stressed syllable beginning with a vowel. This gives the syllable a very abrupt start, which, added to extra stress, is very effective :

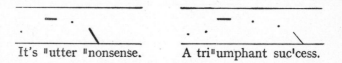

It's "utter "nonsense.   A tri"umphant suc'cess.

(The glottal plosive[1] is inserted before *utter* and before the second syllable of *triumphant*.)

240.   Repetition, e.g.

> I shall "never, "never give "in.
> That will be "much, "much "better.
> I'm "very, "very "tired.
> He's "quite, "quite "mad.

241.   A difference from the normal in the order of the words, e.g.

A"gain and a"gain it a'ppeared, instead of *It a'ppeared a'gain and a'gain. "Never shall I for'get it. "There I 'stood. It's "here that I 'want you to 'help me. . . . 'brown, 'bright 'eyes that 'peep from 'out the 'brake.*

242.   Addition of words, e.g.

> *I* personally. *My* personal *opinion. My* own *view. The* very same. *He* himself *saw it. He'll go far,* that man. *A* tiny *little* bit of a *thing.* Right *in the* very *middle. On the* very extreme *edge.*

[1] Phonetic symbol ?.

243. Use of pauses. A pause made before or after the emphasised word or before the group containing the intensified word has an intensifying effect.

244. Facial expression, gesture.

245. Special kind of voice. Many speakers are capable of introducing a special quality into their voices which helps to reveal (or hide) the degree and nature of their feeling; a voice may be made harsh, or smooth; thin, or rich and full; etc.

There may be a variety of causes for these special qualities. For example, pharyngal contraction gives rise to harshness; limitation of the vibration of the vocal cords to part only of their length gives rise to thinness of quality; extension of the vibrating length results in fullness of quality.

246. In all cases of intensity the *trend* of the intonation is the same as in unemphatic speech, and the effect of intensity is produced mainly by increase of stress together with such devices as those mentioned above.

247. Notice that in English it is the syllable bearing the *normal* stress which is reinforced for intensity.

Chapter XIX

INTENSITY IN FRENCH

248. The French intensify words and sentences much in the same way as the English do, but often to a greater degree. They have also the additional and extremely effective device of "shifted"[1] stress which generally brings with it a difference in the intonation form.

I. Devices Common to both English and French.

249. More than normal stress is used in pronouncing the emphasised syllable. In English it is usually the normally stressed syllable which is reinforced. In French stress for intensity is in most cases placed upon some syllable other than that which is normally stressed. The position of stress for intensity is dealt with in §§ 261–279.

250. The range of intonation may be widened or narrowed according to the particular kind of emotion expressed. The depth is sometimes so great that voiceless sounds replace voiced ones in the last syllables of the group.

251. A glide, instead of a leap, up to the level pitch of the emphasised syllable from that of the previous syllable adds intensity :

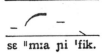

sɛ ‖mːa ɲi ˈfik.

It is difficult to say whether this device is as commonly used in French as in English.

252. Length may be added to certain sounds. (See § 282, footnote 2.)

[1] Not a very good term, since there is no shifting. The term intensive (or emphatic) is used in this book. Intensive stress does not replace normal stress.

253. Sounds may be shortened to suggest hastiness and irritation.

254. The glottal plosive may be used. (See §§ 265-271.)

255. Words may be repeated:

Je suis très, très, très ennuyé. C'était un vieux, vieux carillon. Nous les avons beaucoup, beaucoup vus. Il est bien, bien usé. Vous avez été si, si gentille. C'est fort, fort beau. Tout ce qu'il disait me semblait facile, facile.

256. The word order may be different from the normal. Words may be added:

C'est ici que je vais les planter, instead of *Je vais les planter ici. C'est à Londres que nous les avons rencontrés*, instead of *Nous les avons rencontrés à Londres. Elle est toute blanche, ma chambre*, instead of *Ma chambre est toute blanche. Jamais les vieux sapins n'avaient rien vu d'aussi joli*, instead of *Les vieux sapins n'avaient jamais rien vu d'aussi joli.*
C'est à moi, ce livre, instead of *Ce livre est à moi. C'est elle-même qui vous l'a dit*, instead of *C'est elle qui vous l'a dit. C'est son travail personnel* instead of *C'est son travail.*

257. A pause may sometimes be made before the emphasised word.

258. Gesture and facial expression play a part—in French a much larger one than in English.

259. A special kind of voice may be used to heighten the effect.

260. In all cases of intensity extra stress is used.

II. THE FRENCH DEVICE OF INTENSIVE STRESS.

(1) Intensive stress on words beginning with a consonant.
   Isolated words.

261. In intensified words of more than one syllable the normal stress may be retained, and a much stronger stress placed on some other syllable. In the case of words beginning with a consonant this strong stress is placed as far from the normal stress as possible,

L

i.e. on the *first* syllable, and, for this reason, it is effective in attracting one's attention. E.g. *magnifique, délicieux, superbe, ravissant,* carry intensive stress on the first syllable : "maɲiˈfik, "deliˈsjø, "syˈpɛrb, "raviˈsã.

Connected speech.

262. Monosyllabic words have their stress reinforced.

263. In intensified words of more than one syllable the first syllable—no matter what its position in the group—carries emphatic stress. The final syllable of the sentence or sense-group in which it occurs may retain its normal stress : s ɛ "maɲiˈfik ; s ɛ "deliˈsjø ; ʒə n vwa pɑ la "mwɛːdrə ʃoz ɛtɛrɛˈsãːt ; "pɛrsɔn nə s ãn ɔˈkyp ; vuz ave "tɔːr ; s ɛ "trɛ difisil a ɛkspliˈke ; s ɛ "ʒystəmã pur vuz ã parˈle | k il ɛ vny iˈsi.

(2) Intensive Stress on words beginning with a vowel.

First Method.

264. The most common way of emphasising for intensity words beginning with a vowel is to place emphatic stress on the first syllable beginning with a consonant : ʃ sɥiz ã"ʃãte d vu ˈvwaːr ; s ɛt ap"sɔlymã ɛpɔˈsibl ; ʒə n ãn e o"kyn iˈde ; sa va ad"mirabləmã ˈbjɛ ; s ɛt ɛ"finimã ply kɔˈmɔd ; s ɛt eg"zaktəmã la mɛm ˈʃoːz ; s ɛt ɛks"trɛməmã difiˈsil ; s ɛt ɛ"sypɔrˈtaːbl. In all the above examples the initial consonant of the emphasised syllable may be lengthened : ʃ sɥiz ã"ʃːãte d vu ˈvwaːr ; s ɛt eg"zːaktəmã la mɛm ˈʃoːz ; s ɛt ɛ"fːinimã ply kɔˈmɔd.

Second Method.

265. It is fairly common to hear French people intensify the *first* syllable of words which begin with a vowel.

266. In the following examples liaison is not possible since the word preceding the intensified syllable ends in a vowel sound : ʒə n ãn e "okyn iˈde ; sa va "admirabləmã ˈbjɛ.

267. It is important to notice that in cases where liaison is possible before the intensified word a Frenchman does not include the linking consonant in the emphasised syllable. He thinks it

absurd and at the same time confusing to say, for example, ʃ sɥi ‖zːɑ̃ʃɑ̃te d vu ˈvwaːr ; s ɛ ‖tːapsɔlymɑ̃ ɛ̃pɔˈsibl, calling special attention to such syllables as zɑ̃ and tap ; although in unemphatic speech it is usual, in pronouncing a stressed syllable, to include the final consonant of the preceding word in the stress impulse : avɛ ˈkø, *avec eux* ; œ̃ ˈnœf, *un œuf*.

268. How does a French speaker avoid carrying over the liaison consonant when he places emphatic stress on the first syllable?   The liaison consonant is pronounced but it does not function as a liaison consonant, the speaker inserting the glottal plosive which starts the emphasised syllable in its stead.   E.g. ʃ sɥiz ‖ʔɑ̃ʃɑ̃te d vu ˈvwaːr ; s ɛt ‖ʔapsɔlymɑ̃ ɛ̃pɔˈsibl ; s ɛt ‖ʔɛ̃sypɔrˈtaːbl ; s ɛt ‖ʔɛ̃finimɑ̃ ply kɔˈmɔd.

269. This second way of intensifying the meaning of a word beginning with a vowel is stronger than that of placing emphatic stress on the first syllable beginning with a consonant, but is not so frequently used. Some French people cannot do it without difficulty.

270. When the word beginning with a vowel occurs initially in a group, the question of liaison does not arise, and intensive stress is frequently placed on the first syllable, which may, or may not, begin with the glottal plosive : ‖ (ʔ)ɛ̃pɔsib də l ˈfɛːr ! ‖ (ʔ)apsɔlyˈmɑ̃ ! ‖(ʔ)ɛkstrɛmˈmɑ̃ ʒɔˈli ! ‖ (ʔ)atɑ̃ˈde ! ‖ (ʔ)atɑ̃ˈsjɔ̃ !

In the case of commands beginning with a verb, the first syllable is generally pronounced with intensive stress even when it begins with a vowel : ‖ (ʔ)ale vuz ˈɑ̃ ; ‖ (ʔ)ɑ̃lve tu vo ˈliːvr.

271. In teaching French to English pupils it is not very wise, even in emphasis, to encourage the use of ʔ, since this sound is troublesome to weed out from unemphatic speech where its presence is not justified by French usage. It is suggested, therefore, that (except in the case of commands) English pupils should be taught to place emphatic stress on the first syllable beginning with a consonant. This is nearly always possible.

272. Frequently intensive stress is placed on some short, normally unimportant word such as *le, la, les, de, du, des, au, aux,*

dans, en, à, et. Thus one may hear ‖dez al‖mã, ‖dez ameri‖kɛ̃;
‖la pi‖tje, ‖la ʒys‖tis; s ɛt ‖ʔa ‖vu a parle; il etɛ ‖dã la ‖bwat. This
intensifying of a word usually of small significance does not appear
to be a device for calling attention to the importance of the following
word by using the word of small significance as an intensity-bearing
prefix.

273. Intensive stress on an article or preposition, etc., has the
effect, not of adding to the meaning of the word following, but of
emphasising some other idea, e.g. that of great number, great
variety, "everywhereness," "withinness." In ‖de ‖kri, ‖de ʒy‖rɔ̃,
‖de ku d pwɛ̃ syr la ‖tabl, ‖lə ʃɔk de ‖vɛːr, ‖lə frakɑ de bi‖jaːr it appears
to be not the noises themselves in which the speaker is specially
interested but the *great number* and *variety* of noises. If the speaker
wanted to call special attention to the different noises he would
place intensive stress on the words naming those noises : de ‖ʒy‖rɔ̃,
de ‖ku d pwɛ̃ syr la ‖tabl, lə ‖ʃɔk de ‖vɛːr, lə ‖frakɑ de bi‖jaːr, etc.
(See §§ 403-7 for the intonation of this example.)

274. Many English words, usually unimportant, may also bear
emphatic stress. It is possible, for example, to say ‖*In the* ‖*box.*
Here there is no intensification of the meaning of *box.* It is the
idea of "withinness" which is emphasised. In *I* ‖*warned him* ‖*at the*
‖*time* what is important is not the warning nor the time, but the
fact that the warning synchronised with so-and-so's decision to
take a certain line of action. In *We searched* ‖*in the* ‖*cupboards,*
be‖*hind the* ‖*doors,* ‖*up the* ‖*chimney,* etc., it is the idea of "everywhereness" which is emphasised.

275. There is nothing in English like ‖dez al‖mã, ‖dez ita‖ljɛ̃,
‖de pɔrty‖gɛ, since the article is not used in the equivalent English
construction.

276. It is often possible in French to place emphatic stress on
all the syllables of a word or on many monosyllabic words in
succession, pronouncing them in a staccato manner; and this is
often done under the influence of strong emotion :

s ɛt ‖ʔɛ̃‖sy‖pɔr‖taːbl; s ɛ ‖de‖gu‖tã; ʒə vu parl ‖trɛ
‖sɛ̃‖sɛːr‖mã; s ɛt ‖ʔɛ̃‖kɔ̃‖tɛs‖taːbl; ʒə n lɥi e ‖rjɛ̃ ‖di ‖dy ‖tu;
s ɛ ‖de‖zɔ‖lã; ɛl ɛt ‖ʔa‖dɔ‖raːbl; sa va ‖ʔad‖mi‖raː‖blə‖mã
‖bjɛ̃; s ɛt ‖ʔe‖pa‖tã.

277. It is impossible in English to say *It's* "*dis*"*gus*"*ting*; *It's* "*aw*"*ful*; "*Mar*"*vel*"*lous* !   *It   was   "e"nor"mous* ; "*Mag*"*ni*"*fi-*"*cent* ! etc.

278. Many words do not normally carry stress for intensity. Such words as *très, fort, bien* carry intensive stress for them.   E.g. "**trɛz ele'gã**.   It is usual also to say s ɛ "**trɛ difi'sil** ; s ɛ "**trɛz** ɛ̃por'tã ; ɛl ɛ "**trɛ ʒã'tiːj** ; instead of s ɛ "**difi'sil**, s ɛt ɛ̃"**por'tã**, ɛl ɛ "**ʒã'tiːj**, which are, however, possible.

279. On the other hand, an enormous number of words are not modified by *très* or *fort*, for they carry the idea of *très* or *fort* within themselves. The most important of these words are *superbe, parfait, excellent, impossible, adorable, épatant, insensé, assommant, interminable, irrévocable, ravissant, accompli, consommé, splendide, idéal, merveilleux, abominable, éternel, inoui, insupportable, incomparable, immobile, immortel, bondé, odieux, divin, suprême, universel, infernal, terrible.* Many of these words may be used with *tout à fait, absolument, parfaitement,* which also denote the maximum degree, but not with any expression which implies that a greater degree is possible.

Chapter XX

INFLUENCE OF INTENSIVE STRESS ON INTONATION IN FRENCH

280. We shall now show the effect of intensive stress on the tonal patterns used in French.

(1) On the Rising-Falling intonation.

281. The Rising-Falling intonation, 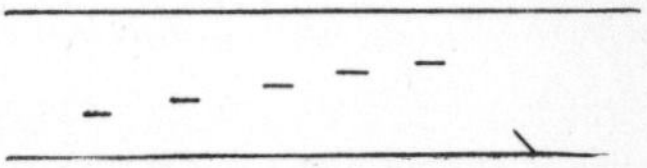

used chiefly for unemphatic assertions, generally has another form when emphatic stress is used.

282. There is no change in the outline of the curve, however, when the final or penultimate syllable bears emphatic stress: the highest pitch is on the penultimate as in unemphatic speech.

Examples:

(i) Intensive word final and monosyllabic; or final and disyllabic beginning with a vowel. Intensive and normal stress then fall on the same syllable:

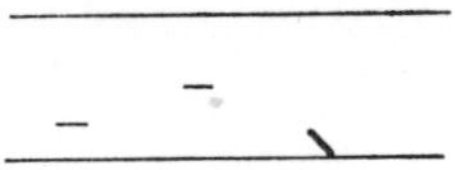

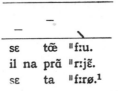

sɛ tœ̃ ‖fːu.
il na prɑ̃ ‖rːjɛ̃.
sɛ ta ‖fːrø.[1]

Notice that extra length is (or may be) used.[2]

[1] It is possible to say **s ɛt ‖ʔaˈfrø.** (See §§ 265–269.)

[2] In most of the examples of intensity given in this book, the initial consonant of the intensified syllable is shown to be lengthened. This length is not essential, though it is often present. In some cases the emphasised syllable could be pronounced with extra shortness or even with normal length.

(ii) Intensified word final and disyllabic, beginning with a consonant sound :

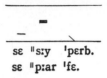

Here again extra length may be used in pronouncing the emphasised syllable. At the same time the range of the intonation may be widened :

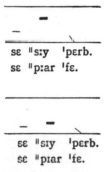

or narrowed

(iii) Intensified word final and of three syllables, the first of which begins with a vowel :

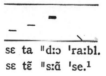

Here again the emphasised syllable may be pronounced with extra length. There may also be a widened or narrowed intonation range.

---

¹ Also

sɛt ‖ʔa dɔ ‖raːbl.
sɛt ‖ʔɛ̃ sɑ̃ ‖se.

(See §§ 265–9).

283.   In other cases the outline of the Rising-Falling intonation varies according to the position of the emphasised word:

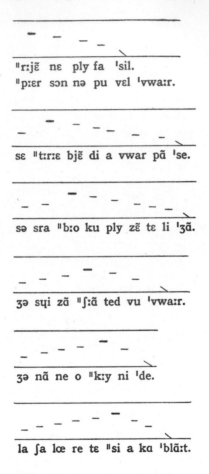

ᵘrːjɛ̃ nɛ ply fa ˈsil.
ᵘpːɛr sɔn nə pu vɛl ˈvwaːr.

sɛ ᵘtːrːɛ bjɛ̃ di a vwar pɑ̃ ˈse.

sə sra ᵘbːo ku ply zɛ̃ tɛ li ˈʒɑ̃.

ʒə sɥi zɑ̃ ᵘʃːɑ̃ ted vu ˈvwaːr.

ʒə nɑ̃ ne o ᵘkːy ni ˈde.

la ʃa lœ re tɛ ᵘsi a kɑ ˈblɑ̃ːt.

284.   The highest pitch is not on the penultimate syllable, but on the syllable bearing intensive stress, whatever its position. The intonation falls from this point, sometimes precipitately, to the end of the sentence. Syllables preceding the emphasised syllable are pronounced quickly and lightly, sometimes on a monotone, thus making more noticeable the length, stress and high pitch of the emphasised syllable.

285. A narrowing of the intonation range is also possible.

(2) ON THE FALLING INTONATION.

286. The Falling intonation,

the typical unemphatic "tune" for questions beginning with a specific interrogative word, for commands and requests, has pretty much the same form when emphasis for intensity is present. There is generally a widening of the range of intonation. A narrowing of the range is also possible.

Specific Interrogative Sentences.

287. Specific interrogative sentences are intensified by placing emphatic stress on the first syllable of the interrogative word which is generally initial in the sentence. The highest pitch is given to this:

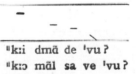

ǁkːi dmɑ̃ de 'vu ?
ǁkːɔ mɑ̃l sa ve 'vu ?

If an unstressed syllable (or syllables) precedes the interrogative word its pitch is generally fairly low so that the interrogative word may have the prominence of the highest pitch:

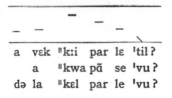

a vɛk ǁkːi par lɛ 'til ?
a ǁkwa pɑ̃ se 'vu ?
də la ǁkɛl par le 'vu ?

288. Note that questions asking for the repetition of an answer have the Rising intonation. Strong stress is generally placed on the initial syllable:

ǁkɛs kə ty 'di ?

The intonation of English questions asking for the repetition of an answer also rises. E.g.

⊔"What do you 'say?

Other examples :

⊔"u va 'ty?
⊔"kɑ̃ lez a ty 'vy?
⊔"u lez a ty aʃ'te?
⊔"d u vjɛ̃ 'ty?
⊔"k ɛ s k il t a 'di?
⊔"purkwa a t il fɛ 'sa?
⊔"kɔ̃'bjɛ̃?

No further examples of this kind will be given.

Commands and Requests.

289. Commands and requests are intensified by placing emphatic stress on the first syllable of the verb since the verb expresses the idea of command or request. The verb generally occurs initially. The pitch falls from the emphasised syllable to the end of the sentence :

⊔"vːjɛ̃   a   vɛk 'mwa.
⊔"nːɛ̃   sis te 'pɑ.
⊔"pːɑ   se pa ri 'si.
⊔ (ʔ)ɑ̃l ve vo 'liːvr.

Exclamations.

290. Exclamations have the same form of intonation as commands :

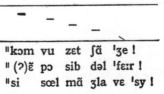

⊔"kɔm vu zɛt ʃɑ̃ 'ʒe !
⊔ (ʔ)ɛ̃ pɔ sib dəl 'fɛːr !
⊔"si   sœl mɑ̃ ʒla vɛ 'sy !

(3) ON THE RISING INTONATION.

291. The emphatic forms of the Rising intonation,

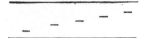

(used chiefly in unemphatic speech in non-final sense-groups, in sentences of a non-final nature : statements with an implication, "yes" and "no" questions, and questions having the grammatical form of statements) are shown in the following examples.

Assertions (non-final groups).

292. The intonation of non-final groups of Assertions may have the forms described below :

(a) In the following non-final groups in which the emphasised syllable is final or followed by one syllable only, the pitch rises continuously to its highest point on the last syllable as in unemphatic speech: there is thus no difference in the intonation :

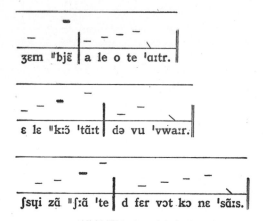

ʒɛm ‖bjɛ̃ | a le o te ˈaːtr. ‖

ɛ lɛ ‖kːɔ̃ ˈtãːt | də vu ˈvwaːr. ‖

ʃsɥi zã ‖ʃːã ˈte | d fɛr vɔt kɔ nɛ ˈsãːs. ‖

(b) In the following examples there is more than one syllable between the intensified syllable and the final one of the sense-group in which it occurs.   In such cases the maximum effect of emphasis is obtained if a fairly high pitch is given to the intensified syllable, and a lowering of pitch to the syllables which intervene between the intensified syllable and the final one, the lowering throwing into relief both the intensified and final syllables :

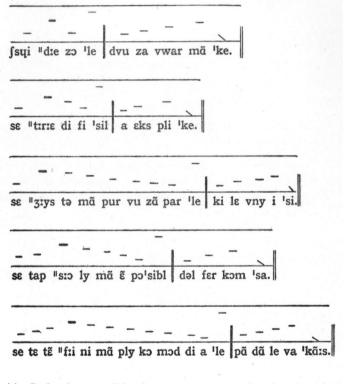

(c) It is also possible, but not so emphatic, for the pitch to rise continuously from syllable to syllable of the sense-group as in unemphatic speech. (If the group is long, a "break" may be made) :

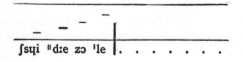

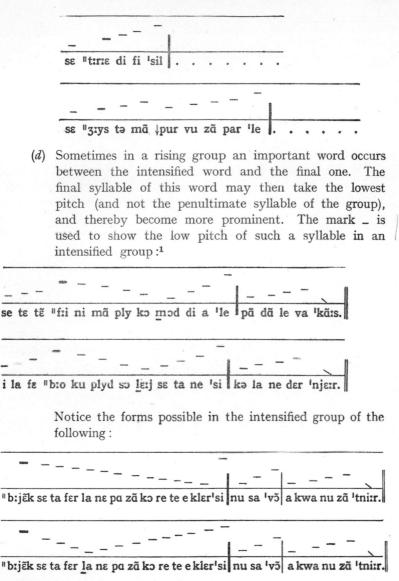

sɛ "tːrːɛ di fi 'sil

sɛ "ɜːys tə mã ↓pur vu zã par 'le

(d) Sometimes in a rising group an important word occurs between the intensified word and the final one. The final syllable of this word may then take the lowest pitch (and not the penultimate syllable of the group), and thereby become more prominent. The mark ‿ is used to show the low pitch of such a syllable in an intensified group :[1]

se tɛ tẽ "fːi ni mã ply kɔ mɔd di a 'le ‖pã dã le va 'kãːs.‖

i la fɛ "bːo ku plyd sɔ lɛːj sɛ ta ne 'si ‖kə la ne dɛr 'njɛːr.‖

Notice the forms possible in the intensified group of the following :

"bːjẽk sɛ ta fɛr la nɛ pɑ zã kɔ re te e klɛr'si‖nu sa 'vɔ̃‖a kwa nu zã 'tniːr.‖

"bːjẽk sɛ ta fɛr la nɛ pɑ zã kɔ re te e klɛr'si‖nu sa 'vɔ̃‖a kwa nu zã 'tniːr.‖

[1] Compare the placing of the highest pitch (marked ‾) on some syllable other than the penultimate in the Rising-Falling intonation. (See § 68 and footnote.) In all orthographic examples and texts the marks are placed *before* the syllables concerned.

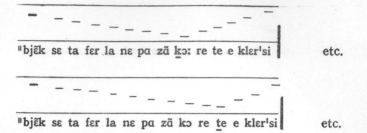

ⁿbjɛ̃k sɛ ta fɛr ˌla nɛ pɑ zã kɔː re te e klɛrˈsi ‖   etc.

ⁿbjɛ̃k sɛ ta fɛr la nɛ pɑ zã kɔ re te e klɛrˈsi ‖   etc.

(e) The intensified word itself may be made still more prominent by giving the lowest tone to its final syllable instead of to the penultimate syllable of the sense-group in which it occurs:

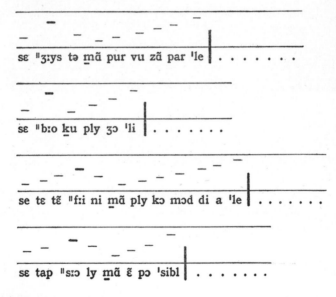

sɛ ⁿʒːys tə m̱ã pur vu zã par ˈle ‖ . . . .

sɛ ⁿbːo ḵu ply ʒɔ ˈli ‖ . . . .

se tɛ tɛ̃ ⁿfːi ni m̱ã ply kɔ mɔd di a ˈle ‖ . . . .

sɛ tap ⁿsːo ly m̱ã ɛ̃ pɔ ˈsibl ‖ . . . .

Statements with an implication.

293. Statements with an implication may have the same intonation, when emphasis for intensity is present, as that of non-final groups just described.[1]   They are, in reality, non-final groups.

[1] See also § 294.

(*a*) The rise is made continuously when the final or pen-ultimate syllable of the group is emphasised:

— — ▬
—

sɛ ta se ‖bjɛ̃.
nu le za vɔ̃ ‖vy.
i nu la di lɥi ‖mɛːm.

— — ▬
—

ɛ lɛ ‖ʒɑ̃ ˈtiːj.
ɛl sɔ̃ ‖ʒɔ ˈli.
i lɛ ‖kɔ̃ ˈtɑ̃.

The following are of an exclamatory nature. The range of intonation is wider in such sentences than in ordinary statements with an implication:

— — ▬
—

i le tɛ ‖bːɔ̃ !

— — ▬ ▬
—

il sɔ̃ dɔ̃ɛ nɑ̃ ‖bːɛ ˈtɑ̃ !

il fɛt ɔ̃ɛ ‖sːɔˈlɛːj !   il fɛt ↓yn də se ‖ʃːaˈlœːr !
il fɛt yn ‖pɹuˈsjɛːr !   ɛl sɔ̃ ↓d ɔ̃ɛ ‖ʒːɔˈli !
il fɛt ↓ɔ̃ɛ d se ‖frwa !   il ɛ ‖kːɔ̃ˈtɑ̃ !
sɛt fiːj ↓ɛ d yn ɛ̃‖pːyˈdɑ̃ːs !   ɛl ɛ d ɔ̃ɛ ‖rːaˈzwaːr !

(*b*) The rise may be made continuously if some syllable other than the final or penultimate is emphasised; but the effect is greater if the emphasised syllable is pronounced with a high pitch and the syllables intervening between that and the final one have a descending pitch:

sɛ ‖di fi ˈsil.

i la ‖bo ku dar ˈʒɑ̃.

The following are of an exclamatory nature:

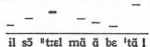

il sɔ̃ ‖tːɛl mɑ̃ ɑ̃ bɛ ˈtɑ̃ !

vuz ɛt ‖sːi ʒɑ̃ˈtiːj !   i fəzɛ ‖tːɛlmɑ̃ ˈbo !
ɛl etɛ ‖sːi ʒɔˈli !   nu vuz ɛmɔ̃ ‖tːɛlmɑ̃ ˈbjɛ̃ !
s ɛt arive ‖sːi sudɛnˈmɑ̃ !   la rɔb ↓ɛ d œ̃ ‖rːey ˈsi !
s etɛ d œ̃ ‖rːaviˈsɑ̃ !

No further examples of statements with an implication will be given for practice.

294. For the help of advanced students it may be pointed out that French speakers often express an implication more strongly than is possible in the way described in § 293 (a) and (b). They do this by raising the pitch *while pronouncing* the final syllable of the group containing the emphasised word.[1] This rise may be marked ′. It is from a fairly high pitch if a rising intonation precedes:

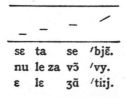

sɛ ta   se ′bjɛ̃.
nu le za vɔ̃ ′vy.
ɛ lɛ ʒɑ̃ ′tiːj.

[1] This rising intonation is also used in pronouncing monosyllabic exclamations with an implication. e.g. ′Oui! ′Non! ′Lui! ′Tiens! ′Vous! ′Moi! ′Toi!

The rise may be from a low or a fairly high pitch if a falling intonation precedes :

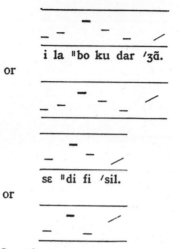

i la "bo ku dar 'ʒã.

or

sɛ "di fi 'sil.

or

"Yes" and "No" Questions.

295. The intonation of emphatic "Yes" and "No" questions (including questions having the grammatical form of statements), may have the following forms :

(a) If the idea of interrogation is emphasised the rise is made in this way :

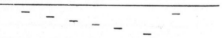

Strong stress is placed on the first syllable, which is pitched fairly high. The intonation then falls, and (unless some intervening word is made prominent) reaches a low level on the penultimate syllable from which a leap is made to the high pitch of the final syllable. The effect of the fall preceding the rise is to intensify the idea of interrogation and at the same time to add to it a suggestion of surprise or authority :

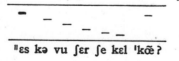

"ɛs kə vu ʃɛr ʃe kɛl 'kœ̃ ?

M

"pu ve vu vni ra sɛ 'tœːr ?

"ɛs kə vu le zɛ me bo 'ku ?

"pɛr sɔn nɛ 'vny ?

(b) If some word is brought into prominence (not for intensity) the final syllable of this word has the lowest pitch and not the penultimate. The idea of interrogation is also emphasised in the following:

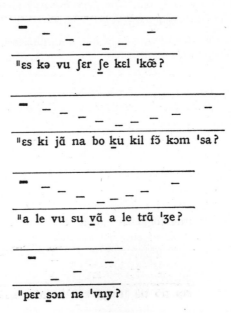

"ɛs kə vu ʃɛr ʃe kɛl 'kœ̃ ?

"ɛs ki jɑ̃ na bo ku kil fɔ̃ kɔm 'sa ?

"a le vu su vɑ̃ a le trɑ̃ 'ʒe ?

"pɛr sɔn nɛ 'vny ?

(c) If some word is emphasised for intensity the appropriate
syllable of this word is strongly stressed and its final
syllable has the lowest pitch, unless, as in the first example
given below, the final syllable of the intensified word is
the final syllable of the sentence. The idea of interrogation is also emphasised in the following :

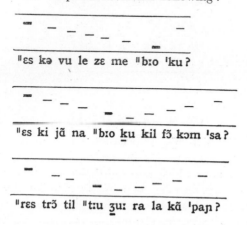

ᶤɛs kə vu le zɛ me ᶤbːo ˈku?

ᶤɛs ki jã na ᶤbːo ku kil fɔ̃ kɔm ˈsa?

ᶤrɛs trɔ̃ til ᶤtːu ʒuː ra la kã ˈpaɲ?

(d) If it is not the idea of interrogation which is emphasised,
but some other idea, the initial syllable need not be
pronounced with a high pitch. The intonation may be
the same as that used for non-final sense-groups of
assertions. (See § 292 (a) and (b).)

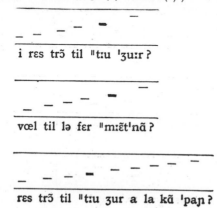

i rɛs trɔ̃ til ᶤtːu ˈʒuːr?

vœl til lə fɛr ᶤmːɛ̃tˈnã?

rɛs trɔ̃ til ᶤtːu ʒur a la kã ˈpaɲ?

or

rɛs trɔ̃ ˙til ‖tːu ʒuː ra la kɑ̃ ˈpaɲ?

i rɔ̃ til ‖ʔa vɛk lə ˈtrɛ̃?

or

i rɔ̃ til ‖ʔa vɛk lə ˈtrɛ̃?

296.   For the help of advanced students it may be pointed out
that there is a very effective intonation form for emphatic "Yes"
and "No" questions which is not included in § 295 above.   It is a
form which involves the use of a *rising* tone for the final syllable
of the question,[1] and is used only when there is a strong implication,
e.g. of surprise, doubt, uncertainty, or reproach.   The rise may be
from a low or from a fairly high pitch :

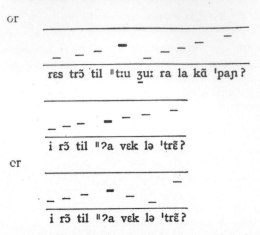

‖ɛs kə vu le zɛ me bo ˈku?

or

‖pɛr sɔn nɛ ˈvny?
‖ɑ̃   nɛt vu ˈsyːr?

or

─────────────────────

[1] Marked thus ʹ.   See also § 294.

Commands.

297. Non-final groups of commands have the same intonation in emphasis as "Yes" and "No" questions.

(a) Idea of command emphasised :

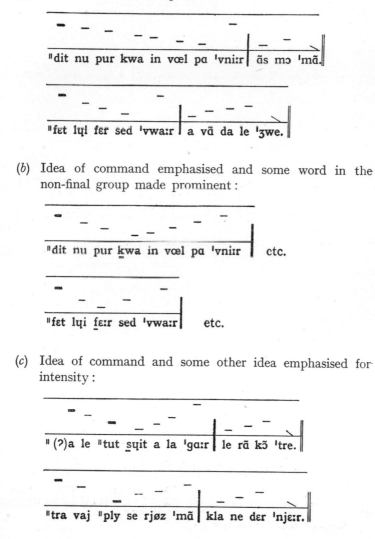

(b) Idea of command emphasised and some word in the non-final group made prominent :

(c) Idea of command and some other idea emphasised for intensity :

(*d*) Idea of command not emphasised, but some other idea :

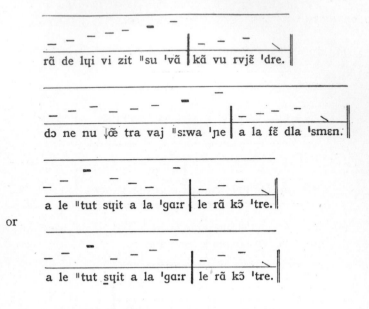

rɑ̃ de lʮi vi zit ‖su ˈvɑ̃ │ kɑ̃ vu rvjɛ̃ ˈdre. ‖

dɔ ne nu ↓œ̃ tra vaj ‖sːwa ˈɲe │ a la fɛ̃ dla ˈsmɛn. ‖

a le ‖tut sʮit a la ˈgɑːr │ le rɑ̃ kɔ̃ ˈtre. ‖

or

a le ‖tut sʮit a la ˈgɑːr │ le rɑ̃ kɔ̃ ˈtre. ‖

(*e*) Double Imperatives.

A double imperative usually has

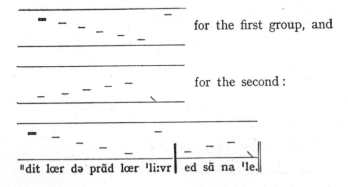

for the first group, and

for the second :

‖dit lœr də prɑ̃d lœr ˈliːvr │ ed sɑ̃ na ˈle. ‖

298. The effect of intensity, then, is created, as in English,
mainly by the use of emphatic stress.

299.   The placing of this emphatic stress on some syllable other than that bearing normal stress together with a different form of the intonation curve which generally gives to the emphasised syllable a higher or lower pitch than normal, (generally a higher), combine to make the French method of emphasising for intensity extremely effective. The other devices used in intensity—a widening or narrowing of the intonation range, extra length, change of word order, etc., are used also in English, so that they present no special difficulty to the English learner.

CHAPTER XXI

SHORT EXAMPLES[1] OF INTENSITY IN FRENCH

(1) FORMS OF THE RISING-FALLING INTONATION.

300. Assertions.

(i) Intensified syllable final:

i lɛ ‖lːa.
sɛ tõ̃ ‖fːu.

il n ira ‖pːa.   ilz ɔ̃t y õ̃ syksɛ ‖fːu.
sa n sɛr a ‖rːjɛ̃.   s ɛt e‖nːɔrm.
ʒə n ã vø ‖pːly.   s ɛt i‖nːwi.
vuz ave ‖tːɔːr.   s ɛt õ̃n ɛ̃‖grːa.
il n aprã ‖rːjɛ̃.   s ɛt ɛ̃‖fːɛkt.
i n sɛ pɑ s kə ‖sːɛ.   s ɛt a‖fːrø.

(ii) Intensified syllable medial:

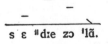

s ɛ ‖dːe zɔ ‖lã.

s ɛ ‖rːidi‖kyl.   ã vwasi le ‖rːezyl‖ta.
s ɛ ‖mːaɲi‖fik.   s etɛt ɛ̃‖tːɛrmi‖naːbl.
s ɛ ‖sːy‖pɛrb.   s ɛt ɛks‖tːrːaɔrdi‖nɛːr.
s ɛ ‖pːar‖fɛ.   ɛl etɛt a‖dːɔ‖raːbl.
s ɛt õ̃ ‖pːarɛ‖sø.   s ɛt e‖pːra‖tã.
i fot ɛtrə ‖rːɛzɔ‖naːbl. s ɛt õ̃n ɛ̃‖bːe‖sil.
s ɛt õ̃ ‖mːize‖raːbl.   s ɛt e‖fːrːwa‖jaːbl.
s ɛ ‖rːepy‖ɲã.   s ɛt ɛ̃‖sːɑ̃‖se.
s ɛ ‖fːɔrmi‖daːbl.   s ɛt ɛ̃‖sːypɔr‖taːbl.

[1] All examples, except those given with a pitch notation are now divided into words, instead of syllables as in Part I.

s ɛt ɛ̃"kɔ̃tɛs'taːbl. s ɛt a"sɔ'mã.
s ɛt ir"rːeme'djaːbl. s ɛt œ̃ rmɛd ɛ̃"fːa'jibl.
s ɛt ir"rːevɔ'kaːbl. s ɛt œ̃ pti mœ↓blə "rːavi'sã.
s ɛt ɛ̃"fːɛr'nal. le vitro ↓d la katedral ↓sɔ̃ "sːy'pɛrb.
s ɛt ɛ̃"kɔ̃sə'vaːbl.

ʒe e te "rːa vid la 'vwaːr.
i le tɛ "fːa ʃe kɔm 'tu.

sa va ad"mirabləmã 'bjɛ̃.
ʒə lez e "tːro 'vy.
ʒə n sɛ "vːirɛmã ply u ʒ ã 'sɥi.
sa m ɛ "tut a fɛt e'gal.
s ɛ "pːarfɛtmã 'vrɛ.
ʒə vɛz ekrir yn lɛt "bːjɛ̃ difi'sil.
s ɛ la "sːœl ʃoz ki m 'mãːk.
ɔ̃n etɛ "sːi trã 'kil.
ɛl ɛ "sːi kɔ̃v'naːbl.
s ɛ "tːɛlmã 'klɛːr.
il ɛ də "tːrːɛ mɔvɛz y'mœːr.
s ɛ "tːru s k il j a d 'ʃik.
s ɛ "bːoku ply difisil a a'prãːdr.
s ɛ "ʒːyst lə kɔ̃'trɛːr.
il ɛ "tːruʒur ã r'taːr.
ʒə n e "ʒːamɛ rjɛ̃ vy d si ʒɔ'li.
ɛl etɛ "pːarfɛtmã o ku'rã.
ʒə vwa "bːoku mjø avɛk se lynɛt 'la.
ʒə n oz "pːly travɛrse le 'ry.
il s ɛ pase "tːrã d ʃoz dəpɥi 'jɛːr.
la mezɔ̃ etɛ "mːːetikyløzmã 'prɔpr.
ʒə truv kə sə sra "bːoku plyz ɛ̃tɛli'ʒã.
s ɛt eg"zːaktəmã la mɛm 'ʃoːz.
s ɛt ap"sːɔlymã ɛ̃pɔ'sibl.
s ɛt ɛ̃"sːyporˈtaːbl.
ʒə mœr "lːːiteralmã d 'frwɑ.

kɛl "ʃːarmɑ̃t ide vuz avez y sə ʒur 'la !
kɛl "ʒɔli ʃapo vuz a've !
s ɛ "tut a fɛ s k i m fa'lɛ.
ʒə n vwa pɑ la "mːwɛ̃ːdrə ʃoz ɛ̃tereˈsɑ̃ːt.
ʒə n truv pɑ sa "rːidikyl dy 'tu.
ɛl ɛ vrɛmɑ̃ "tːut a fɛ ʃar'mɑ̃ːt.
ʒ e kury le magazɛ̃ "tːut la ʒur'ne.
il kɔnɛ "tːut se ʃoz 'la.
ʒə sɥi "dːeʒɔle d vuz avwar mɑ̃'ke.
ʒə "mːœːr də 'fɛ̃.
ʒə sɥi "rːavi d vuz ɛtr agre'aːbl.
ʒə vu parl "tːrːɛ sɛ̃sɛr'mɑ̃.
ʒ avɛ "ʒːɔlimɑ̃ tɔr də m ɔkype d 'sa.
ʒə vɛ "tːu lɥi 'diːr.
ʒə n lɥi e "rːjɛ̃ di dy 'tu.
s ɛt ɛks"tːrːɛmmɑ̃ difi'sil.
s ɛt ap"sːɔlymɑ̃t ɛ̃pɔ'sibl.
s ɛt yn ɛk"sːɛlɑ̃t i'de.
il n i aprɑ̃ ap"sːɔlymɑ̃ 'rjɛ̃.
s ɛt ɛ̃"fːinimɑ̃ ply kɔ'mɔd.
ʒə srɛz ɑ̃"ʃːɑ̃te d vuz akɔ̃pa'ɲe.
sa va ad"mːirabləmɑ̃ 'bjɛ̃.
ʒə n ɑ̃n e o"kːyn i'de.
s etɛt ap"sːɔlymɑ̃ ɛ̃pɔsib də l kɔ̃'prɑ̃ːdr.
s ɛt ɑ̃"nːɥijø kɔm 'tu.

(iii) Intensified syllable initial :

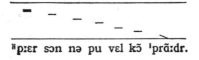

"pːɛr sɔn nə pu vɛl kɔ̃ 'prɑ̃ːdr.

"rːjɛ̃ n mə 'tɑ̃ːt.
"tːu s arɑ̃ʒ'ra.
"rːjɛ̃ n ɛ ply fa'sil.
"ʒːamɛ nu n i rturn'rɔ̃.
"tːu l mɔ̃d etɛ 'la.

"rːjɛ̃ n i 'fɛ.
"tːuʒur il nuz ɑ̃ 'parl.
"rːjɛ̃ n lez ɛ̃te'rɛs.
"pːɛrsɔn nə s ɑ̃n ɔ'kyp.

(iv) Intensified syllable final, medial or initial. Parenthetical
expression appended :

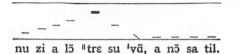

nu zi a lɔ̃ ‖trɛ su ‖vã, a nɔ̃ sa til.

il s ãn ɔkyp ‖trɛ serjøz‖mã, lɥi dit ɛl.
il vjɛn ‖suvã ã vwa‖tyːr, deklara ʒɑːk.
s ɛt yn ‖ʃːarmãt ã‖fã, nuz anɔ̃sa t il.
ʒə mãkrɛ ‖nː ɛ̃pɔrtə ‖kwa, pur i ale.
vu m fɛt ‖bːjɛ̃ d la ‖pɛn, məsjø 1 dirɛktœːr.
ʒ ɛm ‖bːoku le tama‖ris, deklara t ɛl avɛk ãtuzjasm.
ilz ɔ̃t œ̃ syksɛ ‖fːu, deklara t il.
nu truvɔ̃ sla a‖fːrø, nu dit ɛl.
sɛt i‖nwi, aʒutɛr t il.

(2) FORMS OF THE FALLING INTONATION.

301. Specific interrogative sentences :

‖pːurkwa ɛt vu i‖si ?

‖kːi a fɛ ‖sa ?
‖kːomã 1 save ‖vu ?
‖pːurkwa n vœlt i pɑ vnir ã ‖frãːs ?
lə‖kɛl de dø prefere ‖vu ?
‖pːurkwa lœr ave vu di ‖sa ?
a ‖kɛl epɔk rəvjɛ̃drɔ̃t ‖il ?
‖u ɛmrɛt il pɑse lœr va‖kãːs ?
‖u fɔdra t il k il vjɛn nu rãkɔ̃‖tre ?
də la‖kɛl parle ‖vu ?

302. Commands :

‖nː ɛ̃siste ‖pɑ.   ‖vːjɛ̃ avɛk ‖mwa.
‖ʃːãte nu yn ʃã‖sɔ̃.   ‖fːɛrme la ‖pɔrt.

‖rːãʒe voz aˈfɛːr.
‖ (ʔ)ale vuz ˈã.
‖ (ʔ)aple lez ãˈfã.
‖ (ʔ)aksɛpte ˈlɛ.
‖ (ʔ)amyze vu ˈbjɛ̃.

‖ (ʔ)arive d bɔn ˈœːr.
‖ (ʔ)apɔrte vo ˈliːvr.
‖ (ʔ)uvre la fˈnɛːtr.
‖ (ʔ)ãlve ˈlɛ.
‖ (ʔ)ɔkype vu œ̃ pø d lœrz aˈfɛːr.

303. Exclamations :

‖kː il ɛ ˈbo !
‖kːœ vuz ɛt naˈif !
‖kːõbjɛ̃ ty ɛ ˈluːr !
‖kɛl ide il a ˈy !
‖kɔm s ɛ ʒɔˈli !
‖kɔm s ɛ bjɛn arã̃ˈʒe !
‖kɛl ˈʃãːs !
‖tã ˈmjø !

‖kɛl dɔˈmaːʒ !
‖kœ s ɛ ˈbo !
‖kœ vuz ɛt ʒã̃ˈtiːj !
‖ (ʔ)ɛ̃krwɑˈjaːbl !
‖ (ʔ)ɛksɛˈlã̃ !
‖ (ʔ)abɔmiˈnaːbl !
‖ (ʔ)ɛ̃beˈsil !
‖ (ʔ)ã̃ʃã̃ˈte !

(3) FORMS OF THE RISING INTONATION.

304. Assertions (non-final groups).

(a) Intensified syllable followed by one syllable only in the
same group.

i lɛ ‖bːjɛ̃ ˈbo ‖kil sã nɔ ˈkyp.‖

il ɛ ‖ʒːɔˈli ‖ kɔm ˈtu. ‖
nuz irõ ‖tːu t ˈsɥit ‖ si vu l vuˈle. ‖
i fɛ ‖tːrːɛ ˈbõ ‖ dã l ʒarˈdɛ̃. ‖
sə tablo ɛ ‖mːwɛ̃ ˈlɛ ‖ kə sõ vwaˈzɛ̃. ‖
vɔt rɔb ɛ ‖pːly ˈprɔpr ‖ kə la ˈmjɛn. ‖
nuz i alõ ‖sːuˈvã ‖ ãn eˈte. ‖
nuz ɛmõ ‖bːɔˈku ‖ ale le ˈvwaːr. ‖
i sõ ‖ʒːã̃ˈti ‖ a krɔˈke. ‖
i travaj ‖bjɛ̃ ˈmjø ‖ pã̃dã le vaˈkã̃ːs. ‖

(*b*) Intensified syllable followed by more than one syllable in the same group.

In the following examples the lowest tone is on the penultimate of the rising group[1] :

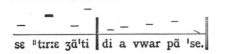

sɛ ‖tːrːɛ ʒã'ti │ di a vwar pã 'se.‖

ʃ sɥi ‖dːezɔ'le │ d vuz avwar mã'ke. ‖
i fɛ ‖tːrːɛz y'mid │ dã l ʒar'dɛ̃. ‖
ʃ sɥi ‖tːrːɛ kɔ̃'tã:t │ kə vu swaje v'ny. ‖
nu n lez avɔ̃ ‖pːɑ vy dy 'tu │ dpɥi lœr rə'tuːr. ‖
s ɛt ɛ̃‖fːinimã ply ʒɔ'li │ kə skə vuz ave 'la. ‖
il i ɔra ‖sːyrmã kɛlkə 'ʃoːz │ ki vuz ɛ̃terɛs'ra. ‖
nuz i alɔ̃ ‖tːrːɛ suvã ã vwa'tyːr │ pãdã la bɔn sɛ'zɔ̃. ‖
‖kːã nu srɔ̃ par'ti │ vu pure vuz ãn ɔky'pe. ‖
ʒə sre ã‖ʃːãte d vuz akɔ̃pa'ɲe │ dəmɛ̃ ma'tɛ̃. ‖
il n aprã ap‖sːɔlymã 'rjɛ̃ │ a sɛt ekɔl 'la. ‖
s etɛt yn ɛk‖sːɛlãt a'fɛːr │ k ilz alɛ kɔ̃'klyːr. ‖
le ʃjɛ̃ s etɛt a‖fːrøːzmã deʃi're │ pãdã la ba'taːj. ‖
s ɛt yn istwar e‖pːuvã'taːbl │ k il nuz a rakɔ̃'te. ‖
nuz avɔ̃z ete a‖greabləmã syr'pri │ d le rãkɔ̃'tre. ‖
il lɥi ɛt ɛks‖tːrɛmmã dezagre'aːbl │ də vwajaʒe la 'nɥi. ‖

(*c*) In the following examples the lowest tone in the rising group is not on the penultimate syllable, but on the final syllable of the important word which intervenes between the intensified and final words. The syllable bearing the lowest tone is marked ‗.

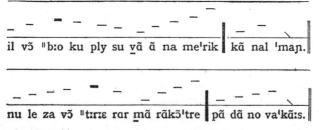

il vɔ̃ ‖bːo ku ply su v‗ã ã na me'rik │ kã nal 'maɲ.‖

nu le za vɔ̃ ‖tːrːɛ rɑr m‗ã rãkɔ̃'tre │ pã dã no va'kãːs.‖

[1] See also § 292(*c*).

s ɛ la ‖dːɛrnjɛr fwa k nu sɔmz ale ɑ̃ ꞌvil | kə nu l avɔ̃ rɑ̃kɔ̃ꞌtre. ‖
lə vwajaʒ ɛ ‖bːoku plyz agreaːbl ɑ̃ deꞌsɑ̃ːbr | k ɑ̃ fevriꞌe. ‖
s ɛ ‖pːɑ̃dɑ̃ k tu l mɔ̃ːd etɛ sɔrꞌti | k lə vɔl s ɔpeꞌra. ‖
s ɛt yn travɛrse ‖bːoku plyz agreaːbl ɑ̃n oꞌtɔn | k ɑ̃n iꞌvɛːr. ‖
‖sː il nə vjɛn pa a nɔt rɑ̃ꞌkɔ̃ːtr | nuz irɔ̃ a ꞌpje. ‖
‖sː il nə vjɛn pa nu ʃɛrʃe avɛk la vwaꞌtyːr | nu prɑ̃drɔ̃ l ꞌtrɛ̃. ‖
‖pːrɛskə ʃak fwa kə ʒ le ꞌvwa | il mə ꞌdiːz | la mɛm ꞌʃoːz. ‖
‖pːɑ̃dɑ̃ k nu rgardjɔ̃ pase l ꞌtrɛ̃ | lə ꞌʃjɛ̃ | dispaꞌry. ‖

305. Statements with an implication.
No further examples are given here.   (See §§ 293-4.)

306. "Yes" and "No" questions.

    (a) Interrogative idea emphasised :

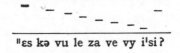

‖ɛs kə vu le za ve vy iꞌsi?

‖kɔ̃prɛnt il s kə sa vø ꞌdiːr? |
‖dœvriɔ̃ nu l kɔ̃sylꞌte? |
‖ire vu le vwar sɛt səꞌmɛn? |
‖ɛ s kə vu kɔnɛse se ʒɑ̃ ꞌla? |
‖save vu purkwa i n sɔ̃ pɑ rɑ̃ꞌtre? |
‖ale vu suvɑ̃ a l etrɑ̃ꞌʒe? |

    (b) Interrogative idea emphasised and a non-final word made prominent :

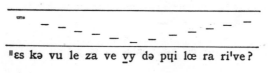

‖ɛs kə vu le za ve vy də pɥi lœ ra riꞌve?

‖kɔ̃prɛnt il bjɛ̃ s kə sa vø ꞌdiːr? |
‖fɔ̃t il suvɑ̃ sɛt ɛrœr ꞌla? |
‖ɛspɛr t il i ale dɑ̃ l kurɑ̃ d l aꞌne? |
‖dœvriɔ̃ nu l kɔ̃sylꞌte? |

ǁfot il kə nu nuz ãn ɔkypjɔ̃ dɛ mɛ̃t'nã? |
ǁire vu la v̱waːr sɛt sə'mɛn? |
ǁɛ s kə vu kɔnɛse se ʒã 'la? |
ǁlez ave vu rãkɔ̃tre la smɛn dɛr'njɛːr? |
ǁsave vu purḵwa in sɔ̃ pɑ rã'tre? |
ǁlez ave vu v̱y dəpɥi 'jɛːr? |
ǁale vu suv̱ã a 1 etrã'ʒe? fit ɛl kyrjøːzmã. |

(c) Interrogative idea emphasised and also some other idea:

ǀi re vu ǁbːjɛ̃ ṯo o ze ta zy'ni?

ǁs ɔkyp t il ǁøm̱ɛːm də 'sa? |
ǁtravajɛt il ǁʃez ø̱ pãdã se ʒur 'la? |
ǁsɔ̃t il vrɛmã ɛ̃ǁfːa'jibl? |
ǁnə sɔ̃t il pɑ aǁsːɔ'mã? |
ǁɛ s kə vuz ale ǁmɛ̃ṯnã ãn ame'rik? |
ǁɛ s kə vu partire sɛt səmɛn ǁs̱i pur 1 etrã'ʒe? |
ǁɛ s kə vuz ɛmərje sɛt etɔf ǁḻa pur fɛr yn 'rɔb? |

(d) Interrogative idea not emphasised, but some other:

sa ve vu ǁpur kwa in sɔ̃ pɑ rã 'tre?

or

sa ve vu ǁpur ḵwa in sɔ̃ pɑ rã 'tre?

s ɔkyp t il ǁøm̱ɛːm də 'sa? |
lez ave vu vy ǁsuv̱ã i'si? |
sɔ̃t il vrɛmã ɛ̃ǁfa'jibl? |
ire vu ǁbjɛ̃ṯo a la kã'paɲ? |

307. Commands.

(a) Command idea emphasised:

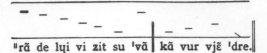

ǁ"rã de lɥi vi zit su ᴵvã ǀ kã vur vjɛ̃ ᴵdre.ǁ

ǁ"rœvne tu t ᴵsɥit ǀ aprɛ vɔt lə'sɔ̃. ǁ
ǁ"ale dus'mã ǀ ã rəvᴵnã. ǁ
ǁ"dɔne nu œ̃ travaj swaᴵɲe ǀ a la fɛ̃ d la ᴵsmɛn. ǁ
ǁ"kup lə gɑto ã ᴵkatr ǀ avã d lə paᴵse. ǁ
ǁ"rœmɛ lə dusᴵmã ǀ a sa ᴵplas. ǁ
ǁ"ale tu t sɥit a la ᴵgɑːr ǀ le rãkɔ̃ᴵtre. ǁ
ǁ"rœvne trãkilᴵmã ǀ a la meᴵzɔ̃. ǁ
ǁ"fɛt lœr vwar tu no ᴵliːvr ǀ avã lœr deᴵpaːr. ǁ
ǁ"ale le vwar ply suᴵvã ǀ kã vu sre d rəᴵtuːr. ǁ
ǁ"rãːʒ tu te ᴵʒwɛ ǀ avã d t ãn aᴵle. ǁ
ǁ"travaj ply serjøzᴵmã ǀ k l ane dɛrᴵnjɛːr. ǁ
ǁ"ʃãte nu yn ʃãᴵsɔ̃ ǀ pur nuz amyᴵze. ǁ
ǁ"ãmne nu avɛk ᴵvu ǀ ʒysk a la ᴵgɑːr. ǁ
ǁ"truve nu yn ᴵplas ǀ ã døzjɛm ᴵklɑːs. ǁ
ǁ"dɔn lɥi tu te ᴵʒwɛ ǀ avã d tãn aᴵle. ǁ
ǁ"va vwar si ɔ̃ lez apɛrᴵswa ǀ o kwɛ̃ d la ᴵry. ǁ

(b) Command idea emphasised and some word in the non-final group made prominent:

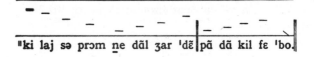

ǁ"ki laj sə prɔm ne dãl ʒar ᴵdɛ̃ǀpã dã kil fɛ ᴵbo.ǁ

ǁ"ʃãte n̲u yn ʃãᴵsɔ̃ ǀ pur nuz amyᴵze. ǁ
ǁ"vu vuz ɔkypre d la meᴵzɔ̃ ǀ pãdã nɔtr apᴵsãːs. ǁ
ǁ"ale tu t s̲ɥit a la ᴵgɑːr ǀ le rãkɔ̃ᴵtre. ǁ
ǁ"fɛt lœr v̲waːr tu no ᴵliːvr ǀ avã lœr deᴵpaːr. ǁ
ǁ"ãmne n̲u avɛk ᴵvu ǀ ʒysk a la ᴵgɑːr. ǁ
ǁ"truve n̲u yn ᴵplas ǀ ã døzjɛm ᴵklɑːs. ǁ

(c) Command idea and some other emphasised for intensity :

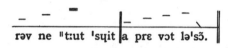

ǁa le le vwar ǁply su ˈvã ǀa vã lœr de ˈpaːr. ǁ

ǁrœvne ǁtrãkilˈmã ǀ a la meˈzɔ̃. ǁ
ǁfɛt lœr vwar ǁtu no ˈliːvr ǀ avã lœr de ˈpaːr. ǁ
ǁrãːʒ ǁtu te ˈʒwɛ ǀ avã d t ãn aˈle. ǁ
ǁrãde lɥi vizit ǁsːu ˈvã ǀ kã vu rvjɛ̃ˈdre. ǁ
ǁrœvne ǁtu t ˈsɥit ǀ aprɛ vɔt lǝˈsɔ̃. ǁ

(d) Command idea not emphasised but some other :

rǝv ne ǁtːut ˈsɥit ǀa prɛ vɔt lǝˈsɔ̃.

ale ǁdusˈmã ǀ ã rǝvˈnã. ǁ

rǝv ne ǁtrã kil ˈmã ǀa la meˈzɔ̃.

rãʒ ǁtu te ˈʒwɛ ǀ avã d t ãn aˈle. ǁ
fɛt lœr vwar ǁtu no ˈliːvr ǀ avã lœr deˈpaːr. ǁ
ale le vwar ǁply suˈvã ǀ kã vu sre d rǝˈtuːr. ǁ
travaj ǁply serjøzˈmã ǀ k 1 ane dɛrˈnjɛːr. ǁ
dɔne lœr le papje iǁmedjatˈmã ǀ pur k il le kɔ̃ˈsylt. ǁ

(e) Double Imperatives :

ǁa le mɛt sɛt lɛ tra la ˈpɔst ǀe rǝv ne tut ˈsɥit. ǁ

N

ꞈmɛ tɔ̃ ʃaꞏpo | e va t prɔmꞏne. ‖

ꞈva ʃɛrʃe te ꞏliːvr | e aprɑ̃ te lꞏsɔ̃. ‖

ꞈrœtjɛ̃ nu yn ꞏplas | e atɑ̃ ꞏnu. ‖

ꞈamne la vwatyr ɑ̃ fas də la meꞏzɔ̃, | e prevne ꞏnu. ‖

ꞈrɑ̃plise le vɑz də ꞏroːz, | e mɛte ꞏlɛ | o saꞏlɔ̃. ‖

ꞈpɔrte lœr le ꞏliːvr | e rəvne tu t ꞏsɥit. ‖

ꞈrɑ̃ːʒ tu te ꞏʒwɛ | e va t kuꞏʃe. ‖

CHAPTER XXII

CONTRAST IN ENGLISH

(1) Contrast word in a group with the Falling intonation.

308. Read the following examples with the intonation indicated :

I'm de"lighted to see you.

The man's an "idiot.

It's ex"tremely difficult.

It's extremely "difficult.

It's "absolutely impossible.

It's absolutely im"possible.

It's forty five shillings a "yard.

309.   In each case the statement is made, not, as in intensity, to express degree—either of delight, stupidity, difficulty, impossibility, high cost, as the case may be—but to put forward an entirely different point of view from that just stated, or from that which you feel exists in the mind of the person to whom you are speaking.   Someone says, for example, *"It's 'not at 'all 'difficult."* You reply, *"On the "contrary, it's ex"tremely difficult,"* extremely offering a contrast to *not at all*.   Or someone says, *"I 'think it will be 'easy."*   You reply, *"I "don't think so : I think it will be "difficult,"* difficult offering a contrast to *easy*.   The statement *"It's forty-five shillings a "yard"* is made, not to impress someone with the high price of the material, but probably to destroy the impression that forty-five shillings is the price of the *dress-length*.

310.   The effect of contrast is produced mainly by the sudden turn in the pitch of the syllable which normally bears stress.   The height of the fall varies according to the degree of emphasis.

311.   Syllables which precede the emphasis are generally short and unstressed and have the intonation of initial unstressed syllables. Those which follow also lack prominence and have the intonation of final unstressed syllables.

312.   It is the word expressing the contrast which attracts the attention of the hearer by the sudden change in pitch given to it.

313.   Generally, the change in pitch is accompanied by an increase of stress, but this is not the important thing.   When intonation and stress work together, the effect is, of course, strengthened.

314.   Other devices, used also in intensity—such as the use of an upward glide on to the pitch of the emphasised syllable, a difference of word order, an enlarging of the construction—may at the same time contribute towards producing a greater effect of emphasis for contrast.

(2) Contrast word in a group with the Falling-Rising intonation :

315.   The following are examples of statements with an implication, requiring a rising intonation finally.   The sudden fall in pitch expresses contrast ; the rise suggests an implication.   The

implication is very strongly suggested when emphatic intonation
is present :

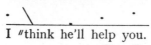

I "think he'll help you.

(But I'm not sure about it.)

Compare the above with

I 'think he'll help you,

where *think* is not pronounced with the intonation of contrast
and the implication is not so strong

I didn't "know "you were the author.

(I thought it was somebody else.)

I didn't "know you were the "author.

(I thought you were the publisher.)

316.   Sometimes this fall-rise occurs in pronouncing one syllable :

You'll "get one "there.[1]

(But you'll have no success here.)

It's a "genuine an"tique.

(So you can't expect to have it at the price
of one of these modern reproductions.)

[1] The dot at the beginning of the fall shows the point of greatest prominence
in the syllable.

317. This type of Fall-Rise intonation does not occur in French in pronouncing a single syllable.[1] It is extremely common in English. English people should be on their guard against using it in French.

---

[1] There *is* a Fall-Rise intonation in French, used in pronouncing a single syllable; for example, in saying *oui*, *non*, in a way which implies doubt or uncertainty:

wi.   nɔ̃.

The prominent part of the syllable, however, is not at the beginning of the fall as in the English Fall-Rise illustrated in § 316.

Chapter XXIII

CONTRAST IN FRENCH

318. Contrast in French is expressed in the same way as in English : mainly by an abrupt change in the pitch of the emphasised word.

319. As in English it is the syllable normally bearing stress which is pronounced with the intonation of contrast. If the contrast concerns *degree*, however, it is the intensity-bearing syllable which is pronounced with the intonation of contrast. (See Chap. XXV.)

320. As in English, the syllables preceding the emphasis may be quickly and lightly pronounced on a monotone, and thus have little prominence. Those that follow may have a low level intonation ; or, if the fall in pronouncing the emphasised syllable is only a small one, the intonation of the syllables which follow may continue to descend instead of being pronounced on a monotone :

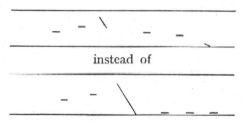

instead of

321. Attention is focussed on the emphasised syllable to the neglect of all others.

322. A reinforcement of stress often accompanies the rapid change in pitch.

INFLUENCE OF EMPHASIS FOR CONTRAST ON INTONATION.

(I) ON THE RISING-FALLING INTONATION.

323. The Rising-Falling intonation

may take the following forms according to the position of the emphasised syllable.

(i) Emphasised syllable final:

sɛ tɛks trɛm mɑ̃ di fi ‖sil.

Contrast
with
facile.

il la aʃ te ɑ̃ na me ‖rik.

Contrast
with
Allemagne.

i lɛ tɛ̃ sy pɔr ‖taːbl.

Contrast
with
agréable.

ʒə sɥi za le a ‖lɔ̃ːdr.

Contrast
with
Leeds.

(ii) Emphasised syllable medial:

sɛ tɛks trɛm ‖mɑ̃ di fi sil.

Contrast
with
pas du tout.

ʃsɥi zɑ̃ ʃɑ̃ ‖te dle vwaːr.

Contrast
with
fâché.

(iii) Emphasised syllable initial:

‖rjɛ̃n mə tɑ̃ːt.

Contrast
with
tout.

‖tu lə de rɑ̃ːʒ.

Contrast
with
rien.

(2) ON THE FALLING INTONATION.

324. The Falling intonation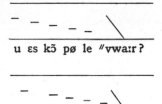

may take the following forms according to the position of the emphasised syllable:

(i) Final syllable emphasised:

u ɛs kɔ̃ pø le ″vwaːr?

pur kwa a til fɛ ″sa?

(ii) Medial syllable emphasised:

a vɛk ″ki a le vu tra va je?

də ″kwa sa ʒi til?

(iii) Initial syllable emphasised:

″kɑ̃ dwav til par tiːr?

″ki vu za di kil fa lɛ fɛr sa?

(3) ON THE RISING INTONATION.

325.　The Rising intonation ———————

or ———————

may take the following forms according to the position of the emphasised syllable:

(i) Final syllable emphasised:

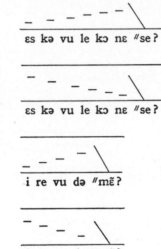

ɛs kə vu le kɔ nɛ ″se?

or

ɛs kə vu le kɔ nɛ ″se?

i re vu də ″mɛ̃?

or

i re vu də ″mɛ̃?

(ii) Medial syllable emphasised:

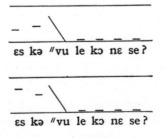

ɛs kə ″vu le kɔ nɛ se?

or

ɛs kə ″vu le kɔ nɛ se?

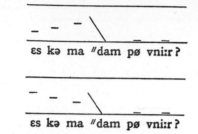

ɛs kə ma ″dam pø vniːr?

or

ɛs kə ma ″dam pø vniːr?

(iii) Initial syllable emphasised :

″fym til, a lɔːr?

The normal way of asking questions like the above, however, is with *Est-ce que.* The emphasised word then occurs medially as under (ii).

326. The change in pitch and increase of stress in pronouncing the emphasised syllable may be reinforced by the presence of other devices which are used also in intensity : repetition, a difference of word order, an enlarging of the construction, the use of an upward glide. But these are not mainly responsible for the effect of contrast : they simply add to the effect produced by the sudden turn in the intonation which is always present.

Chapter XXIV

SHORT EXAMPLES WITH CONTRAST IN FRENCH

327. It must be taken into account in reading the examples given below that such sentences can never occur as isolated statements; they must always be considered as expressing a contrast to some opinion either stated or felt. The reader must imagine the context in order to read them with conviction.

SHORT EXAMPLES WITH CONTRAST.

(1) Forms of the Rising-Falling intonation.

328. Assertions:

(i) Emphasised syllable final:

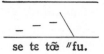

se tɛ tœ̃ ″fu.

rjɛ̃ n mə ″tãːt.	s ɛt efrwa″jaːbl.
s ɛ parfɛtmã ″vrɛ.	s ɛ par″fɛ.
ʒə vɛ lɥi ″rãːdr.	s ɛ dezas″trø.
me ʒ l e ″vy.	s ɛ ʒyst lə kɔ̃″trɛːr.
s ɛ l ″voːtr.	s ɛt œ̃n ɛ̃be″sil.
ʃ truv kə vuz ave ″tɔːr.	s ɛt ɛkstrɛmmã difi″sil.
i j ãn a ″sis.	s ɛ maɲi″fik.
ʒə n truv pɑ sa ridikyl dy ″tu.	s ɛ deli″sjø.
ʒ ire le vwar kã ″mɛːm.	s ɛt œ̃ parɛ″sø.
ʒə n tjɛ̃ pɑ a le ″vwaːr.	sa s fɛ fasil″mã.
ʒə n lez e ʒamɛ ″vy.	s ɛt inimaʒi″naːbl.
rjɛ̃ n ɛ ply fa″sil.	s ɛt ɛkstraɔrdi″nɛːr.
s ɛ l kɔ̃″trɛːr.	ɛl etɛt adɔ″raːbl.
s ɛt ɛ̃tɛrmi″naːbl.	s ɛ dezɔ″lã.
sa m ɛt e″gal.	s ɛ dife″rã.
s ɛt ɛ̃pɔ″sibl.	s ɛt yn otr a″fɛːr.
s ɛ trɛ ʒɔ″li.	ɛl ɛ ʃar″mãːt.
s ɛt epa″tã.	tu s arãʒ″ra.

s ɛ ridi″kyl.

il ɛt ɛ̃sypɔr″taːbl.

s ɛt ɛ̃sɑ̃″se.

s ɛ ravi″sɑ̃.

s ɛt ɑ̃ɥi″jø.

s ɛ sy″pɛrb.

ilz ɔ̃ de ʃoz deli″sjøːz.

i n vjɛn pɑ su″vɑ̃.

ʒ ɛm mjø n pɑ le rɑ̃kɔ̃″tre.

vu vu trɔ̃″pe.

ʒə l e ″fɛ.

(ii) Emphasised syllable medial:

ʒə˙vɛ ″tu lɥi diːr.

mɛ ″rjɛ̃ n i fɛ.

ɛ ɔ lɑ ″ɔœl ʃoz ki m mɑ̃ːk.

il ɛ d ″trɛ mɔvɛz ymœːr.

s ɛ ″sa ki m ɛt egal.

ʒə truv kə vuz ave ″tɔːr də fɛr sa.

ʒə vwa bɔku ″mjø avɛk se lynɛt la.

ɔ̃ n oz ″ply travɛrse la ry.

s ɛt a ″nu d vuz ɛ̃terɔʒe.

s ɛ ″mwa lə kupaːbl.

s ɛ ″mwa ki e di d lə fɛːr.

s ɛ ″twa ki sra pyni.

ʒə sɥiz ɑ̃ʃɑ̃″te d le vwaːr.

s ɛt ɛkstrɛm″mɑ̃ difisil.

ʒə sɥi dezɔ″le d vuz avwar mɑ̃ke.

il ɛ tu″ʒuːr ɑ̃ rtaːr.

ʒə srɛ ra″vi d vu vwaːr.

ʒə n ɑ̃n e o″kyn ide.

s ɛt yn ɛksɛ″lɑ̃ːt ide.

s ɛt ɛ̃fini″mɑ̃ ply kɔmɔd.

s ɛt yn vil ɛkstrɛm″mɑ̃ ɛ̃terɛsɑ̃ːt.

s ɛt egzaktə″mɑ̃ la mɛm ʃoːz.

s ɛt admirablə″mɑ̃ kɔ̃pri.

pɛr″sɔn nə puvɛ l fɛːr.

ʃa″kœ̃ s ɑ̃ ɔkypra.

ʒə sɥiz a″le a lɔ̃ːdr.   (Reply to: *Vous n'avez sans doute jamais vu Londres.*)

(iii) Emphasised syllable initial:

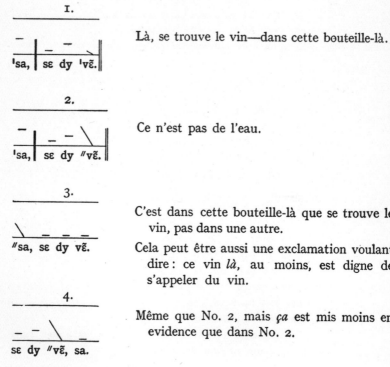

〃tu sa rɑ̃ʒ ra.

〃rjɛ̃ n ɛ ply fasil.
〃ʒɑːk i ɛt ale.
〃ø sɔ̃ parti.
〃mwa ʒ le vø.

(iv) Other examples.

   Study the following:

1.

ˈsa,│ sɛ dy ˈvɛ̃.‖   Là, se trouve le vin—dans cette bouteille-là.

2.

ˈsa,│ sɛ dy 〃vɛ̃.‖   Ce n'est pas de l'eau.

3.

〃sa, sɛ dy vɛ̃.   C'est dans cette bouteille-là que se trouve le vin, pas dans une autre.

Cela peut être aussi une exclamation voulant dire: ce vin *là*, au moins, est digne de s'appeler du vin.

4.

sɛ dy 〃vɛ̃, sa.   Même que No. 2, mais *ça* est mis moins en evidence que dans No. 2.

5.

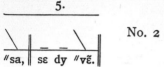

No. 2 et No. 3.

″sa, ‖ sɛ dy ″vɛ̃.‖

Say, in the same five ways, **nu, nuz irɔ̃ ; mwa, ʒ lez e vy,**
and notice the difference in meaning expressed by each
different intonation form.

(2) FORMS OF THE FALLING INTONATION.

329. Specific interrogative sentences and commands.

(i) Emphasised syllable final :

kə kɔ̃ te vu fɛr də ″mɛ̃?

u ɛt vu ale jɛr ″swaːr?
ki dezire vu ″vwaːr?
k ɛ s k ɛl pɑs də sɛt afɛr ″la?
ki ɛ ɛ ki ɛɛt oktypo d ″oa?
kə vule vu g ʒə vu ″diːz?
kɔmɑ̃ dit ɔ̃ sa ɑ̃ frɑ̃″sɛ?
ki vuz a di k il falɛ fɛr ″sa?
k ɛ s kə vuz ave vy la smɛn dɛr″njɛːr?
ekute s k il a a vu ″diːr.
vɑ̃de la me″zɔ̃.

(ii) Emphasised syllable medial :

kɔ̃ bjɛ̃d ″liː vra ve vu?

ʃe ″ki ɛt ɛl ale?
kɛl ″œːr ave vu?
a ″kwa travaj t il?

kɔ″mã sa s fɛ t il?

kɔmã dit ɔ̃ ″sa ã frãsɛ?

la″kɛl prefere vu?

kɛl ku″lœːr prefere vu?

k ɛ s kə ″sɛ k sɛt istwaːr?

a ″ki vule vu parle?

u ɛt vu a″le jɛr swaːr?

kə kɔ̃te vu ″fɛːr dəmɛ̃?

ki ″ɛ s ki s ɛt ɔkype d sa?

pur″kwa dit vu de ʃoz parɛːj?

dã kɛl dirɛk″sjɔ̃ ale vu?

a ″ki ale vu le dɔne?

avɛk ″ki kɔ̃te vu rəvniːr?

ki ɛ s ki vuz a ″di d rãtre?

kɔmã s fɛt ″il kə vu n swaje paz ãkɔr **parti**?

k ɛ s kə vuz ave ″fɛ dpɥi tãto?

ki ʋuz a ″di k il falɛ fɛr sa?

purkwa n ave vu pɑ vã″dy sɛt mezɔ̃?

purkwa n vø t il pɑ nu ″diːr s ki s ɛ pase?

pur″kwa n vø t il pɑ nu diːr s ki s ɛ pase?

k ɛ s kə vuz ave ″vy la smɛn dɛrnjɛːr?

k ɛ s k ɛl ″pãːs də sɛt afɛr la?

nə lɥi mɔ̃tre ″pɑ s kə ʒ vuz e dɔne.

n ale ″pɑ avɛk ɛl.

eku″te s k il a a vu diːr.

nə lɥi rakɔ̃te ″rjɛ̃ d sɛt afɛr la.

vã″de la mezɔ̃.

(iii) Emphasised syllable initial :

″ki de zi re vu vwaːr?

″u ɛt vu ale jɛr swaːr?

″kã va t il partiːr?

″d u ɛ s k i vjɛ̃?

″d u vjɛ̃t il?

(3) FORMS OF THE RISING INTONATION.

330. "Yes" and "No" questions.

(i) Emphasised syllable final:

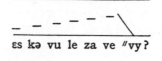

ɛs kə vu le za ve ″vy?

or

ɛs kə vu le za ve ″vy?

vjɛ̃drɔt il sə ″swaːr?
s ɔkypt il boku d ″lɥi?
irɔ̃t il avɛk ″ø?
lez ave vu rɑ̃kɔ̃″tre?
vu lez ɔ̃t il rɑ̃″dy?
ɛ s kə vu lez ave ɑ̃tɑ̃″dy?
rəvjɛ̃dre vu bjɛ̃″to?
vjɛ̃t il su″vɑ̃?

(ii) Emphasised syllable medial:

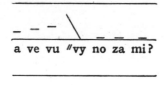

a ve vu ″vy no za mi?

or

a ve vu ″vy no za mi?

ɛ s kə vu l ave ″vy ɑ̃ frɑ̃ːs?
ɛ ty kɔ̃″tɑ̃ d tɔ̃n aprɛmidi?
ɛ s kə vuz ave kɔ̃″fjɑ̃ːs ɑ̃ lɥi?
ɛ s kə pɛr″sɔn n a ete arɛte?
lɥi ave vu rɑ̃″dy sɔ̃ paraplɥi?
vɔ̃t il su″vɑ̃ a l etɑ̃ʒe?

o

CHAPTER XXV

INTENSITY AND CONTRAST IN SAME GROUP OR WORD

331. Intensity and contrast may occur in the same sense-group. They may even occur in pronouncing the same word. Intensity and contrast in relation to *degree* may occur in the same syllable.

332. Below are examples of groups containing

(*a*) A word the meaning of which is generally intensified by *très* or *fort* or *bien*, e.g. *gentille*. (See § 278.)

(*b*) A word which is not modified by *très*, etc., e.g. *ridicule*. (See § 279.)

(*c*) A word of type (*b*) used with an expression denoting the maximum degree, e.g. *absolument ridicule, tout à fait ridicule, parfaitement ridicule*. (See § 279.)

Example of (*a*) : *Elle est très gentille.*

333. *Gentille* does not often carry stress for intensity ; this is generally borne by *très*. The above sentence may be pronounced emphatically in the following ways :

I. Intensity.

ɛ lɛ ⁿtɪːɛ ʒɑ̃ ˈtiːj.

This expresses the speaker's experience of many degrees of niceness in the child under discussion. The speaker does not contradict, but merely states his own opinion, using certain of the intensity devices in pronouncing *très*: strong stress, raised pitch, added length of t and r, with perhaps a facial expression which indicates great appreciation, and some kind of gesture. *She's ⁿvery ˈnice* has a similar intonation :

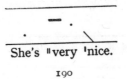

She's ⁿvery ˈnice.

2.

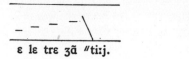

ε lε trε ʒɑ̃ ″tiːj.

Contrast
with
vilaine.

This intonation, with a high falling tone on the final syllable
of *gentille* shows that the speaker is not specially concerned
with his own appreciation of the niceness of the child.
His object is flatly to contradict the hearer who has probably
just described her as *vilaine.*

She's very nice may express the same thing in the same
way :

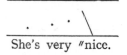

She's very ″nice.

3.

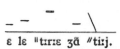

ε lε ″tːrːε ʒɑ̃ ″tiːj.

Intensity and
contrast with
vilaine.

Here the strength of the speaker's reaction to the niceness
of the child is expressed by intensifying *très* as in 1. His
contradiction of the listener's opinion that she is *vilaine*
is expressed as in 2 by the high falling tone given to the
final syllable of *gentille*. Note the lowered pitch of *gen-*.
This throws both *très* and *gentille* into greater relief.
Compare

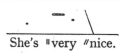

She's ″very ″nice.

4 (*a*).

ε lε ″tːrːε ʒɑ̃ tiːj.

Contrast in
relation to
degree.

Here there is contradiction of the other person's opinion, not that the child is *vilaine* (as in 3), but that *Elle n'est pas gentille du tout* or *Elle n'est pas très gentille*. This is shown by the falling pitch of *très*. It is the other person's opinion that there are no degrees of niceness, or very few, which is contradicted.

Compare

She's ʺvery nice.

At the same time the speaker may use intensive stress and other intensity devices in pronouncing *très*, and thus express, *"Non seulement je contredis votre opinion qu'elle n'est pas gentille du tout, mais moi, je la trouve extrêmement gentille."* To show this intensity and contrast in pronouncing *très* the mark ʺ could be used:

4 (*b*).

ɛ lɛ ʺtːrːɛ ʒɑ̃ tiːj.

Compare

She's ʺvery nice.

5.

ɛ lɛ ʺtːrːɛ ʒɑ̃ ʺtiːj.

Intensity and "double" contrast.

This adds to 4 (*b*) a definitely expressed contradiction of *vilaine*.

Compare

She's ʺvery ʺnice.

334. Examples of (a) for practice.

C'est bien important.

1.	s ε ‖bjẽn ɛ̃pɔr‖tɑ̃.
2.	s ε bjẽn ɛ̃pɔr‖tɑ̃.
3.	s ε ‖bjẽn ɛ̃pɔr‖tɑ̃.
4 (b).	s ε ‖bjẽn ɛ̃pɔrtɑ̃.
5.	s ε ‖bjẽn ɛ̃pɔr‖tɑ̃.

The English sentence *It's very important* can be emphasised in the same way except that *important* bears both normal stress and emphasis for contrast on the *second* syllable.

Elle est très élégante.

1.	εl ε ‖trɛz ele‖gɑ̃:t.
2.	εl ε trɛz ele‖gɑ̃:t.
3.	εl ε ‖trɛz ele‖gɑ̃:t.
4 (b).	εl ε ‖trɛz elegɑ̃:t.
5.	εl ε ‖trɛz ele‖gɑ̃:t.

The English sentence, *She's very elegant,* can be emphasised in the same way except that *elegant* bears both normal stress and emphasis for contrast on the *first* syllable.

335. Thus when there is a separate word for expressing intensity the French way of emphasising is much the same as the English way : *très* (or whatever the intensity word is) shows emphasis concerning degree ; the following word shows emphasis for contrast with some other idea.

336. The meaning of those words which cannot be modified by *très* or *fort* (see § 279) can also be intensified. In fact, these words can in themselves express both intensity and contrast.

337. This double emphasis *within* a word can be expressed more effectively in French than in English, since in French intensity and contrast (unless of degree) are expressed in pronouncing different syllables of a word. In English they are generally expressed in the same syllable. E.g. *parfait, superbe, ridicule* show intensity in the first syllable, contrast in the last; *abominable, impossible,* show intensity in the second (or first) syllable, contrast in the last. In

the English word *perfect* the first syllable has to express both intensity and contrast. In *superb, ridiculous, abominable, impossible,* the second syllable has to show both intensity and contrast.

Example of (*b*): *C'est ridicule.*

338. This can be pronounced in such a way that it expresses the speaker's strong feeling as to the degree of absurdity:

1.

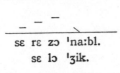

        Intensity.

      sɛ "ri di 'kyl.
Cf. sɛ "trɛ ʒɑ̃ 'ti.

The first syllable of *ridicule* bears stress for intensity which in the case of *gentil* is borne by *très*.

339. The other person may have said about the thing under discussion

      sɛ rɛ ɔ 'naːbl.
      sɛ lɔ 'ʒik.

The answer, *C'est ridicule,* may be said in such a way (i.e. by giving a high falling pitch to the final syllable of *ridicule*) that it contradicts the above opinion:

2.

        Contrast.

      sɛ ri di ″kyl.
Cf. sɛ trɛ ʒɑ̃ ″ti.

340. *C'est ridicule* may be so pronounced that the speaker expresses 1 and 2 at the same time:

3.

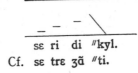

Intensity and contrast in the same word.

      sɛ "rːi di ″kyl.
Cf. sɛ "tːrːɛ ʒɑ̃ ″ti.

341. The other person may feel the absurdity of the thing differently: his impression of it may be much weaker; or he may feel that it is not absurd at all. He may say, for example,

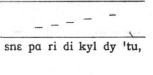

sɛ ta s̄e sã 'se,
sɛ ta s̄e lɔ 'ʒik,

(admitting some degree of reasonableness), or

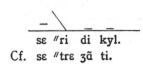

snɛ pɑ ri di kyl dy 'tu,

or

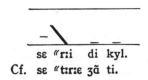

snɛ pɑ ri di kyl dy ʺtu

(denying that there is any degree of absurdity at all). This opinion as to *degree* can be contradicted by giving a high falling pitch to the first syllable of *ridicule*:

4 (*a*).

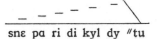

sɛ ʺri di kyl.
Cf. sɛ ʺtrɛ ʒã ti.

Contrast in relation to degree.

342. At the same time the speaker may place intensive stress, etc., on **ri,** thus expressing intensity and contrast of degree in the same syllable:

4 (*b*).

sɛ ʺrːi di kyl.
Cf. sɛ ʺtːrːɛ ʒã ti.

Intensity and contrast in relation to degree.

343. At the same time may be expressed a very definite contradiction of *raisonnable* :

5.

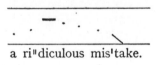

se ⁗rːi   di ⁗kyl.
Cf. se ⁗tːrːe ʒɑ̃ ⁗ti.

Intensity and
"double"
contrast.

344. Compare the above five ways with the emphatic ways of saying *It's ridiculous* where the effect of both intensity and contrast has to be made in pronouncing the second syllable of *ridiculous* :

1.

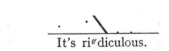

It's ri⁗diculous.

Intensity.

(The pitch falls on the second syllable of *ridiculous* because it happens to be the last stressed syllable in the group. In *a ri⁗diculous mis'take* the intonation is

a ri⁗diculous mis'take.

2.

It's ri⁗diculous.

Contrast.

Here there need only be an abrupt change of pitch in pronouncing the second syllable.

3.

It's ri⁗diculous.

Intensity and
contrast.

Here the abrupt change of pitch is accompanied by a reinforcement of stress and as many of the other intensity devices as are suitable.

345.   Examples of (b) for practice:

C'est ravissant.

1.   s ε ‖ravi'sã.
2.   s ε ravi″sã.
3.   s ε ‖ravi″sã.
4 (b).   s ε ″ravisã.
5.   s ε ″ravi″sã.

C'est superbe, c'est parfait, c'est splendide.

1.   s ε ‖sy'pεrb.
2.   s ε sy″pεrb.
3.   s ε ‖sy″pεrb.*
4 (b).   s ε ″sypεrb.
5.   s ε ″sy″pεrb.*

* These forms are possible, but not very usual. The speaker would probably prefer to chose a three syllabled word such as *merveilleux, épatant, ravissant, excellent,* in order to avoid the two kinds of emphasis in successive syllables.

C'est excellent.

1.   s εt εk″sε'lã   or   s εt ‖ʔεksε'lã.
2.   s εt εksε″lã.
3.   s εt ‖ʔεksε″lã.
4 (b).   s εt εk″sεlã   or   s εt ″ʔεksεlã.
5.   s εt ″ʔεksε″lã.

Forms with emphasis on two successive syllables can easily be avoided in the case of three syllabled words beginning with a vowel by placing emphasis on the *first* syllable as in 3 and 5 above.

C'est insupportable.

1.   s εt ε̃″sypɔr'taːbl   or   s εt ‖ʔε̃sypɔr'taːbl.
2.   s εt ε̃sypɔr″taːbl.
3.   s εt ε̃″sypɔr″taːbl   or   s εt ‖ʔε̃sypɔr″taːbl.
4 (b).   s εt ε̃″sypɔrtaːbl   or   s εt ″ʔε̃sypɔrtaːbl.
5.   s εt ε̃″sypɔr″taːbl   or   s εt ″ʔε̃sypɔr″taːbl.

Example of (c):   *C'est absolument ridicule.*

346. In saying this, various devices for emphasis may be used on either or on both words. Many forms are possible.

347. Only *ridicule* emphasised.

Ridicule, spoken with exactly the same stress and intonation forms as those described under (*b*), can express degree of absurdity and contrast with *raisonnable*. The presence of *absolument* adds to the effect of intensity :

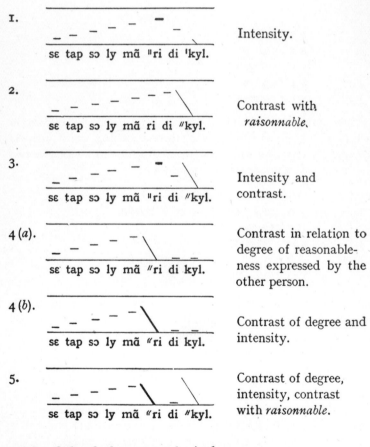

1.   sɛ tap sɔ ly mã "ri di 'kyl.   Intensity.

2.   sɛ tap sɔ ly mã ri di "kyl.   Contrast with *raisonnable*.

3.   sɛ tap sɔ ly mã "ri di "kyl.   Intensity and contrast.

4 (*a*).   sɛ tap sɔ ly mã "ri di kyl.   Contrast in relation to degree of reasonableness expressed by the other person.

4 (*b*).   sɛ tap sɔ ly mã "ri di kyl.   Contrast of degree and intensity.

5.   sɛ tap sɔ ly mã "ri di "kyl.   Contrast of degree, intensity, contrast with *raisonnable*.

348. Only *absolument* emphasised.

The speaker is in this case concerned only with degree of

absurdity (intensity or contrast in relation to degree) and not directly with any contrast with *raisonnable*.

1.

sɛ tap ‖sɔ ly mã ri di ꞌkyl.   Intensity.

or

sɛt ‖ʔap sɔ ly mã ri di ꞌkyl.

2.

sɛ tap sɔ ly ″mã ri di kyl.   Contrast of degree.

3.

sɛ tap ‖sɔ ly ″mã ri di kyl.   Intensity and contrast
                                   of degree.

or

sɛt ‖ʔap sɔ ly ″mã ri di kyl.

4.

sɛ tap ″sɔ ly mã ri di kyl.   Intensity and contrast
                                 of degree expressed in
or   one syllable.

sɛt ″ʔap sɔ ly mã ri di kyl.

5.

sɛ tap ″sɔ ly ″mã ri di kyl.   Intensity and "double"
                                  contrast of degree.

349. Similar forms are also possible for *It's absolutely ridiculous*, since *absolutely* is an exceptional word that may be emphasised on two syllables, the first and third:

I.

It's "absolutely ri'diculous.

Intensity.

or

It's "abso"lutely ri'diculous.

Intensity.

2.

It's "absolutely ridiculous.

Contrast of degree.

or

It's abso"lutely ridiculous.

3.

It's "abso"lutely ridiculous.

Intensity and contrast of degree.

4.

It's "absolutely ridiculous.

Intensity and contrast of degree in one syllable.

5.

It's "abso"lutely ridiculous.

Very strong intensity and contrast of degree.

350. In other words of the *absolutely* type, e.g. *completely,
utterly, entirely, perfectly,* it is impossible to show emphasis in more
than in one syllable:

1.

Intensity.

It's "utterly ri'diculous.

2.

Contrast of degree.

It's "utterly ridiculous.

If intensity and contrast of degree are both present, the second
intonation form is used, the emphasised syllable being pronounced
with intensive stress and possibly other intensity devices.

351. Both *absolument* and *ridicule* emphasised, the emphasis
relating to degree (intensity or contrast of degree).

In this case *absolument* simply reinforces *ridicule*:

1.

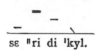

sɛ tap "sɔ ly mã "ri di 'kyl.

This is a very emphatic way of saying

sɛ "ri di 'kyl.

2.

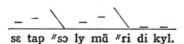

sɛ tap "sɔ ly mã "ri di kyl.

This is a very emphatic way of saying

sɛ "ri di kyl.

3.

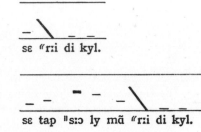

sɛ tap ⟨sɔ ly mã ⟨rːi di kyl.

This is a very emphatic way of saying

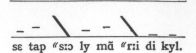

sɛ ⟨rːi di kyl.

4.

se tap ‖sɔ ly mã ⟨rːi di kyl.

This shows less contrast than 3.

352. *Absolument* emphasised as in § 348 and § 351, *ridicule* emphasised for contrast with *raisonnable* :

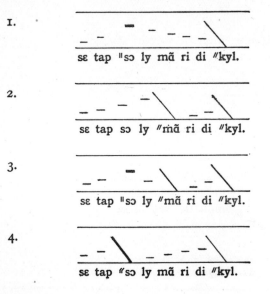

I.

sɛ tap ‖sɔ ly mã ri di ⟨kyl.

2.

sɛ tap sɔ ly ⟨mã ri di ⟨kyl.

3.

sɛ tap ‖sɔ ly ⟨mã ri di ⟨kyl.

4.

sɛ tap ⟨sɔ ly mã ri di ⟨kyl.

5.

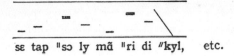

sɛ tap ʺsɔ ly ʺmã ri di ʺkyl.

Similar forms are possible for *It's absolutely ridiculous.*

353.   It is also possible to emphasise *absolument* as above, and *ridicule* for both intensity and contrast with *raisonnable.*   E.g.

sɛ tap ʺsɔ ly mã ʺri di ʺkyl,   etc.

354.   Examples of (*c*) for practice.   Some of the most usual forms only are suggested.

C'est absolument merveilleux.

1.   s ɛt apsɔlymã ʺmɛrvɛˈjø.
2.   s ɛt apsɔlymã mɛrvɛʺjø.
3.   s ɛt apsɔlymã ʺmɛrvɛʺjø.
4.   s ɛt apsɔlymã ʺmɛrvɛʺjø.
5.   s ɛt apʺsɔlymã mɛrvɛˈjø.
6.   s ɛt apʺsɔlymã ʺmɛrvɛˈjø.
7.   s ɛt apʺsɔlymã mɛrvɛʺjø.
8.   s ɛt apʺsɔlymã mɛrvɛʺjø.
9.   s ɛt apʺsɔlymã mɛrvɛʺjø.

C'est tout à fait impossible.
1.   s ɛ tut a fɛ ɛ̃ʺpɔˈsibl.
2.   s ɛ tut a fɛ ɛ̃pɔʺsibl.
3.   s ɛ tut a fɛ ʺɛ̃pɔʺsibl.
4.   s ɛ tut a fɛ ɛ̃ʺpɔsibl.
5.   s ɛ tut a fɛ ʺʔɛ̃pɔʺsibl.
6.   s ɛ ʺtut a fɛ ɛ̃pɔˈsibl.
7.   s ɛ tut a ʺfɛ ɛ̃pɔsibl.
8.   s ɛ ʺtut a fɛ ɛ̃pɔsibl.
9.   s ɛ ʺtut a ʺfɛ ɛ̃pɔsibl.

10.   s ɛ ⟨tut a ⟨fɛ ɛ̃pɔsibl.
11.   s ɛ ‖tut a fɛ ɛ̃‖pɔsibl.
12.   s ɛ ⟨tut a fɛ ɛ̃⟨pɔsibl.
13.   s ɛ ‖tut a fɛ ɛ̃⟨pɔsibl.
14.   s ɛ ‖tut a fɛ ɛ̃pɔ‖sibl.
15.   s ɛ tut a .⟨fɛ ɛ̃pɔ‖sibl.
16.   s ɛ ‖tut a ⟨fɛ ɛ̃pɔ‖sibl.
17.   s ɛ ⟨tut a fɛ ɛ̃pɔ‖sibl.
18.   s ɛ ⟨tut a ⟨fɛ ɛ̃pɔ‖sibl.

355. It will have been noticed that the question of *degree* in French, whether it be an expression of the speaker's feeling regarding degree, or contradiction of the other person's opinion regarding degree, affects the syllable bearing intensive stress, either by adding stress to it (intensity of degree, ‖),[1] or by giving to it a rapidly falling pitch (contradiction of degree, ⟨), or by both, ⟨.

356. The question of suggesting the *opposite* of the thing named (contrast, ⟨) affects the intonation of the syllable bearing normal stress, i.e. of the final syllable of the emphasised word.

[1] Other intensity devices may also be present.

CHAPTER XXVI

INTONATION OF LONG APPENDED EXPRESSIONS AND OF REAL PARENTHESES

I. APPENDED.

(a) To sentences with the Rising-Falling or the Falling intonation.

357. *Long* expressions of a parenthetical nature may generally be divided into two or more sense-groups. The intonation of these sense-groups appended to sentences with the Rising-Falling or the Falling intonation is as follows:

358. Sense-groups of small significance like *dit-il, répliqua-t-il, je trouve, voyons, madame, enfin, cependant, vous savez, il me semble, on m'a dit, vous comprenez, je suppose, je crois, en effet, peut-être,* etc., which form the first part of the appended expression, may be pronounced on a monotone. The intonation of such groups does not therefore constitute one of the typical tonal patterns of French (see § 123), and may be regarded as forming the non-prominent tail-end of the preceding intonation group (see § 50). Although the final syllable of a sense-group of small significance may bear more stress than the syllables preceding, it is convenient not to mark it as stressed.[1]

359. The remainder of the parenthetical expression, since it adds new matter, generally has an intonation more distinctive than a level one. As a rule the intonation is not *continued* on a monotone (though it may be, in very quick speech), but develops into the Rising intonation for non-final sense-groups and into the Rising-Falling for final sense-groups, the intonation of these groups generally having a narrowed range:

sa srɛ ɛ̃ pɔ 'sibl, re pɔ̃ diːʒ, ‖ a vɛ kɔ̃ɛ̃ sɑ̃ ˉɪrwɑ kry 'ɛl.‖

---

[1] This applies also to the final syllables of all unimportant groups of this kind.

P

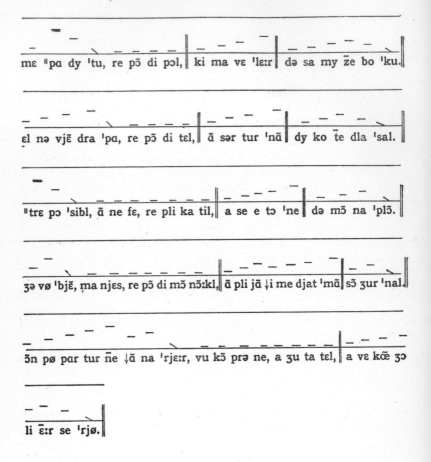

mɛ ‖pɑ dy ꞌtu, re pɔ̃ di pɔl, ‖ ki ma vɛ ꞌlɛːr ‖ də sa my z̄e bo ꞌku.‖

ɛl nə vjɛ̃ dra ꞌpɑ, re pɔ̃ di tɛl, ‖ ɑ̃ sər tur ꞌnɑ̃ ‖ dy ko t̄e dla ꞌsal. ‖

‖trɛ pɔ ꞌsibl, ɑ̃ ne fɛ, re pli ka til, ‖ a se e tɔ ꞌne ‖ də mɔ̃ na ꞌplɔ̃. ‖

ʒə vø ꞌbjɛ̃, ma njɛs, re pɔ̃ di mɔ̃ nɔ̃ːkl, ‖ ɑ̃ pli jɑ̃ ↓i me djat ꞌmɑ̃ ‖ sɔ̃ ʒur ꞌnal.‖

ɔ̃n pø pɑr tur n̄e ↓ɑ̃ na ꞌrjɛːr, vu kɔ̃ prə ne, a ʒu ta tɛl, ‖ a vɛ kɶ̃ ʒɔ

li ɛ̄ːr se ꞌrjø.‖

Other Examples:

ʒə vu rmɛrꞌsi, mə di mɔ̃ nuvɛl ami, ‖ kɑ̃t il sə truva ꞌsɶl ‖ avɛk ꞌmwa. ‖

s ɛt ɑ̃tɑ̃ꞌdy, deklara mɔ̃ pɛːr, ‖ ɑ̃ fəzɑ̃ tɔ̃ꞌbe ‖ la s̄ɑ̃ː↓drə də sɔ̃ siꞌgaːr. ‖

s ɛt ɶ̃ povr ꞌɔm, fi mɔ̃n ɔ̃ːkl, ‖ ki kry dəvwar p̄rɑ̃ː↓dr ɶ̃n ɛːr ↓atrisꞌte. ‖

ʒə ꞌpaːr, dit il ɑ̃ s ləvɑ̃, ‖ e ɑ̃ ʒtɑ̃ syr la ꞌtabl ‖ tu le paꞌpje ‖ k ɔ̃ vn̄ɛ
  d ↓lɥi aporꞌte. ‖

ʒə kɔ̃ꞌprɑ̃, dit il o bu d ɶ̃ mɔmɑ̃, ‖ ɑ̃ dɔnɑ̃ o paꞌpje ‖ yn ꞌtap ‖ dy
  rv̄ɛːr ↓də la ꞌmɛ̃. ‖

il a vɛ̃t døz 'ɑ̃, mɔ̃n ami, dit ɛl, ‖ ɑ̃ mɛlɑ̃ ↓kɛlk ɔr'gœːj | a boꭓu
↓də melɑ̃kɔ'li. ‖

k ɛ s 'dɔ̃ːk? repeta mɔ̃ pɛːr, ‖ ki avɛt œ̃ pø pɑ'li. ‖

dɔne 'mwa | s k i ja dɑ̃ vɔt 'sak, mə dit il, ‖ d œ̃ 'tɔ̃ | ki n admɛtɛ
pɑ̄ d re'plik. ‖

ʃ sɥiz ɑ̃"ʃɑ̃'te | də fɛr la kɔnɛ'sɑ̃ːs | d yn osi "ʃarmɑ̃t ku'zin, mə
dit ɛl d œ̃ tɔ̃ kɔ̃vɛ̃ky ‖ ɑ̃ m tɑ̄dɑ̄ la 'mɛ̃. ‖

kɔmɑ̃ s apɛl sɛt 'ɔm? dəmɑ̃da t ɛl, ‖ avɛk œ̃ muvmɑ̃ 'brysk | də
la 'tɛːt. ‖

tɛze 'vu ! dit il ɑ̃ s ləvɑ̃ a dmi, ‖ e ɑ̃ pɔrtɑ̃ la 'mɛ̃ | a sɔ̃ 'frɔ̃. ‖

kə fɛt vu 'la? mə di mɔ̃ pɛːr, ‖ ki s etɛt aprɔʃe d 'mwa, | sɑ̃ kə ʒ
l ys ɑ̄tɑ̄dy mar'ʃe. ‖

purkwa lə lœr ave vu dɔ'ne? me dit il, ‖ syr œ̃ tɔ̃ d rə'prɔʃ | ki m
ɛ̃timi'da | prɔfɔ̃de'mɑ̃. ‖

360. In English the intonation of long expressions appended
to sentences pronounced with the Falling intonation is developed
in a similar way. The sense-groups containing matter of little
importance are pronounced on a monotone and their intonation may
be regarded as belonging to the preceding intonation group. The
remaining intonation groups of parenthetical expressions, if pronounced with separate tonal patterns, have a narrowed range.
Non-final groups rise finally[1] ; the final group falls :

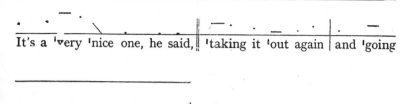

¹ They may fall if the sense permits.

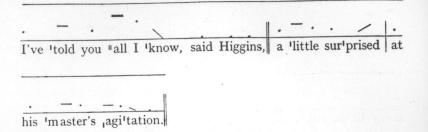

I've 'told you "all I 'know, said Higgins,‖ a 'little sur'prised ⎪ at

his 'master's ˌagi'tation.‖

(b) To sentences with a Rising or Falling-Rising intonation.

361. The intonation of a long expression of a parenthetical
nature appended to a sentence with a rising intonation is generally
as follows.   The intonation of those groups of the expression which
have little significance[1] may be considered as part of the previous
intonation group.   It continues the rise, generally after an introductory break, and, if necessary, may be broken in one or more
places :

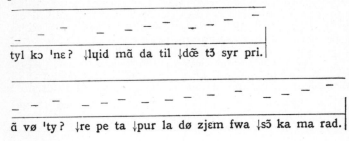

tyl kɔ 'nɛ? ↓lɥid mɑ̃ da til ↓dœ̃ tʒ syr pri.⎪

ɑ̃ vø 'ty? ↓re pe ta ↓pur la dø zjɛm fwa ↓sɔ̃ ka ma rad.⎪

362. If the parenthetical expression lengthens out into matter
which is too important or too long to be included in the preceding
intonation group, a separate rising group (or groups) is formed with,
if necessary, a break or breaks.

Examples :

sa ve vud ↓kwa i sa 'ʒi? ↓də mɑ̃ dal ljøt nɑ̃⎪ ɑ̃s kwa fɑ̃d ↓sɔ̃ ke 'pi.⎪

[1] See § 358 and footnote concerning the stress of the final syllables of such
groups.

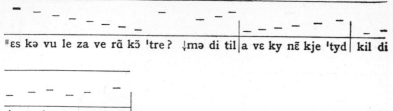

"ɛs kə vu le za ve rã kɔ̃ 'tre? ↓mə di til|a vɛ ky nɛ̃ kje 'tyd| kil di

si my lɛt ↓a vɛk 'pɛn.|

Other Examples:

ɛs 'vrɛ ↓mɔ̃ kuzɛ̃? ↓dit ɛl, | syrmɔ̃tã ase rapidmã ↓sɔ̃n ãba'rɑ. |

ty m aprãdra a dã'se? di:ʒ, | ã sotã deʒa ↓syr ma 'ʃe:z. |

save vu d u il 'vjɛn? |dəmãda t ɛl | avɛk yn pwɛ̈:t ↓də kyrjozi'te |
    ki n eʃapa ↓a pɛr'sɔn. |

il sɔ̃t i'si[1] ↓lɥi repɔ̃dit il ↓bryskəmã, | sã sɔ̃ʒe a la 'pɛn | k il puvɛ
    lɥi 'fe:r. |

363. It is also possible, in the case of long parenthetical expressions appended to sentences with a Rising or Falling-Rising
intonation, to use for those sense-groups which are sufficiently
important to have separate intonation groups the intonation which
is given to similar groups appended to sentences with the Rising-
Falling or the Falling intonation.   (See § 359.)

Example:

il sɔ̃ ti 'si ↓lɥi re pɔ̃ di til ↓brys kə mã,| sã sɔ̃ ʒe a la 'pɛn| kil pu

v̄ɛ lɥi 'fe:r.|

364. In English, the intonation of that part of the parenthetical
expression not included in the preceding Falling-Rising group is

¹ Implication.

developed into a series of Falling-Rising groups with narrowed range :

'Do you 'know what I 'want?   she asked, | 'going 'up to them,

and 'looking 'eagerly | from. 'one to the 'other.‖

2. MEDIAL (Short and Long).

(*a*)   Parenthesis casual.

365. Real parenthetical expressions, if thrown in casually, generally have a rising intonation (broken if necessary) if the preceding group rises. It is convenient to regard the intonation of expressions of this kind as forming part of the previous intonation group, unless they are very long, when a division may be made at a convenient place, as in the last example given below. The intonation of the group following the parenthesis is not influenced by the insertion of the parenthesis :

sɛ pur 'kwa, ↓ã ve ri te, | vum vwa'je | dã zœ̃ ḡrã ↓tã ba 'ra.‖

si ʒe fɛ ty nɛ 'rœːr, ↓mə di til ↓sã za sy rãːs, | ʒə vu sy 'pli | dəm

par dɔ 'ne.‖

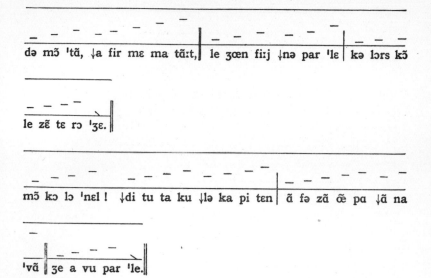

də mɔ̃ 'tɑ̃, ↓a fir mɛ ma tɑ̃ːt,‖ le ʒœn fiːj ↓nə par 'lɛ| kə lɔrs kɔ̃

le zɛ̃ tɛ rɔ 'ʒɛ.‖

mɔ̃ kɔ lɔ 'nɛl ! ↓di tu ta ku ↓lə ka pi tɛn| ɑ̃ fə zɑ̃ œ̃ pɑ ↓ɑ̃ na

'vɑ̃ ‖ ʒe a vu par 'le.‖

366. Medial parenthetical expressions, if thrown in casually, have a level or slightly falling intonation if the previous group falls. Here again it is convenient to regard the intonation of short parenthetical groups of this kind as forming part of the preceding intonation group. Long ones are developed in the way described in § 359. The intonation of the groups following the parenthesis is not influenced by the insertion of the parenthesis :

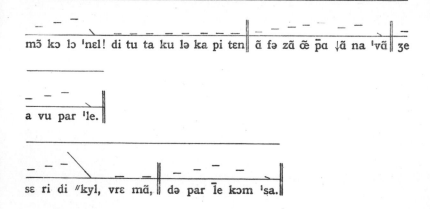

mɔ̃ kɔ lɔ 'nɛl! di tu ta ku lə ka pi tɛn‖ ɑ̃ fə zɑ̃ œ̃ p̄ɑ ↓ɑ̃ na 'vɑ̃‖ ʒe

a vu par 'le.‖

sɛ ri di "kyl, vrɛ mɑ̃,‖ də par l̄e kɔm 'sa.‖

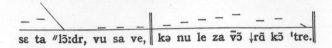

sɛ ta ″lɔːdr, vu sa ve,‖ kə nu le za v̄ɔ̃ ↓rɑ̃ kɔ̃ ′tre.‖

367. If the words following the parenthesis are also unimportant, then they, like the parenthesis, are pronounced with a fairly level intonation :

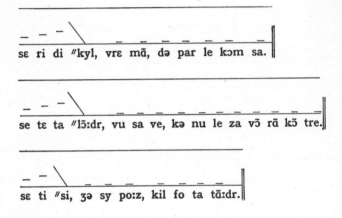

sɛ ri di ″kyl, vrɛ mɑ̃, də par le kɔm sa.‖

se tɛ ta ″lɔːdr, vu sa ve, kə nu le za vɔ̃ rɑ̃ kɔ̃ tre.‖

sɛ ti ″si, ʒə sy poːz, kil fo ta tɑ̃ːdr.‖

368. Other examples of casual parentheses :

e s ɛ pur′kwa, ↓vu kɔ̃prəne, ❘ ʒə n l e ʒamɛ ′vy. ‖

il ɛ ′vrɛ, ↓səpɑ̃dɑ̃, ❘ k il ɛ bjɛ̃ ma′lad. ‖

e mɛ̃t′nɑ̃, ↓dit il grɑvmɑ̃, ❘ il fo lə ′fɛːr ❘ də nu′vo. ‖

ʒə sɥi v′ny, ↓dit ɛl ↓o bu d œ̃ mɔmɑ̃, ❘ vuz ɛksplike tu ′sa. ‖

lə lɑ̃d′mɛ̃, ❘ madam lə′blɑ̃, ↓avɛk yn pətit fjɛː↓vrə d emosjɔ̃, ❘ sə rɑ̃′di ❘ ry rɔ′dɛ̃. ‖

(b) Parenthesis important.

369. Certain parenthetical expressions like *c'est vrai, j'en suis bien sûr, après tout, je sais bien, tout de même,* etc., are not as a rule thrown in in a casual way ; they are nearly always pronounced with an assurance which demands the Falling intonation, no matter whether the previous group rises or falls. Such parentheses, then,

have their own tonal pattern, which may be modified for either intensity or contrast or both.

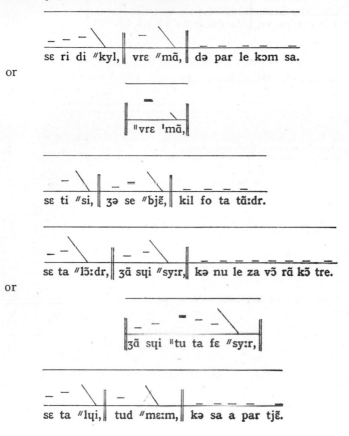

370. Some parenthetical expressions like *vous savez, vous comprenez, allez,* are often important because they express a warning, a doubt, or some other implication ; and are then pronounced with the Rising intonation, no matter whether the preceding group rises or falls :

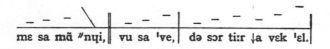

371. In English, medial parenthetical expressions are similarly treated. Unimportant parentheses do not introduce another tonal pattern into the intonation of the sentence into which they are interpolated. Important parentheses introduce another tonal pattern.

372. Examples of casual parentheses:

'All you 'have to 'do, he explained, │ is to 'fill in a 'form. ‖

And ″now, ladies and gentlemen, │ I'm going to 'show you a most

″marvellous 'thing. ‖

It's ri″diculous, I think, ‖ to ex'pect 'anything 'different. ‖

″That sort of work, you know, │ is ″useless. ‖

373. Examples of important parentheses:

It's ri″diculous, ‖ 'all the 'same, ‖ to behave like that.

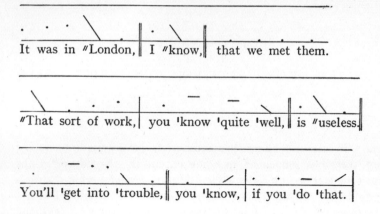

It was in ″London, ‖ I ″know,‖ that we met them.

″That sort of work, │ you 'know 'quite 'well, ‖ is ″useless.

You'll 'get into 'trouble, ‖ you 'know, │ if you 'do 'that. │

CHAPTER XXVII

INTONATION OF GROUPS INTRODUCING DIRECT SPEECH

1. IN FRENCH.

(a) Reading Aloud.

374. In reading aloud the intonation of groups introducing direct speech is influenced to some extent by the nature of the subject matter and by the style. But it would perhaps always be possible to use the Rising-Falling intonation. English learners are often tempted to use an intonation which rises finally. (See §378.)

375. In serious, deliberate styles the Rising-Falling intonation is invariably used, the pitch descending rather low. It is general also to use the Rising-Falling intonation if the introductory group is long.

Examples :

a'lɔːr | piῑat lчi 'di : ‖ ty ɛ dɔ̃k 'rwɑ? |
il lчi repɔ̃'diːr : ‖ ɛ ty osi ↓galile'ɛ̃? |
il dit ↓ɑ̃sчit ↓a œ̃n 'oːtr : ‖ e 'twa, ‖ "kɔ̃bjɛ̃ dwa 'ty? ‖
il lœr dit ɑ̃'kɔːr : ‖ œ̃n ɔ̄m ↓avɛ dø 'fis. ‖
e il lœr dəmɑ̃'da : ‖ kɔ̃bjɛ̃ ave vu də 'pɛ̃? ‖
ɛl repɔ̃'di | tristə'mɑ̃ : ‖ ʒə l e "tut a fɛ pɛrdy d 'vy. ‖
la 'rɛːn | ekri'vi : ‖ lə kɔ̃sjɛrʒ ↓də la prizɔ̃ ↓də sɛ̃ ʒɛr'mɛ̃ | mɛtra
    ɑ̃ libɛr'te | lə kɔ̃sɛ'je | bru'sɛl. ‖
də tɑ̃z ↓ɑ̃ 'tɑ̃ | il mə di'zɛ : ‖ s ɛt etɔ"nɑ̃, tu se pwasɔ̃ ! ‖
e il 'kri | d yn vwa ↓enɛr'ʒik : ‖ vuz ɛt "ʒɔlimɑ̃ grɔ'ɲɔ̃, terɛːz. ‖
œ̃n ɔm ↓sivili'ze | sə 'tjɛ̃ | dəvɑ̄t ↓œ̃ pei'zɑ̃ ‖ 'e, | lə salчɑ̃ trɛ
    'bɑ, | lчi 'di : ‖ geri 'mwa, mɔ̃ pti pɛːr, ‖ ʒə 'mœːr | də
    mala'di. ‖ lə pei'zɑ̃, | a sɔ̃ 'tuːr, | saly ↓œ̃bləmɑ̃ ↓l ɔm
    sivili'ze, | e lчi 'di : ‖ eklɛre 'mwa, mɔ̃sɛɲœːr, ‖ ʒə pe'ri |
    fot də ly'mjɛːr. ‖
lə rənaːr ↓s ɑ̃ sɛ'zi | e 'di : ‖ mɔ̃ bɔ̃ mə'sjø | aprəne ↓kə tu
    fla'tœːr | vit o de'pɑ̃ | də səlчi ↓ki l e'kut. ‖

216

376. In the following examples in quick conversational style the Rising intonation is more suitable than the Rising-Falling, though the latter is possible, provided that the fall is not to a very low pitch :

εl s ekria ↓tut a 'ku : | e le para'plчi ! ‖ ma'ri, | "u sɔ̃ le para'plчi ? ‖
alɔːr, ↓εl nu 'di : | i j ɔra d l ɔ'raːʒ | avã la f̄ε̃ ↓d la ʒur'ne. ‖
ɔ̃ ʃyʃɔ'tε : | kεl "ʒɔli ma'rje ! ‖
i s dit ↓osi'to : | səlчi 'si ‖ n ε 'pɑ | kɔm lez 'oːtr. ‖
i r'vε̃ | ã di'zã : | məsjø ↓εt ɔkype ↓a deʒœ'ne ‖ dã sa 'ʃãːbr. ‖
εl lчi di ↓tut a 'ku : | rə'gard, ʒã ! ‖
εl dəmã'da, | etɔ'ne : | "pur'kwa ? ‖
εl s ekri'a : | ʒə n lə "vø 'pɑ. ‖
me ʒã re'pɔ̃ : | 'ʋ ! ‖ "si ! mari, ‖ vu saṽe ↓dez is'twaːr. ‖
kãt i m vi ε̃sta'le | dã l elegã lãdo d ↓mɔ̃n 'ɔːkl, | i s ekri'a : | "kə ʒ .sчi kɔ̃'tã ‖ d vu saṽwaːr ↓a vɔt 'plas. ‖

(b) In Actual Conversation.

377. The intonation of the group introducing direct speech usually rises slightly in quick conversation. It may, if the group is short, be level :

pчi i m 'di : | le vwa'la ! ‖
e alɔr εl 'di : | ʒə n pø pɑ l 'fεːr. ‖
e aprε ↓il a 'di : | i fo le 'vwaːr, mɔ̃ ʃεːr. ‖

2. IN ENGLISH.

(a) Reading Aloud.

378. In serious, deliberate, literary styles the intonation of groups introducing direct speech is generally Falling-Rising. In the case of very short groups the intonation may be level :

'Pilate 'therefore 'said unto him, | 'Art thou a 'king then? |
They 'answered and 'said unto him, | 'Art 'thou 'also of Galilee? |
'Then said 'he to a'nother,[1] | And 'how much 'owest 'thou? |

---

[1] If *another* were emphasised for contrast, the group would have a falling intonation : '*Then said 'he to a''nother* : ‖ . Similarly : '*Then he 'asked a''gain* : ‖ *Does* '*anyone* '*here know* '*Rip Van* '*Winkle ?* |

And he 'said, | A 'certain 'man | had 'two 'sons. ‖
And he 'asked them, | 'How many 'loaves have ye? ‖
And at 'length the 'King 'said to him, | 'Help me to my 'horse. ‖
His 'first 'words on the 'subject 'were, | I 'told you so ! ‖
And 'now and 'then she would 'say, | 'What a 'pity you 'never 'knew him ! ‖

379.   In quick conversational style the intonation of the introductory group is either Falling-Rising or level, the latter being
very common in the case of short groups :

'Then he 'said : | Why I'd 'quite for'gotten you! ‖
So I 'said to him : | Well if you 'can't do it 'better than 'that, | 'don't do it at 'all.‖
Then he 'grinned ‖ and 'said : | You're 'so in'quisitive, you know! ‖
'Some one was 'saying : | 'Why should we 'worry? ‖ We 'can't 'change anything. |

(b)   In Actual Conversation.

380.   In conversation the intonation of the introductory group
is like that described in § 379.

381.   Note that, in both reading aloud and in conversation, if
the introductory group is grammatically complete the intonation
is a falling one :

He 'made the 'following 'statement : ‖
He a'ddressed the 'audience in 'these 'words : ‖
'Then he 'asked 'this 'question : ‖
'This is 'what I 'said to him : ‖

CHAPTER XXVIII

INTONATION OF ENUMERATIONS

382. There are various modifications possible in the intonation used in giving lists of things.

383. If the list is a complete one, there is generally a falling intonation in the final sense-group. A rising intonation in the final group suggests that the list is incomplete, either because the speaker cannot remember the other items, or because it is not worth while stating them : the rising intonation suggests that the other items exist.

384. The following example is given with the intonations most commonly heard : *Il y avait des Anglais, des Allemands, des Turcs, des Arabes, des Portugais, des Américains.*

UNEMPHATIC ENUMERATIONS.

385.   Intonation 1 (*a*).

i ja vɛ de zã ˈglɛ, | de zal ˈmã, | de ˈtyrk, | de za ˈrab, | de pɔr ty ˈgɛ |

de za me ri ˈkɛ̃.‖

Note that each intonation group except the last, begins on the same pitch and ends on the same pitch.   (The heavy upright line is placed only after the last rising group.)

Compare the intonation with that of the corresponding English sentence : *There were English people, Germans, Turks, Arabs, Portuguese, Americans* :

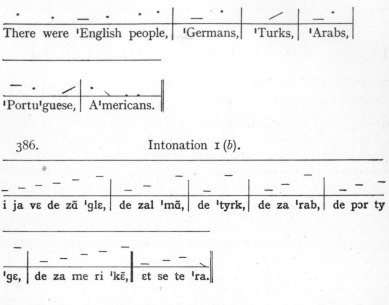

386.   Intonation 1 (*b*).

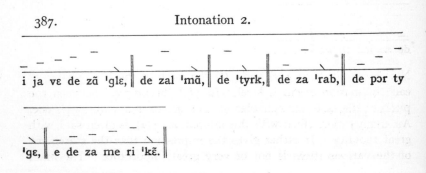

In this case the intonation of the final sense-group rises and the words *et cætera* are added to make it quite plain to the hearer that there were other nationalities represented. The speaker would probably pause before adding *et cætera*.

1 (*a*) or 1 (*b*) is the usual intonation for an ordinary enumeration.

387.   Intonation 2.

i ja vɛ de zɑ̃ 'glɛ, ‖ de zal 'mɑ̃, ‖ de 'tyrk, ‖ de za 'rab, ‖ de pɔr ty

'gɛ, ‖ e de za me ri 'kɛ̃. ‖

Here the addition of the word *et* and the fact that each intonation group falls finally suggest a complete list. Compare it with the corresponding English intonation:

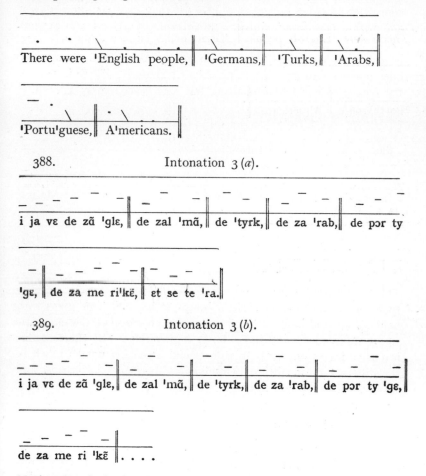

'Portu'guese, A'mericans.

388.   Intonation 3 (*a*).

i ja vɛ de zɑ̃ 'glɛ, de zal 'mɑ̃, de 'tyrk, de za 'rab, de pɔr ty

'gɛ, de za me ri'kɛ̃, et se te 'ra.

389.   Intonation 3 (*b*).

i ja vɛ de zɑ̃ 'glɛ, de zal 'mɑ̃, de 'tyrk, de za 'rab, de pɔr ty 'gɛ,

de za me ri 'kɛ̃ . . . .

Notice that in both 3 (*a*) and 3 (*b*) the pitch of the last syllable of each intonation group is level. In 3 (*a*) the interval between the pitch of the last two syllables of each group is a very small one. An enumeration given with this intonation, 3 (*a*), is often said with great rapidity. It rather gives the impression that the statement of the various items is not of very great importance. The main

Q

thing is to suggest a very large number, only a few of which are given as examples.   In 3 (*b*), the interval being greater between the last two syllables of each intonation group, the suggestion of incompleteness is not so strong.   This list may be given more slowly and with a certain amount of deliberation.   3 (*a*) and 3 (*b*) are not heard in English, but are extremely common in French, not only in giving enumerations, but also in many cases where the speaker does not want to give the impression of finality.   There is always the choice of another intonation, but this is extremely French.

EMPHATIC ENUMERATIONS.

390.   Intonation 4 (*a*).

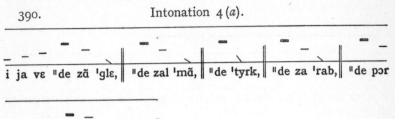

This intonation, with a fall in each intonation group suggests that the speaker has in mind a complete list which he gives with deliberation and assurance.   The *des* of each group carries emphatic stress (marked "), and has a fairly high pitch.   The effect of this intensive stress on *des* is to call special attention not so much to the different nationalities themselves as to their *great number* and *variety*.   (See §§ 272, 273.)

The last syllable of each group could be pronounced on a low level pitch instead of on a low falling one.

391.   It is also possible to draw special attention to the great number of nationalities represented by using the following stress and intonation :

Intonation 4 (*b*).

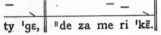

and by using a slightly modified form of the above:

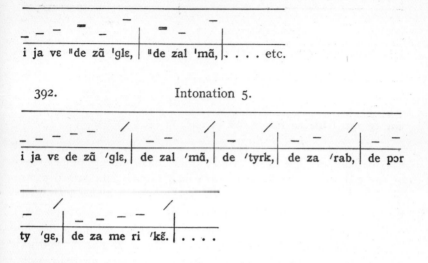

392.   Intonation 5.

This is a modification of 1.   More prominence is given to the final words of each sense-group by the change in pitch which occurs in pronouncing their final syllables.[1]   This change implies rather strongly *Que vous faut-il de plus?*   Because of the tendency of English speakers to pronounce syllables with a rising instead of a level intonation in cases where it is not possible, this intonation is not recommended to any but advanced students.

393.   Intonation 6 (*a*).

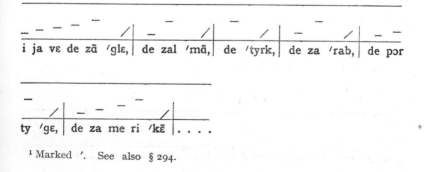

[1] Marked ´.   See also § 294.

394.   Intonation 6 (b).

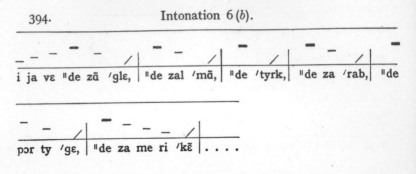

i ja vɛ "de zã 'glɛ, | "de zal 'mã, | "de 'tyrk, | "de za 'rab, | "de

pɔr ty 'gɛ, | "de za me ri 'kɛ̃ | . . . .

6 (a) is like 3 (b), but has a rise in pitch during the pronunciation of the last syllable of each group which implies emphatically, as in 5, *Que vous faut-il de plus?* The rise is from a rather low pitch instead of from a high one, as in 5.

6 (b) is like 4 (a), but the last syllable in each group has a rise in pitch which implies, as in 5, *Que vous faut-il de plus?* Neither 6 (a) nor 6 (b) is recommended for English beginners, for the reason given under 5.

I. EXAMPLES OF ENUMERATIONS IN PHONETIC TRANSCRIPTION WITH PITCH NOTATION.

395.   Intonation 1 (a).   (See § 385.)

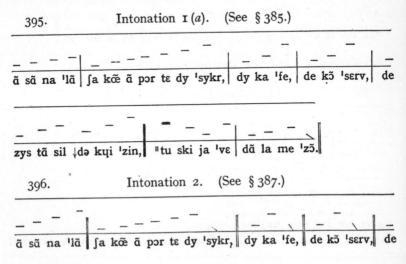

ã sã na 'lã | ʃa kɶ̃ ã pɔr tɛ dy 'sykr, | dy ka 'fe, | de kɔ̃ 'sɛrv, | de

zys tã sil ↓də kɥi 'zin, | "tu ski ja 'vɛ | dã la me 'zɔ̃.‖

396.   Intonation 2.   (See § 387.)

ã sã na 'lã ‖ ʃa kɶ̃ ã pɔr tɛ dy 'sykr, ‖ dy ka 'fe, ‖ de kɔ̃ 'sɛrv, ‖ de

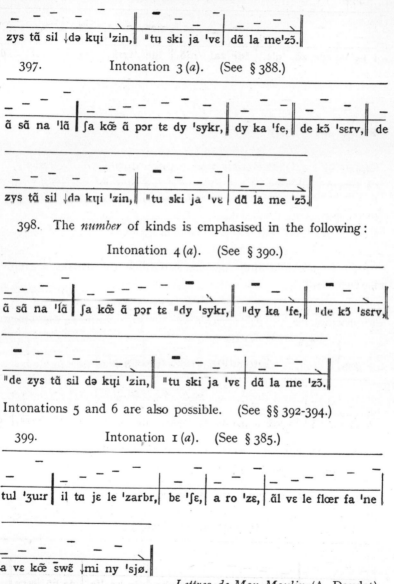

zys tã sil ↓də kɥi 'zin,‖ "tu ski ja 'vɛ| dã la me'zɔ̃.‖

397.   Intonation 3 (a).   (See § 388.)

ã sã na 'lã‖ ʃa kœ̃ ã pɔr tɛ dy 'sykr,‖ dy ka 'fe,‖ de kɔ̃ 'sɛrv,‖ de

zys tã sil ↓də kɥi 'zin,‖ "tu ski ja 'vɛ| dã la me 'zɔ̃.‖

398. The *number* of kinds is emphasised in the following:

Intonation 4 (a).   (See § 390.)

ã sã na 'lã‖ ʃa kœ̃ ã pɔr tɛ "dy 'sykr,‖ "dy ka 'fe,‖ "de kɔ̃ 'sɛrv,‖

"de zys tã sil də kɥi 'zin,‖ "tu ski ja 'vɛ| dã la me 'zɔ̃.‖

Intonations 5 and 6 are also possible.   (See §§ 392-394.)

399.   Intonation 1 (a).   (See § 385.)

tuʃ 'ʒuːr| il tɑ jɛ le 'zarbr,| bɛ 'ʃɛ,| a ro 'zɛ,| ãl vɛ le flœr fa 'ne|

a vɛ kœ̃ swɛ̃ ↓mi ny 'sjø.‖

Lettres de Mon Moulin (A. Daudet).

400.   Intonation 2.   (See § 387.)

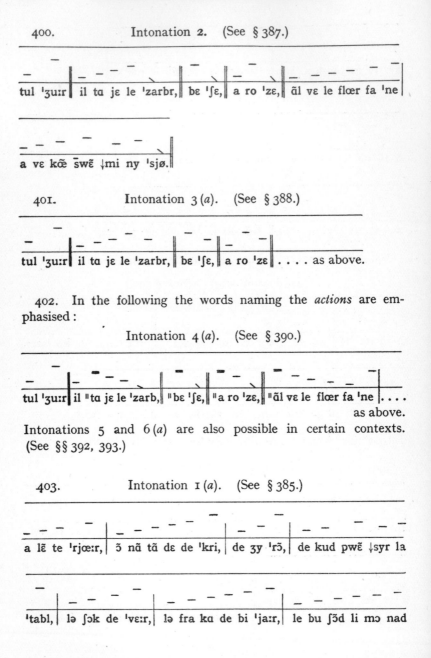

tul 'ʒuːr | il tɑ jɛ le 'zarbr, ‖ bɛ 'ʃɛ, ‖ a ro 'zɛ, ‖ ãl vɛ le flœr fa 'ne |

a vɛ kõ̃ s̄wɛ̃ ↓mi ny 'sjø. ‖

401.   Intonation 3 (a).   (See § 388.)

tul 'ʒuːr | il tɑ jɛ le 'zarbr, ‖ bɛ 'ʃɛ, ‖ a ro 'zɛ ‖ . . . . as above.

402. In the following the words naming the *actions* are emphasised :

Intonation 4 (a).   (See § 390.)

tul 'ʒuːr ‖ il ‖tɑ jɛ le 'zarb, ‖ ‖bɛ 'ʃɛ, ‖ ‖a ro 'zɛ, ‖ ‖ãl vɛ le flœr fa 'ne | . . . .
                                                              as above.
Intonations 5 and 6 (a) are also possible in certain contexts.
(See §§ 392, 393.)

403.   Intonation 1 (a).   (See § 385.)

a lɛ̃ te 'rjœːr, | ɔ̃ nã tã dɛ de 'kri, | de ʒy 'rɔ̃, | de kud pwɛ̃ ↓syr la

'tabl, | lə ʃɔk de 'vɛːr, | lə fra kɑ de bi 'jaːr, | le bu ʃɔ̃d li mɔ nad

↓ki so 'tɛ, │ 'e, │ dɔ mi nɑ̃ ↓tus ty 'mylt, │ yn vwa ʒwa 'jøːz, │ e

kla 'tɑ̃ːt, │ ki ʃɑ̃ 'tɛ │ a fɛr trɑ̃ b̄le le 'vitr. ‖

Lettres de Mon Moulin (A. Daudet).

404.　　　　　Intonation 2.　(See § 387.)

a lɛ̃ te 'rjœːr, │ ɔ̃ nɑ̃ tɑ̃ dɛ de 'kri, ‖ de ʒy 'rɔ̃, ‖ de kud pwɛ̃ ↓syr

la 'tabl, ‖ lə ʃɔk de 'vɛːr, ‖ lə fra kɑ ↓de bi'jaːr, ‖ le bu ʃɔ̃d li mɔ

nad ↓ki so 'tɛ, ‖ . . . . as above.

405.　　　　　Intonation 3 (a).　(See § 388.)

a lɛ̃ te 'rjœːr, │ ɔ̃ nɑ̃ tɑ̃ dɛ de 'kri, ‖ de ʒy 'rɔ̃ ‖ de kud pwɛ̃ ↓syr

la 'tabl, ‖ lə ʃɔk de 'vɛːr, ‖ lə fra kɑ ↓de bi 'jaːr, ‖ le bu ʃɔ̃d li mɔ

nad ↓ki so 'tɛ, ‖ . . . . as above.

406. In the following the *number* of different noises is emphasised :

Intonation 4 (*a*).   (See § 390.)

a lɛ̃ te 'rjœːr, ‖ ɔ̃ nɑ̃ tɑ̃ dɛ "de 'kri, ‖ "de ʒy 'rɔ̃ ‖ "de kud pwɛ̃ syr

la 'tabl, ‖ "lə ʃɔk de 'vɛːr, ‖ "lə fra kɑ de bi 'jaːr, ‖ "le bu ʃɔ̃d li

mɔ nad ki so 'tɛ, ‖ . . . . as above.

Intonations 5 and 6 are also possible. (See §§ 392-4.)

407. In the following the words naming the noises are emphasised :

Intonation 7.

a lɛ̃ te 'rjœːr, ɔ̃ nɑ̃ tɑ̃ dɛ de "kri, ‖ de "ʒy 'rɔ̃, ‖ de "kud pwɛ̃ syr

la 'tabl, ‖ lə "ʃɔk de 'vɛːr, lə "fra kɑ de bi 'jaːr, ‖ le "bu ʃɔ̃d li

mɔ nad ki so 'tɛ, ‖ . . . . as above.

408. In enumerations of a less ordinary and concrete type than those previously given, the intonations described are not all suitable. Whether the intonation rises or falls finally in each non-final group

often depends on the nature of the things enumerated. If they
are gay, stimulating, hopeful, etc., there is a tendency to use rising
intonation groups. If they are sad, depressing, dignified, etc.,
there is a tendency to use falling groups.

409. Examples of non-final rising groups :
1.

"pɛr sɔn na rjɛ̃ 'vy | o mi ljø ↓dla my 'zik, | də la 'dɑ̃ːs, | de 'riːr, | dy gu 'te.

2.

tul tɑ̃ ↓kəʒ par 'lɛ | se tɛ tɑ̃ trø ↓de ɔʃ mɑ̃ də 'tɛːt, | də pti rir 'fɛ̃,

də kliɲ mɑ̃ 'djø | de ʒɛːr ↓ɑ̃ tɑ̃ 'dy.

Lettres de Mon Moulin (A. Daudet).

410. Examples of non-final falling groups :
1.

se tɛl mɔ 'mɑ̃ | dy grɑ̃ 'frwa, | dy bɔ̃ bar də 'mɑ̃, | de ze pi de 'mi,

də la fa 'min.

Contes du Lundi (A. Daudet).

2.

ʒəl tru ve "vjɛ 'ji, | "a mɛ̃ 'si | "dːe se 'ʃe, | "dːyr 'si | par lə sɔ 'lɛːj.

3.

il klak de ˈdɑ̃ ‖ də ˈfrwɑ, ‖ de mo ˈsjɔ̃, ‖ də frɛ ˈjœːr, ‖ də rə ˈmɔːr.‖

4.

n tur də ˈmwa,‖ se tɛ tɔ̃ si lɑ̃ sap ‖ˈsɔ ˈly,‖ ‖ˈfe e ˈrik,‖ œ̃ si ĩɑ̃ːs ↓dɑ̃ ʃɑ̃t ˈmɑ̃.‖

411. Notice in the following passage the effect of falling groups in enumerating the vices and of rising groups in enumerating the virtues :

mɛ ki ˈkɔ̃ːk │ a vwa ja ʒe ↓ɑ̃ nœ ˈrɔp │ e ɑ̃ ˈʃin, ‖ ɔ ra sɑ̃ ˈti │ la di

fe ˈrɑ̃ːs ; ‖ ‖vyl ga ri ˈte, ‖ ‖gro sjɛr ˈte, ‖ ‖ve na li ˈte, ‖ ‖fur bə

ri e̱ sal ˈte, ‖ ʃe ˈnu ; ‖ dis tɛ̃k ˈsjɔ̃, │ pɔ li ˈtɛs, │ de zɛ̃ te rɛs ˈmɑ̃,

drwɑ tyːr ↓e prɔ prə ˈte, ‖ ʃe le ˈzoːtr.‖

II. EXAMPLES OF ENUMERATION IN ORDINARY ORTHOGRAPHY. INTONATION SUGGESTED BY MARKS.

412. In the enumerations of ordinary things given below in § 413 all the intonations described for the example *Il y avait des Anglais, des Allemands, des Turcs, des Arabes, des Portugais, des*

Américains (§ 384) may be used.   That is why no intonation group-marks are shown.   In the examples in §§ 414-416 the most natural intonation is suggested.

413.   Enumerations of a very simple nature :

1.   J'ai acheté des o'ranges, des 'pommes, des 'poires, des ba'nanes, des ana'nas, des 'prunes, des rai'sins.

2.   Il y avait des hiron'delles, des a'louettes, des 'merles, des fau'vettes, des mé'sanges, des moi'neaux.

3.   J'ai vu un hippopo'tame, une gi'raffe, un élé'phant, un 'tigre, un 'lion, un 'phoque, un cha'meau.

4.   C'était un encombrement ↓de véhicules ↓de toutes 'sortes, ‖ 'fiacres, ta'xis, auto'bus, ca'mions, tra'mways.

5.   Puis viennent les major'domes, les 'pages, les pi'queurs, les inten'dants, les ser'vantes, les méta'yers, les marmi'tons.

6.   On y 'vend | des tapis d'o'rient, des armoires ↓an'ciennes, des 'vases, de la vai'sselle, des co'lliers, des 'perles, des brace'lets.

414.   Enumerations of a less simple nature :

1.   Ce 'coin | est deve'nu | à la 'mode : ‖ ar'tistes, | sports'men, | chasseurs de gazelle ↓et de mou'fflon, | 'snobs, | mondains fati'gués, | "tout ce peuple e'rrant, | cosmopo'lite, | qui promène in"lassable- ment sa curiosi_té ou son en'nui, | débarque i'ci | chaque 'jour | plus nom'breux. ‖

Note.—The heavy line could be placed after *fatigués* instead of after *ennui*.

2.   Il fallait traverser ↓la première 'cour, | pleine de ca'rrosses, | de va'lets, | de chaises à por'teurs, | "toute claire du feu des 'torches, | et de la flam‾bée ↓des cui'sines. ‖

3.   Les fonctions ↓de l'agent d'a'ffaires | sont "très va'riées : ‖ tour à tour ↓avo'cat, | a'voué, | cour'tier, | ex'pert, | inter'prète, | teneur de 'livres, | commissio'nnaire, | écrivain pu'blic, | c'est le maître 'Jacques | de la colo'nie. ‖

Lettres de Mon Moulin (A. Daudet).

4.   Pour bien connaî↓tre les o'ranges, | il faut les avoir ‾vues chez 'elles ; ‖ aux îles ↓Balé'ares, ‖ en Sar'daigne, ‖ en 'Corse, ‖ en Algé'rie, ‖ dans l'air 'bleu | do'ré, | l'atmosphère 'tiède | de la Méditerra'née. ‖

Lettres de Mon Moulin (A. Daudet).

5. Il avait l'œil 'clair, | le geste 'libre, | la parole 'nette, | et "juste assez d'agrément de tour‿nure et d'es'prit | pour se glisser ↓inaper'çu | dans les 'foules. ‖

Dominique (E. Fromentin).

Note.—The heavy line could be placed after *nette* instead of after *esprit.*

6. C'était un esprit bien 'fait, | 'simple, | di'rect, | pré'cis, | nourri de lec'tures, | ayant un avis sur 'tout, | prompt à a'gir, | mais "jamais avant d'avoir discu'té | les mo‾tifs ↓de ses 'actes, ‖ très pra'tique, | et forcé'ment | "très ↓ambi'tieux. ‖

Dominique (E. Fromentin).

415. In the following examples it is the "everywhereness" which is emphasised :

1. Il y en avait "dans la salle à man'ger, ‖ "dans le sa'lon, ‖ "dans le vesti'bule, ‖ "dans l'esca'lier, ‖ "dans la 'cour, ‖ et "jusque dans le jar'din. ‖

2. Ils sont allés "en Ita'lie, ‖ "en Es'pagne, ‖ "au Dane'mark, ‖ "en 'Suède, ‖ "aux États-U'nis, ‖ "en 'Chine, ‖ "au Ja'pon, ‖ enfin "par'tout. ‖

416. In the following examples it is the great number of different varieties which is emphasised :

1. Ils ont un étalage de fleurs "su'perbes : ‖ "des 'roses, ‖ "des œ'illets, ‖ "des giro'flées, ‖ "des pi'voines, ‖ "des gla'ïeuls, ‖ "des i'ris ; | l'ensem↓ble des cou'leurs | est "ravi'ssant. ‖

2. Il a eu "toutes les maladies imagi'nables, | auxquelles les en'fants | sont su'jets : ‖ "la rou'geole, ‖ "la vari'celle, ‖ "la scarla'tine, ‖ "la diphté'rie, ‖ "la fièvre typho'ïde. ‖

3. Elles avaient ↓des ba'gages | à n'en "plus fi'nir : ‖ "douze va'lises, ‖ "huit 'malles, ‖ "six cartons à cha'peaux, ‖ "deux 'chiens, ‖ "des couvertures de vo'yage, ‖ "des para'pluies, ‖ en'fin | c'était "presque un déménage'ment! ‖

417. Other examples of enumeration will be found amongst the connected texts which follow.

CHAPTER XXIX

CONNECTED TEXTS[1] WITH EMPHASIS

418. TEXTS IN PHONETIC TRANSCRIPTION WITH PITCH
NOTATION.

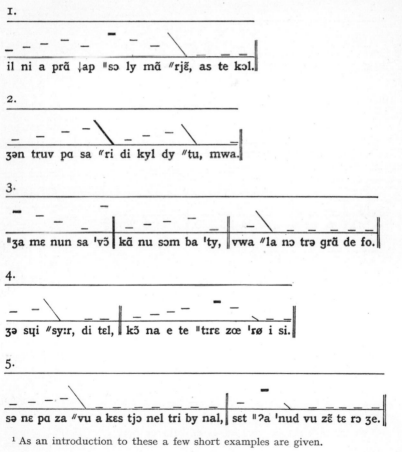

1.

il ni a prã ↓ap "sɔ ly mã "rjɛ̃, as te kɔl.

2.

ʒən truv pɑ sa "ri di kyl dy "tu, mwa.

3.

"ʒa mɛ nun sa 'vɔ̃ ‖ kɑ̃ nu sɔm ba 'ty, ‖ vwa "la nɔ trə grɑ̃ de fo.

4.

ʒə sɥi "syːr, di tɛl, ‖ kɔ̃ na e te "tːrɛ zœ 'rø i si.

5.

sə nɛ pɑ za "vu a kɛs tjɔ nel tri by nal, ‖ sɛt "ʔa 'nud vu zɛ̃ tɛ rɔ ʒe.

___

[1] As an introduction to these a few short examples are given.

6.

il nə sɔ̃ "ʒa mɛ za "le ɑ̃ na me rik.

7.

sə nɛ pɑ ↓za prɛd "mɛ̃ kəʒ vu za tɑ̃, ‖ sɛ "dːə 'mɛ̃. ‖

8.

in sɔ̃ pɑv "ny sɛ ta ne, ‖ sɛ "nu ki sɔm za le le 'vwaːr ɑ̃ no 'triʃ. ‖

9.

— vu nɛt pɑv ny ↓di rɛk tə mɑ̃ i 'si ɑ̃ ki tɑ̃ pa 'ri?

— 'nɔ̃, ‖ ʒe pɑ se ↓par la bɛl 'ʒik e la ɔ 'lɑ̃ːd. ‖

— ɛ me vu ly 'sɛrn?

— "bːo 'ku.

— vu kɔ̃ te i rɛs te ↓ʒys ka la fɛ̃ ↓dla se 'zɔ̃?

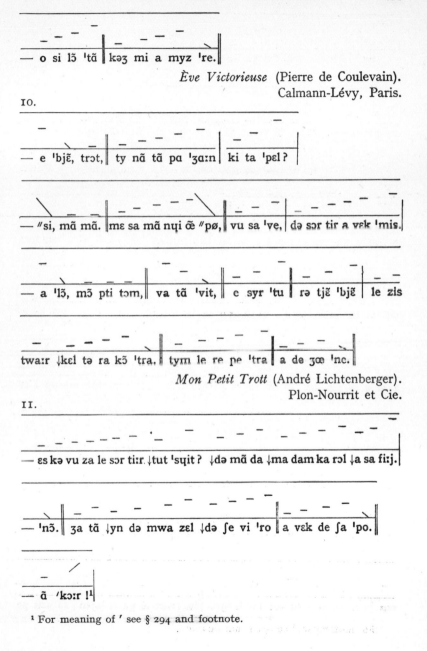

— o si lɔ̃ 'tɑ̃ ‖ kəʒ mi a myz 're.‖

Ève Victorieuse (Pierre de Coulevain).
Calmann-Lévy, Paris.

10.

— e 'bjɛ̃, trɔt, ‖ ty nɑ̃ tɑ̃ pɑ 'ʒɑːn | ki ta 'pɛl ?

— ″si, mɑ̃ mɑ̃. ‖mɛ sa mɑ̃ nɥi œ̃ ″pø, ‖ vu sa 've, | də sɔr tir a vɛk 'mis.|

— a 'lɔ̃, mɔ̃ pti tɔm, ‖ va tɑ̃ 'vit, ‖ e syr 'tu | rə tjɛ̃ 'bjɛ̃ | le zis

twaːr ↓kɛl tə ra kɔ̃ 'tra. ‖ tym le re pe 'tra | a də ʒœ 'ne.‖

Mon Petit Trott (André Lichtenberger).
Plon-Nourrit et Cie.

11.

— ɛs kə vu za le sɔr tiːr ↓tut 'sɥit ? ↓də mɑ̃ da ↓ma dam ka rɔl ↓a sa fiːj.|

— 'nɔ̃. ‖ ʒa tɑ̃ ↓yn də mwa zɛl ↓də ʃe vi 'ro ‖ a vɛk de ʃa 'po.‖

— ɑ̃ 'kɔːr !‖

[1] For meaning of ' see § 294 and footnote.

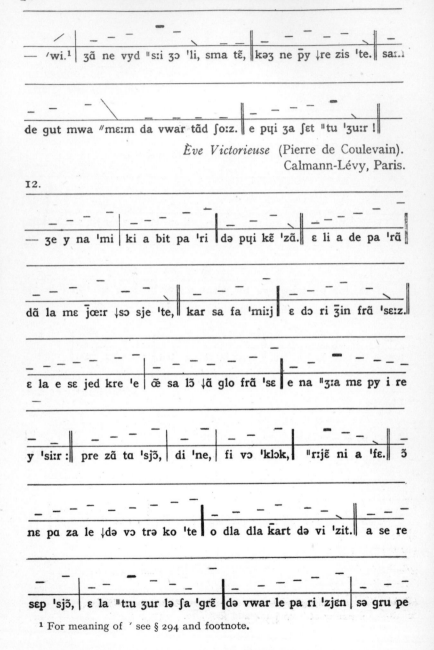

— 'wi.¹ | ʒɑ̃ ne vyd "siːɾ ʒɔ 'li, sma tɛ̃, ‖ kəʒ ne p̄y ↓re zis 'te. ‖ saɾ.ɪ

de gut mwa "mɛːm da vwar tɑ̃d ʃoːz. ‖ e pɥi ʒa ʃɛt "tu 'ʒuːr !‖

Ève Victorieuse (Pierre de Coulevain).
Calmann-Lévy, Paris.

12.

— ʒe y na 'mi | ki a bit pa 'ri | də pɥi kɛ̃ 'zɑ̃. ‖ ɛ li a de pa 'rɑ̃

dɑ̃ la mɛ j̄œːr ↓sɔ sje 'te, ‖ kar sa fa 'miːj ‖ ɛ dɔ ri ʒin frɑ̃ 'sɛːz.‖

ɛ la e sɛ jed kre 'e | œ̃ sa lɔ̃ ↓ɑ̃ glo frɑ̃ 'sɛ | e na "ʒːa mɛ py i re

y 'siːr :‖ pre zɑ̃ tɑ 'sjɔ̃, | di 'ne, | fi vɔ 'klɔk, | "ːjɛ̃ ni a 'fɛ. ‖ ɔ̃

nɛ pɑ za le ↓də vɔ trə ko 'te ‖ o dla dla k̄art də vi 'zit.‖ a se re

sɛp 'sjɔ̃, | ɛ la "tːu ʒur lə ʃa 'grɛ̃ ‖ də vwar le pa ri 'zjɛn | sə gru pe

¹ For meaning of ′ see § 294 and footnote.

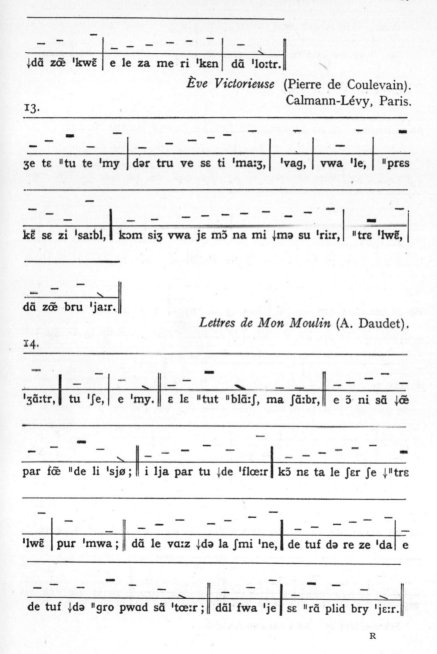

↓dã zœ̃ 'kwɛ̃ | e le za me ri 'kɛn | dã 'loːtr.‖

Ève Victorieuse (Pierre de Coulevain).
Calmann-Lévy, Paris.

13.

ʒe tɛ "tu te 'my | dər tru ve sɛ ti 'maːʒ, | 'vag, | vwa 'le, | "prɛs

kɛ̃ sɛ zi 'saːbl, ‖ kɔm siʒ vwa jɛ mɔ̃ na mi ↓mə su 'riːr, ‖ "trɛ 'lwɛ̃,

dã zœ̃ bru 'jaːr.‖

Lettres de Mon Moulin (A. Daudet).

14.

'ʒãːtr, ‖ tu 'ʃe, | e 'my. ‖ ɛ lɛ "tut "blãːʃ, ma ʃãːbr, ‖ e ɔ̃ ni sã ↓œ̃

par fœ̃ "de li 'sjø; ‖ i lja par tu ↓de 'flœːr | kɔ̃ nɛ ta le ʃɛr ʃe ↓"trɛ

'lwɛ̃ | pur 'mwa; ‖ dã le vaːz ↓də la ʃmi 'ne, | de tuf də re ze 'da | e

de tuf ↓də "gro pwad sã 'tœːr; ‖ dãl fwa 'je | sɛ "rã plid bry 'jɛːr.‖

R

Note.—The three first intonation groups could also be:

ˈʒɑ̃ːtr ‖ tu ˈʃe, ‖ e ˈmy.‖

15.

yn de ˈʃoːz │ kim sɔ̃ ˮpar ti ky ljɛr mɑ̃ de za gre aː blɑ̃ vwa

ˈjaːʒ, │ sɛ la fa ˈsɔ̃ │ dɔ̃ sɔ̃ de kɔ ˈre │le ʃɑ̃ː ↓brə do ˈbɛrʒ :‖ le ri do

ˈʒoːn │ a vɛk de ga lɔ̃ ˈruːʒ, │ le fo tœj ˈruːʒ │ a vɛk de ga lɔ̃ ˈʒoːn ;‖

se ku ˈlœːr │ ˮsi ɔr di nɛr ˈmɑ̃ │ e ˮsi bry tal mɑ̃ re y n̩i par lə ta

pi ˈsje │ mə koz de zɛ̃ prɛ ˈsjɔ̃ │ ˮtu ta ˈfɛ │ de za gre ˈaːbl.‖

Voyage Autour de Mon Jardin (A. Karr).

16.

kɑ̃ la ʃɛ vrə ˈblɑ̃ːʃ │ a ri ↓va[1] dɑ̃ la mɔ̃ ˈtaɲ, │ sə fy tœ̃ ˮra vis

[1] See Appendix 2.

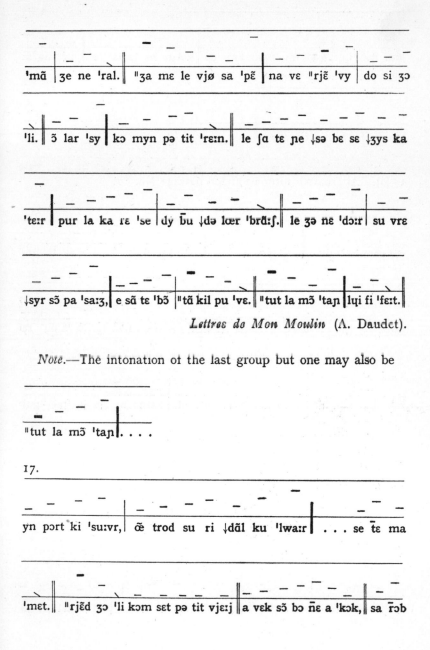

'mã │ ʒe ne 'ral. ‖ "ʒa mɛ le vjø sa 'pɛ̃ │ na vɛ "rjɛ̃ 'vy │ do si ʒɔ

'li. ‖ ɔ̃ lar 'sy │ kɔ myn pə tit 'rɛːn. ‖ le ʃɑ tɛ ɲe ↓sə bɛ sɛ ↓ʒys ka

'teːr │ pur la ka ɾɛ 'se │ dy bu ↓də lœr 'brɑːʃ. ‖ le ʒə ne 'dɔːr │ su vrɛ

↓syr sɔ̃ pa 'saːʒ, │ e sɑ̃ tɛ 'bɔ̃ ‖ "tɑ̃ kil pu 've. ‖ "tut la mɔ̃ 'taɲ │ lɥi fi 'fɛːt. ‖

Lettres de Mon Moulin (A. Daudet).

Note.—The intonation of the last group but one may also be

"tut la mɔ̃ 'taɲ‖. . . .

17.

yn pɔrt ki 'suːvr, │ œ̃ trod su ri ↓dɑ̃l ku 'lwaːr │ . . . se tɛ ma

'mɛt. ‖ "rjɛ̃d ʒɔ 'li kɔm sɛt pə tit vjɛːj ‖ a vɛk sɔ̃ bɔ ɲɛ a 'kɔk, ‖ sa r̄ɔb

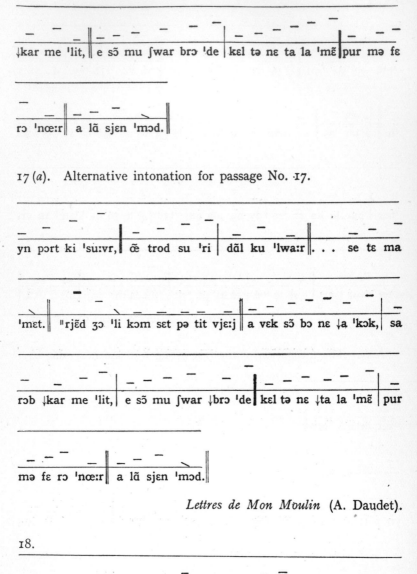

↓kar me 'lit, ‖ e sɔ̃ mu ʃwar brɔ 'de │ kɛl tə nɛ ta la 'mɛ̃ │ pur mə fɛ

rɔ 'nœːr ‖ a lɑ̃ sjɛn 'mɔd. ‖

17 (a).   Alternative intonation for passage No. 17.

yn pɔrt ki 'suːvr, │ œ̃ trod su 'ri │ dɑ̃l ku 'lwaːr ‖ . . . se tɛ ma

'mɛt. ‖ "rjɛ̃d ʒɔ 'li kɔm sɛt pə tit vjɛːj ‖ a vɛk sɔ̃ bɔ nɛ ↓a 'kɔk, │ sa

rɔb ↓kar me 'lit, │ e sɔ̃ mu ʃwar ↓brɔ 'de │ kɛl tə nɛ ↓ta la 'mɛ̃ │ pur

mə fɛ rɔ 'nœːr ‖ a lɑ̃ sjɛn 'mɔd. ‖

Lettres de Mon Moulin (A. Daudet).

18.

a prɛ za 'vwaːr │ a se de 'by │ a bɔr del te 'aːtr, │ pur lə kɛl ↓il nə

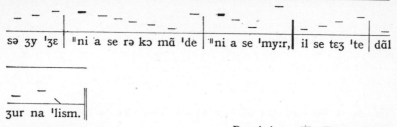

sə ʒy ˈʒɛ | ‖ni a se rə kɔ mã ˈde | ‖ni a se ˈmyːr, | il se tɛʒ ˈte | dãl

ʒur na ˈlism. ‖

Dominique (E. Fromentin).

Note.—The pitch could rise to its greatest height at the end of the third intonation group, instead of at the end of the sixth.

19.

ɔ̃ na pɛr sə vɛ ↓sɛ̃ ku si ˈfɛrm, | də lɔ̃g grã:ʒ ↓a twa tyr ˈruːʒ, | œ̃

na brœ vwaːr ↓sã ˈzo ‖ dã zœ̃ bu k̄ɛ ↓də fi gje ˈmɛːgr, ‖ ˈe, | ‖tu to

bu dy peˈi, ‖ ‖dø grãd zo ˈbɛrʒ | ki sə rə gard fa ↓sa ˈfas | də ʃak

ko te dyʃ ˈmɛ̃. ‖

Lettres de Mon Moulin (A. Daudet).

20.

ˈmwa, | ʒə re pɔ̃ dɛ ↓də mɔ̃ ˈmjø | a ‖tut lœr kɛs ˈtjɔ̃, ‖ dɔ nã syr

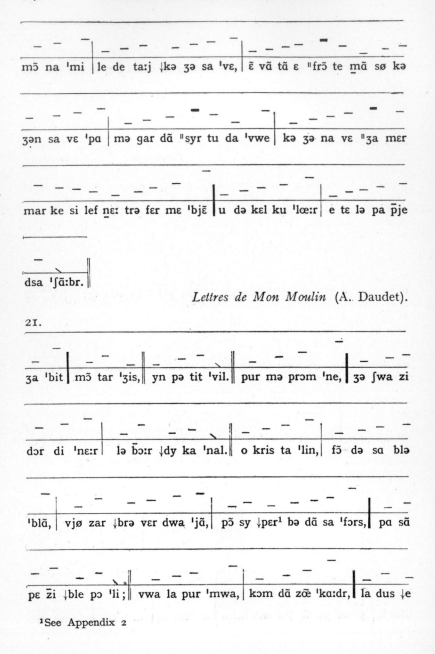

mɔ̃ na ˈmi │ le de taːj │↓kə ʒə sa ˈvɛ, │ ɛ̃ vɑ̃ tɑ̃ ɛ "frɔ̃ te mɑ̃ sø kə

ʒən sa vɛ ˈpɑ │ mə gar dɑ̃ "syr tu da ˈvwe │ kə ʒə na vɛ "ʒa mɛr

mar ke si lef nɛː trə fɛr mɛ ˈbjɛ̃ │ u də kɛl ku ˈlœːr │ e tɛ lə pa p̄je

dsa ˈʃɑ̃ːbr. ‖

Lettres de Mon Moulin (A. Daudet).

21.

ʒa ˈbit │ mɔ̃ tar ˈʒis, ‖ yn pə tit ˈvil. ‖ pur mə prɔm ˈne, │ ʒə ʃwa zi

dɔr di ˈnɛːr │ lə b̄ɔːr ↓dy ka ˈnal. ‖ o kris ta ˈlin, │ fɔ̃ də sɑ blə

ˈblɑ̃, │ vjø zar ↓brə vɛr dwa ˈjɑ̃, │ pɔ̃ sy ↓pɛr[1] bə dɑ̃ sa ˈfɔrs, │ pɑ sɑ̃

pɛ z̄i ↓ble pɔ ˈli ; ‖ vwa la pur ˈmwa, │ kɔm dɑ̃ zœ̃ ˈkɑːdr, │ la dus ↓e

[1]See Appendix 2

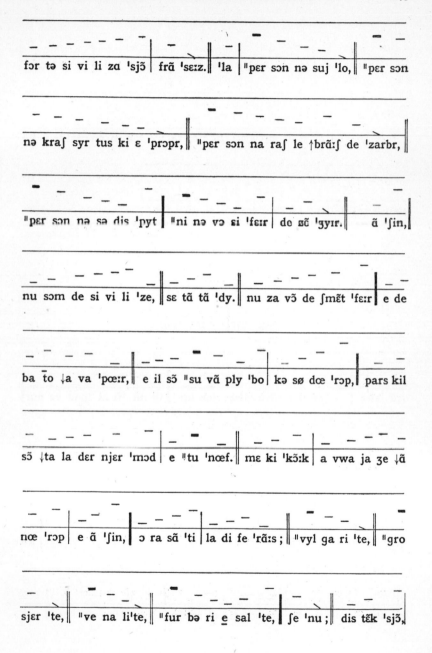

for tə si vi li za 'sjɔ̃ | frã 'sɛːz.‖ 'la | "pɛr sɔn nə suj 'lo,‖ "pɛr sɔn

nə kraʃ syr tus ki ɛ 'prɔpr,‖ "pɛr sɔn na raʃ le ↑brã:ʃ de 'zarbr,‖

"pɛr sɔn nə sə dis 'pyt | "ni nə vɔ si 'fɛır | də sã 'ʒyır.‖ ã 'ʃin,|

nu sɔm de si vi li 'ze,‖ sɛ tã tã 'dy.‖ nu za vɔ̃ de ʃmɛ̃t 'fɛːr | e de

ba ᴛo ↓a va 'pœːr,‖ e il sɔ̃ "su vã ply 'bo | kə sø dœ 'rɔp,| pars kil

sɔ̃ ↓ta la dɛr njɛr 'mɔd | e "tu 'nœf.‖ mɛ ki 'kɔ̃:k | a vwa ja ʒe ↓ã

nœ 'rɔp | e ã 'ʃin,| ɔ ra sã 'ti | la di fe 'rã:s;‖ "vyl ga ri 'te,‖ "gro

sjɛr 'te,‖ "ve na li'te,‖ "fur bə ri e sal 'te,| ʃe 'nu;‖ dis tɛ̃k 'sjɔ̃,

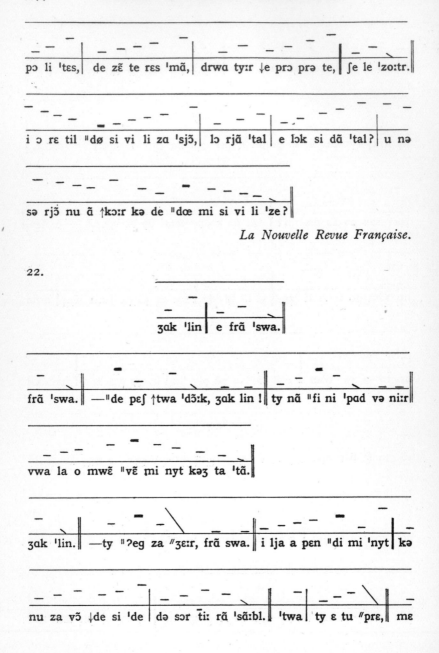

pɔ li ˈtɛs, | de zɛ̃ te rɛs ˈmã, | drwɑ tyːr ↓e prɔ prə te, ‖ ʃe le ˈzoːtr.‖

i ɔ rɛ til ‖dø si vi li zɑ ˈsjɔ̃, | lɔ rjã ˈtal | e lɔk si dã ˈtal? | u nə

sə rjɔ̃ nu ã ↑kɔːr kə de ‖dœ mi si vi li ˈze?‖

La Nouvelle Revue Française.

22.

ʒɑk ˈlin | e frã ˈswa.‖

frã ˈswa.‖ —‖de pɛʃ ↑twa ˈdɔ̃ːk, ʒɑk lin ! ‖ ty nã ‖fi ni ˈpɑd və niːr‖

vwa la o mwɛ̃ ‖vɛ̃ mi nyt kəʒ ta ˈtã.‖

ʒɑk ˈlin.‖ —ty ‖ʔeg za ‖ʒɛːr, frã swa. ‖ i lja a pɛn ‖di mi ˈnyt | kə

nu za võ ↓de si ˈde | də sɔr t̄iː rã ˈsãːbl.‖ ˈtwa | ty ɛ tu ‖prɛ, ‖ mɛ "mwa, | i fok ʒə ʃãːʒ ↓də twa 'lɛt, | ek ʒə mɛt ↓mɔ̃ ʃa 'po | e mɔ̃

mã 'to. ‖ dy 'rɛst, | nu za vɔ̃ "bjɛ̃l 'tã. ‖

frã 'swa. ‖ —"na ty ↑rɛl 'mã, ‖ ty a ã "kɔːr rɛ 'zɔ̃. ‖ ty a "tu ʒur

rɛ 'zɔ̃ ! ‖ a 'lɔ̃ ! ‖ "de pɛʃ 'twa. ‖ o trə 'mã | nu na riv rɔ̃ "mɛːm

'pa | o mi 'ljø | dy prə mje 'rakt ! ‖ e ʒã sre "trɛ fa 'ʃe; ‖ kar ʒə

tjɛ̃ ap "sɔ ly 'mã | a vwar sɛt 'pjɛs. ‖

ʒak 'lin. ‖ —mɛ "mwa o "si, ʒvø la vwaːr. ‖ ɔ̃ di rɛ "vrɛ mã a tã

'tãːdr | kəʒ tã 'pɛʃ | di a 'le. ‖ im sãːb ↓kə sɛ "mwa ki vu lɛ i

a le, da bɔːr. ‖ tu ta 'lœːr, | ty e tɛ "trɛ zɛ̃ di fe ↑rã ! | e mɛt 'nã,

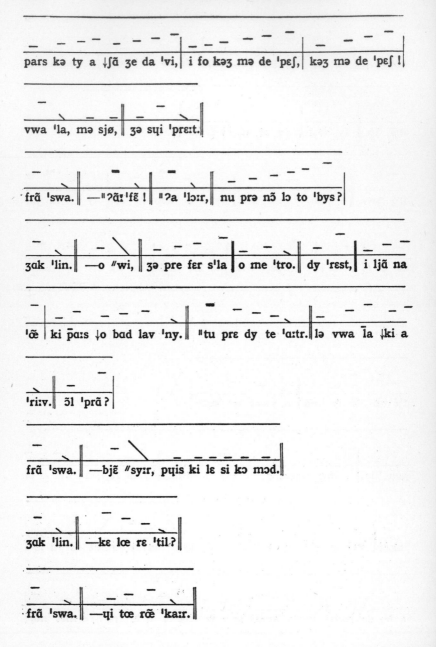

pars kə ty a ↓ʃɑ̃ ʒe da 'vi, | i fo kəʒ mə de 'pɛʃ, | kəʒ mə de 'pɛʃ !|

vwa 'la, mə sjø, ‖ ʒə sɥi 'prɛːt.‖

frɑ̃ 'swa.‖ —"ʔɑ̃ː'fɛ̃ ! ‖ "ʔa 'lɔːr, ‖ nu prə nɔ̃ lɔ to 'bys ?

ʒɑk 'lin.‖ —o "wi, ‖ ʒə pre fɛr s'la | o me 'tro. ‖ dy 'rɛst, | i ljɑ̃ na

'ɛ̃ | ki pɑːs ↓o bad lav 'ny. ‖ "tu prɛ dy te 'aːtr.‖ lə vwa la ↓ki a

'riːv.‖ ɔ̃l 'prɑ̃ ?|

frɑ̃ 'swa.‖ —bjɛ̃ "syːr, pɥis ki lɛ si kɔ mɔd.‖

ʒɑk 'lin.‖ —kɛ lœ rɛ 'til ?‖

frɑ̃ 'swa.‖ —ɥi tœ rɛ̃ 'kaːr.‖

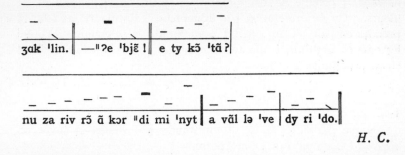

ʒɑk 'lin.‖ —"ʔe 'bjɛ̃ !‖ e ty kɔ̃ 'tɑ̃ ?

nu za riv rɔ̃ ɑ̃ kɔr "di mi 'nyt | a vɑ̃l lə 've | dy ri 'do.‖

H. C.

419. TEXTS IN ORDINARY ORTHOGRAPHY. INTONATION SUG-
GESTED BY MARKS.

1.

Vous accepterez 'bien | un verre ↓de mon mus"cat? proposa-t-il. ‖
Je vous 'l'offre | à la bonne fran'quette. ‖ Il est 'pur. ‖ Je vous
le garan'tis. ‖ La vigne 'pousse | sur notre 'sol. ‖ "Oui, madame,
poursuivit-il, ‖ en s'adre'ssant | à ma 'mère, ‖ ce vin ↓a été cu'vé |
"chez 'nous ‖ et j'en suis ↓orgue"illeux. ‖

> *Régine et Nous* (Albert-Émile Sorel).
> Tiré de la Petite Illustration.

2.

"Ah ! ‖ "que j'aime cette 'femme ! ‖ Vrai'ment, | je la trou↓ve
ex"traordi'naire ! ‖ Elle a un "goût ! |[1] Tu as remar"qué sa robe? ‖
"Cette brode'rie ! ‖ Elle "sait ce qui lui "va ! ‖ Et 'puis, | "j'aime
sa conversa'tion. ‖ Elle "parle de "tout ! ‖ Elle a "tout 'vu ! ‖ Elle
est "rensei'gnée ! |[1] J'a"dore 'ça ! ‖[2] Et 'puis, | "quelle personnali'té ! ‖
Quoi qu'elle 'fasse, | quoi qu'elle 'dise, | ce n'est "jamais ba'nal. ‖
"Ah ! | c'est quel"qu'un ! . . . . ‖ Tu ne trouves 'pas? |

3.

Oh ! "oui, ‖ ça va me sembler "bon de prendre pied quelque
part, ‖ de faire 'halte. ‖ Ils disent ↓que là-'bas | j'au‾rai ↓un bout
de te'rrain, ‖ des ou'tils, ‖ une petite mai'son. . . . ‖ "Une
"pe"tite "mai"son ! ‖ Nous en avions rêvé "une, ma femme et moi, ‖
du cô'té | de Saint-Man'dé : ‖ 'basse, | avec un petit jardin ↓étalé

---

[1] See § 293.   [2] Also J'a"dore ça!

de'vant, | comme un tiroir ou'vert | "plein de lé'gumes | et de
'fleurs. ‖ On serait venu 'là | le di'manche, ‖ du ma⁻tin au 'soir, ‖
prendre de l'air ↓et du so'leil | pour "toute la se'maine. ‖ 'Puis, |
les enfants gran'dis, | mis au co'mmerce, | on s'y serait reti'ré |
"bien tran'quille. ‖

Contes du Lundi (A. Daudet).

4.

Tout en par'lant | "sans disconti'nuer, | il mangeait ↓avec un
appé'tit | et un en'train | "sans pa'reils. ‖

Les morceaux ↓s'empilaient ↓sur son a'ssiette | et disparai'ssaient |
avec une vélocité "si remar'quable | qu'il arriva un mo'ment |
où ma 'tante, | le curé ↓et 'moi | nous res'tâmes, | la fourchette
en 'l'air, | à le "contem'pler | dans un ⁻muet ↓étonne'ment. ‖

« Je vous avais "bien préve'nus, ↓nous dit-il ↓en riant, | que
j'avais une 'faim | de "canni'bale, ‖ ce qui m'a'rrive, | du 'reste, |
"trois cent soixante-cinq 'fois | par 'an. ‖

— "Quel ar'gent | vous devez dépen'ser | pour votre 'table !
s'écria ma tante, ‖ qui avait la spéciali'té | de saisir le côté mercantile
↓des 'choses | et de 'dire | ce qu'il ne fallait "pas 'dire. ‖

— "Vingt-trois mille trois cent soixante-dix-sept 'francs, madame, ‖
répondit M. de Con'prat | avec un ⁻grand sé'rieux. ‖

— "Pas po'ssible ! marmotta ma tante stupéfaite. ‖

— Vous semblez "parfaitement heu'reux, monsieur, ‖ dit le
cu'ré | en se fro⁻ttant les 'mains. ‖

— Si je suis heu'reux, ↓monsieur le curé? | Je crois ″bien ! ‖ Et
vo'yons, ‖ 'là, ‖ "franche'ment, ‖ est-il bien natu'rel d'être
malheureux? ‖

— Mais "quelque'fois,[1] répondit le curé en souriant. |

— 'Ah ! ‖ les gens malheu'reux | le 'sont | le plus sou'vent | par
leur 'faute, ‖ parce qu'ils prennent la 'vie | à l'en'vers. ‖ Voyez-
'vous, | le ma'lheur | n'existe 'pas, ‖ c'est la bêtise hu'maine
qui existe. ‖

— Mais voilà dé'jà | un "ma'lheur, répliqua le curé. ‖

— Assez néga'tif | en lui-″même, monsieur le curé, ‖ 'et, | "de
ce que mon voi_sin est 'bête, | il ne s'ensuit 'pas | que je ⁻doive
↓l'imi'ter. ‖

[1] See § 294 for meaning of '.

— Vous ai'mez | le para'doxe, monsieur? ‖

— "Point ; ‖ mais j'en"rage | quand je vois "tant de 'gens | assombrir ↓leur exis'tence | par une imagina'tion | mala'dive. ‖ Je su'ppose | qu'ils ne mangent pas a'ssez, | qu'ils "vivent ↓d' a'louettes | ou "d'œufs ↓à la 'coque, | et se "dé‿traquent la cer'velle | en même 'temps | que l'esto'mac. ‖ J'a"dore la 'vie, ‖ je 'pense | que chacun ↓devrait la trouver 'belle | et qu'elle n'a "qu'un dé'faut : ‖ c'est de fi'nir, | et de finir "si 'vite ! » ‖

Le din'don, | la sa'lade, | le 'lait, | "tout était dévo'ré, ‖ et ma tante ↓regar'dait, | avec une physiono'mie | qui n'était "plus du tout gra'cieuse, | la carcasse ↓du vola'tile | sur lequel elle avait comp'té | pour festo'yer | durant "plusieurs 'jours. ‖

Nous allions ↓quitter la 'table | quand Su'zon | entr'ouvrit la 'porte ‖ 'et, | passant la tête ↓dans l'ouver'ture, | nous 'dit | d'un ton 'rogue : ‖

« J'ai fait du ca'fé, | faut-il l'appor'ter? |

— "Qui vous a per'mis . . . , commença ma tante. ‖

— "Oui, ‖ "oui, dis-je en l'interrompant vivement, ‖ "apporte-le tout de 'suite. » ‖

Je l'aurais "bien embra'ssée | pour cette "bonne i'dée, ‖ mais ma 'tante | ne partageait pas ↓mon a'vis. ‖ Elle dispa'rut | pour aller se disputer ↓avec Su'zon, | et nous ne la re'vîmes | que dans le sa'lon. ‖

« Vous avez une ex"cellente cui↑si'nière, ma cousine, ‖ dit Paul de Con'prat, | en siro‾tant ↓son ca'fé. ‖

— 'Oui, ‖ mais "si gro'gnon ! ‖

— C'est un "dé'tail, cela. ‖

— "Et ma 'tante, ‖ comment la trouvez-'vous? demandai-je d'un ton confidentiel. ‖

— 'Mais . . . | assez majes"tueuse, répondit M. de Conprat un peu embarrassé. ‖

— 'Ah ! | majes'tueuse[1] . . . | vous voulez 'dire | "désagré"able? ‖

— "Reine ! murmura le curé. ‖

— Eh 'bien, | "parlons d'autre 'chose, monsieur le curé, ‖ mais je voudrais bien a'voir | "l'heureux carac‿tère de mon cou'sin | et décou'vrir | le bon cô‾té de ma 'tante. ‖

[1] For the meaning of ' see §§ 294, 296.

— "Ayez un peu de philosophie pra'tique, charmante cousine, ‖ c'est 'là | une base sérieuse ↓pour le bo'nheur | et la "seule philoso'phie | qui me paraisse a'voir | le ⁻sens co'mmun. » ‖

Mon Oncle et mon Curé (Jean de la Brète).
Plon-Nourrit et Cie.

5.

Le profe'sseur | monta dans sa 'chaire | et se ⁻mit ↓à dic'ter. ‖ C'était une composi'tion | de dé'but. ‖ Pour la "première 'fois | mon amour-propre ↓avait à lu'tter | contre des ambi⁻tions ri'vales. ‖ J'examinai ↓mes nouveaux cama'rades, | et me sentis "parfaitement 'seul. ‖ La 'classe | était 'sombre ; ‖ il pleu'vait. ‖ A travers la fenê↓tre à petits ca'rreaux, | je voyais des ar↓bres agités ↓par le 'vent | et dont les ra'meaux | "trop à l'é'troit | se fro'ttaient | contre les murs noi⁻râ↓tres du pré'au. ‖ Ce bruit fami'lier | du vent pluvieux ↓dans les 'arbres | se répan'dait | comme un murmure ↓intermi'ttent | au milieu du si⁻lence des 'cours. ‖ Je l'écoutais ↓sans trop d'amer'tume | dans une sorte ↓de tris'tesse | "frisso_nnante et recue'illie | dont la dou'ceur | par mo'ment | deve⁻nait ex'trême. ‖

Dominique (E. Fromentin).

6.

"Nul ani'mal | n'est plus ↓propre que le re'nard | au ⁻rôle ↓du courti'san. ‖ Il n'a 'pas | la physionomie bé↓ate et per'fide | du 'chat. ‖ Son long mu'seau | effilé ↓et fen'du, | ses yeux brillants ↓et intelli'gents, | indiquent "tout d'a'bord | un fri'pon, ‖ mais un fripon ↓de quali'té | et de mé'rite. ‖ Il est a'gile | et in"fati'gable, ‖ et l'on de'vine, | en voyant ses membres a↓lertes et dis'pos, | qu'il n'attendra pas ↓chez 'lui | la for'tune. ‖ Sa fourrure ↓est 'riche, | et sa ⁻queue ↓magni'fique. ‖ Ce sont là ↓de "beaux ha'bits | qui lui siéront 'bien | dans une anti'chambre. ‖

La Fontaine et ses Fables (H. Taine).
Librairie Hachette, Editeur.

7.

Il avait une 'voix | admi'rable ‖ — une voix 'chaude, | 'jeune, | 'riche, | so'nore, | hu'maine, | émou'vante. . . . ‖ Elle mon'tait | et s'épan'dait | sans e'ffort. ‖ "Tous les senti'ments | s'y 'jouaient. ‖ "Nul de ceux qui l'ont enten'due | ne l'oublie'ra. ‖ C'était un magnifique ↓instru'ment | et qui inspirait con'fiance | et a'mour. ‖ "Rien de pe'tit | ni d'étri'qué. ‖ Une chose ↓comme do'rée | et

lumi'neuse. ‖ Elle couvrait "toutes les 'voix | et sans qu'il eût
be'soin | de forcer le 'ton. ‖

Il avait ↓à la tri'bune | un geste ↓et un vi'sage | d'une extra-
ordi⁻naire ↓expre'ssion : ‖ la 'face | au relief pui'ssant ; ‖ les deux
trous ⁻d'om↓bre de ses 'yeux ; ‖ le dos 'large | et tra'pu ; ‖ les bras
↓qui semblaient pé'trir | et lu'tter. . . . ‖

* Il descendait ↓de la tri'bune | pour aller s'a⁻sseoir ↓à son 'banc ‖
et il sem'blait | emporter le regard ↓avec 'lui | comme si un "ra‿yon
lumi'neux | n'eut éclai'ré | que lui 'seul. . . . . ‖ *

Alternative intonation for passage between asterisks :

Il descendait ↓de la tri'bune | pour aller s'asseoir ↓à son 'banc |
et il sem'blait | emporter le regard ↓avec 'lui | comme si un rayon
↓lumi'neux | n'eut éclai'ré | que lui 'seul. . . . ‖

Extrait d'un article sur Clemenceau par Jean Martet.
Tiré de L'Illustration.

8.

Je dois a'vouer | que je 'fume, mon ami. ‖ J'ai pris ↓cette
habi'tude | avec les pê'cheurs | et les ma'rins ‖ et au'ssi | pour
une rai'son. ‖ Il m'arrivait fréque'mment | autre'fois | de me trouver
↓avec des 'gens | qui m'ennu'yaient ; ‖ je voulais bien être 'là |
pendant qu'ils par'laient, | mais je ne voulais 'pas | leur par'ler ; ‖
je n'avais ab"solument 'rien | à leur 'dire ; ‖ je trouvais commode
↓et po'li | de les faire fu'mer | et de fu'mer ; ‖ ils parlaient 'moins |
et je ne parlais "pas du 'tout. ‖ Du 'reste, | je "fume quelquefois ; ‖
je suis au'ssi | "quelque'fois | des "mois en'tiers | sans décro⁻cher
ma 'pipe ; ‖ je ne fume 'pas | dans mon jar'din ; ‖ je ne veux pas
mê'ler | l'odeur du ta'bac | aux par⁻fums de mes 'fleurs. ‖

Voyage Autour de Mon Jardin (A. Karr).
Calmann-Lévy, Paris.

9.

Le 'chat | est tou⁻jours ↓compo'sé, ‖ ⁻maî↓tre de 'soi. ‖ Il
n'avance la 'patte | qu'avec réfle'xion ; ‖ il ne la 'pose | qu'en
essa⁻yant le che'min ; ‖ il ne hasar↓de ja'mais | sa sage ↓et dis⁻crète
per'sonne. ‖ Il est pro'pret, | dédai'gneux, | méticu'leux, | et dans
"tous ses mouve'ments | a⁻droit ↓au mi'racle. ‖ Pour s'en faire
une i'dée, | il faut l'avoir 'vu | se promener ↓d'un air ai'sé, | sans

ꞮꞮrien reꞮmuer, ‖ sur une ta↓ble encombrée de couꞮteaux, │ de ꞮꞮverres, │ et de bouꞮteilles. ‖

La Fontaine et ses Fables (H. Taine).
Librairie Hachette, Editeur.

Note.—In the last sentence the highest pitch could be on *idée* instead of on *remuer*.

10.

Paris tout entier ↓dorꞮmait, ‖ comme il Ɪdort │ entre trois ↓et six Ɪheures │ du maꞮtin. ‖ La lune ↓éclairait les quais déꞮserts ‖ à ⌐per↓te de Ɪvue. ‖ Il ne faisait ꞮꞮpresque plus Ɪfroid : ‖ c'é⌐tait en Ɪmars. ‖ La rivière ↓avait des frissons de luꞮmière │ qui la blanchi-Ɪssaient, ‖ et couꞮlait, │ sans faire le ꞮꞮmoindre Ɪbruit, │ entre ses ꞮꞮhautes ↓bordures Ɪd'arbres │ et de paꞮlais. ‖ * Au Ɪloin │ s'enfonçait la ville ↓popuꞮleuse, │ avec ses Ɪtours, │ ses Ɪdômes, │ ses Ɪflèches, │ où les éꞮtoiles │ avaient l'air d'être allumées ↓comme des faꞮnaux, ‖ et le Paris du cen↓tre sommeꞮillait, │ confusément ↓étenꞮdu │ sous des Ɪbrumes. ‖ *

Alternative intonation for passage between asterisks :

Au Ɪloin │ s'enfonçait la ville ↓popuꞮleuse, │ avec ses Ɪtours, │ ses Ɪdômes, │ ses Ɪflèches, ‖ où les éꞮtoiles │ avaient l'air ↓d'être alluꞮmées │ comme des faꞮnaux, ‖ et le Paris du cen↓tre sommeꞮillait, ‖ confusément ↓étenꞮdu │ sous les Ɪbrumes. ‖

Dominique (E. Fromentin).

11.

— ParꞮdÓn, dit-il, ‖ comme le Ɪtrain ‖ franchi⌐ssait le caꞮnal. ‖ SiꞮꞮmon, ‖ n'est-ce Ɪpas? │ L'œil surꞮpris, ‖ l'au↓tre réponꞮdit │ sans ⌐trop d'éléꞮgance : ‖

— Excusez-Ɪmoi, ‖ mais je ne ⌐vous remets Ɪpas. . . . ‖

— ꞮꞮCerꞮnay. ‖ ꞮꞮJacques CerꞮnaÿ. ‖ Tu te raꞮꞮppelles? ‖ ꞮꞮAu lyꞮcée ! ‖

— ꞮꞮAh ! . . . ‖ Mais ꞮꞮoui. ‖ MainteꞮnÁnt, ‖ j'y ꞮꞮsuis ! ‖ C'est ꞮqÛe . . . │ ça ne date pas ꞮꞮd'hier. ‖ Excuse-ꞮꞮmoi. ‖

Jacques CerꞮnay │ s'étonnait ↓qu'un camarade de Ɪclasse ‖ pût lui pa⌐raî↓tre si Ɪvieux. ‖

— Ne t'excuse Ɪpas. ‖ Il est ꞮꞮbien natuꞮrel ‖ que j'aie chanꞮꞮgé. ‖

— Mais ꞮꞮnon ! ‖ Mais ꞮꞮnon ! ‖ Tu es resꞮté, │ au conꞮtraire, ‖ éꞮꞮtonnamment ꞮꞮjeune, affirma Simon ‖ qui se hâ⌐ta de Ɪdire : ‖

Et a'lors, ‖ "comment vas-'tu? ‖ 'Moi, | je suis venu à 'Reims |
pour "deux mai'sons | que j'y po‾ssède en'core. ‖
— Tu n'y habites 'plus? |
— 'Non. ‖ "Oh! 'non. ‖ Je suis fixé ↓à Su'resne | depuis long-
'temps. ‖
— Ma"rié, probablement? ‖
— Grand-'père, | le mois pro'chain! ‖ Par ma "fille, comme de
bien entendu. ‖ Mon 'fils | va pa'sser | son ba'chot. ‖ Et 'toi? ‖
Dans les a'ffaires? | 'Où? ‖
— A Pa'ris, dit Jacques Cernay. ‖ Mais je ‾suis ↓avo'cat. ‖

> *La Jeune Fille du Yacht* (Maurice Renard).
> Tiré de la Petite Illustration.

12.

"Ah! les fées de 'France, ‖ "où sont-'elles? ‖ "Toutes 'mortes,
mes bons messieurs. ‖ Je suis la der'nière; ‖ il ne reste "plus que
'moi. . . . ‖ En véri'té, | c'est "grand do'mmage, ‖ car la France
↓était "bien plus 'belle | quand elle avait en‾core ses 'fées. ‖ Nous
é'tions | la poé‾sie ↓du pa'ys, ‖ sa 'foi, ‖ sa can'deur, ‖ sa jeu'nesse. ‖
"Tous les en‗droits que nous han'tions, | les fonds de parc
↓embroussa'illés, | les pierres des fon'taines, | les tourelles ↓des
vieux châ'teaux, | les brumes d'é'tangs, | les grandes landes
↓maréca'geuses | recevaient ↓de notre pré'sence | je ne sais quoi
↓de ma'gique | et d'agran'di. ‖ A la clarté ↓fantastique ↓des
lé'gendes, | on nous voyait passer ↓un peu par'tout | traînant nos
jupes ↓dans un rayon de 'lune, | ou courant sur les 'prés | à la
‾pointe des 'herbes. ‖

> *Contes du Lundi* (A. Daudet.)

13.

Je revenais ↓par ce che'min | au commencement ↓de l'au'tomne, |
et je me ra'ppelle | combien le changement ↓de pay'sage | me
fra'ppa. ‖ "Plus de gran'deur | ni de pui'ssance; ‖ l'air sauvage
↓ou 'triste | s'e'fface; ‖ la monotonie ↓et la poé'sie | s'en 'vont; ‖
la variété ↓et la gai'té | co'mmencent. ‖ "Point trop de 'plaines |
ni de mon'tagnes; ‖ "point trop de so'leil | ni d'humidi'té. ‖ "Nul
ex'cès | et "nulle éner'gie. ‖ "Tout y semblait ma'niable | et
civili'sé; ‖ "tout y é‗tait un petit mo'dèle, | en proportions
co'mmodes, | avec un air ↓de fi'nesse | et d'agré'ment. ‖

Les mon'tagnes | étaient devenues ↓co'llines, | les 'bois | n'étaient plus 'guère | que des bos'quets ; ‖ *les ondulations du te'rrain | rece'vaient, | "sans disconti'nuer, | les cul'tures. ‖*

Alternatives intonation for passage between asterisks :

les ondulations ↓du te'rrain | recevaient "sans disconti'nuer, | les cul'tures. ‖

La Fontaine et ses Fables (H. Taine).
Librairie Hachette, Editeur.

14.

Les boule'vards | sont ⁻pleins de 'monde. ‖ On 'sort | des thé'âtres.‖ Je me 'croise | sans 'doute | avec des 'gens | qui ont ⁻vu ma 'pièce. ‖ Je vou⁻drais deman'der, ‖ sa'voir, ‖ et en même 'temps | je passe 'vite | pour ne pas enten↓dre les réflexions ↓à haute 'voix | et les feuille'tons | en pleine 'rue. ‖ 'Ah ! | "comme ils sont heu'reux, tous ceux-là ‖ qui rentrent chez 'eux | et qui n'ont pas ⁻fait de 'pièces. . . . ‖ Me voi'ci | devant le thé'âtre. ‖ "Tout est fer'mé, ‖ é'teint. ‖ Décidé'ment, | je ne saurai "rien | ce 'soir ; ‖ *mais je me sens ↓une immense tris'tesse | devant les affiches mou'illées | et les ifs ↓à lam'pions | qui clignotent en'core | à la 'porte. ‖* Ce grand bâti'ment | que j'ai vu tout à 'l'heure | s'étaler en bruit ↓et en lu'mière | à "tout ce coin de boule'vard | est 'sourd, ‖ 'noir, ‖ dé'sert, ‖ ruisse'lant ‖ comme a⁻près ↓un incen'die. . . . ‖ *A'llons ! ‖ C'est fi'ni. ‖ "Six mois de tra'vail, | de 'rêves, | de fa'tigues, | d'espé'rances, ‖ "tout cela s'est brû'lé, ‖ per'du, ‖ en"volé à la flam_bée de 'gaz. | d'une soi'rée. ‖*

Alternative intonation for passages between asterisks :

Mais je me 'sens | une immense tris'tesse | devant les affiches mou'illées | et les ifs ↓à lam'pions | qui clignotent en'core | à la 'porte. ‖

A'llons ! ‖ C'est "fi'ni. ‖ "Six mois de tra'vail, ‖ de 'rêves, ‖ de fa'tigues, ‖ d'espé'rances, ‖ "tout cela s'est brû'lé, | per'du, | en"volé à la flam_bée de 'gaz | d'une soi'rée. ‖

Contes du Lundi (A. Daudet).

15.

En auto'bus, | je m'a⁻ssieds au 'fond, ‖ et d'a'bord, | je fixe ↓le conduc'teur | pour ne pas cé⁻der ma 'place. ‖ Une jeune femme ⁻monte ↓sur la plate-'forme. ‖ Jo'lie, | et de bonne san'té, ‖ elle

"peut | se tenir de'bout. ‖ 'Puis, | c'est une vieille 'dame. ‖ Elle
sem↓ble distin'guée | et 'riche. ‖ "Que ne prend-'elle | une voi'ture? ‖
Plus 'loin, | c'est une ouvrière ↓du peuple | avec un en'fant | et un
pa'nier. ‖ L'idée ↓d'une bonne ac'tion | me sé'duit. ‖ Mais "où
placer le pa'nier? ‖ D'a'illeurs, | il y a ↓dans l'auto'bus | des
me'ssieurs | plus jeunes que 'moi. ‖ Tout à 'coup, | "sans rai'son |
(car la dernière ve'nue | n'est "ni 'vieille, | "ni 'jeune, | "ni 'bien, |
"ni 'mal, | et elle ne demande 'rien, | elle ne penche pas la tête ↓à
l'inté'rieur | comme les effrontées ↓qui dévi'sagent), | je me 'dresse, |
j'écarte le double obs'tacle | des pieds ↓et des ge'noux | et je 'dis |
d'un 'ton | autori'taire : ‖ « Ma'dame, ‖ "prenez ma 'place.» ‖
— Non, "Mer'ci », répond la dame, ‖ po'lie | et 'sèche. ‖ ⁄Oui, |
"elle re ⁄fuse.[1] | C'est son ⁄⁄droit ‖ et elle n'admet au"cune ré'plique. ‖
Il ne me 'reste | qu'à rega'gner | "piteuse ment ma 'place, | au
milieu des ⁻jambes hos'tiles. ‖ Je pré⁻fère des'cendre. ‖

Le Vigneron dans sa Vigne (Jules Renard).
Mercure de France.

16.   Le bi'jou. ‖

Francine ↓se pro'mène | et ne ⁻pense à 'rien, ‖ quand sou'dain |
son pied 'droit | refuse de dépa'sser | son pied 'gauche. ‖
    Et la voilà plan'tée, | in"déraci'nable, | de⁻vant ↓une vi'trine. ‖
    Elle ne s'est pas arrê'tée | pour se mirer ↓dans les 'glaces | ou
se tapo⁻ter les che'veux. ‖ Elle ⁻fixe ↓un bi'jou. ‖ Elle le 'fixe |
obs"tiné'ment, ‖ et "s'il avait des 'ailes, | il irait "tout 'seul, | ainsi
qu'une mouche ↓fascinée, | se po'ser, | 'bague, | sur le ⁻doigt de
Fran'cine, ‖ ou 'broche | à son cor'sage, ‖ ou 'boucle | au ⁻lobe
↓de son o'reille. ‖
    Pour mieux le 'voir, | elle clôt ↓à de'mi | les 'yeux, ‖ et 'même, |
pour le possé'der | au "moins sous ses pau'pières, | elle les 'ferme. ‖
Il ⁻sem↓ble qu'elle 'dort. ‖

---

[1] For meaning of ⁄ see § 294.

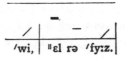

Mais derrière la vi'trine, | "ve‿nue du fond de la bou'tique, | une ⁻main pa'raît. ‖ Elle 'sort, | "blanche et 'fine | de ⁻sa man-'chette. ‖ On di'rait | qu'elle entre adroite'ment | dans une vo'lière. ‖ Elle ⁻est ↓habi'tuée. ‖ Elle se fau'file, | "sans se brû'ler | aux feux ↓des dia'mants, | "sans éve‿iller les pierres assou'pies, | et du bout ↓de ses doigts 'prestes, | comme faisant les cornes ↓à Fran'cine | qui l'observe ↓avec inquié'tude, | elle lui ⁻vole ↓le bi'jou. ‖

Le Vigneron dans sa Vigne (Jules Renard).
Mercure de France.

17. Le por'trait. ‖

Afin de prendre une pose ↓natu'relle, | je m'a'ssieds | comme j'ai l'habi'tude, ‖ j'allonge la jambe 'droite | et la 'gauche | reste plo'yée, ‖ j'écarte une 'main | et ferme 'l'autre | sur mes 'cuisses, ‖ je me tiens 'raide | et de trois 'quarts, ‖ je fixe un 'point | et je sou'ris. ‖ — Pourquoi souriez-'vous? dit le photographe. ‖

— Est-ce que je souris trop 'tôt? |

— "Qui vous prie de sou'rire? ‖

— Je vous é'vite | de me le deman'der. ‖ Je 'sais | les u'sages. ‖ Je ne me fais pas ↓photogra'phier | pour la "première "fois. ‖ Je ne suis plus ↓un en'fant | auquel on 'dit : ‖ «"regarde le petit oi'seau.» ‖ Je souris "tout 'seul, ‖ "d'avance, ‖ et je peux sou'rire | "longtemps ain'si. ‖ Ça ne me fatigue 'pas. ‖

— "Monsieur, dit le photographe, ‖ c'est bien une "vraie photogra"phie que vous désirez, ‖ et "non quelque i'mage | impersonnelle ↓et 'vague, | dont les fla'tteurs | ne pourraient que 'dire | poli'ment : ‖ «'Oui, |¹ "il y a quelque 'chose.» |¹

— Je "veux une photogra'phie, dis-je, | où il y ait "tout, ‖ ressem'blante, | vi'vante, | fra'ppante, | près de par'ler, | de cri'er, | de sortir du 'cadre, | et cæte'ra, | et cæte'ra. ‖

— "Qui que vous so'yez, me dit alors le photographe, | cessez 'donc | de sou'rire. ‖ Le "plus heureux des 'hommes | pré'fère | grima'cer. ‖ Il gri'mace | dès qu'il 'souffre, | dès qu'il s'en'nuie | et ⁻dès ↓qu'il tra'vaille. ‖

Il grimace d'a'mour | comme de 'haine, | et il gri⁻mace de 'joie. ‖ Sans 'doute, | vous souriez par'fois | aux étran'gers, ‖ et il vous a'rrive | de souri↓re à votre 'glace, | quand vous êtes 'sûr | que

¹ For meaning of ' see § 294 and footnote.

per‾sonne n'est 'là. ‖ Mais vos parents ↓et vos a'mis ❘ ne connaissent
guère de 'vous ❘ qu'une fi‾gure mau'ssade, ‖ et si vous tenez ↓à
leur o'ffrir ❘ un por'trait ❘ que je garan'tisse, ❘ "croyez-'moi,
Monsieur, ‖ "faites la gri'mace. ‖

Le Vigneron dans sa Vigne (Jules Renard).
Mercure de France.

18.

Mon père ↓s'interrom'pit ❘ pour questio'nner ❘ Madame Val'bert. ‖
— Vous êtes du 'nord, vous, ↓Madame? ❘
— Je suis Nor'mande, répliqua-t-elle avec une pointe d'orgueil. ‖
— Nor″mande, répéta mon père, ‖ "beau recrute″ment. ‖ J'ai
vu à 'l'œuvre ❘ les ‾gars ↓de chez ″vous. ‖
Cet éloge ↓fut sen'sible ❘ à la jeune 'femme. ‖ Elle renversa la
'tête ❘ et souffla la fumée ↓de sa ciga'rette ❘ qui se dissi'pa. ‖ 'Puis, ❘
re‾nouant ↓la conversa'tion : ‖
— Vous ne connaissez pas ↓la Norman'die? ↓interrogea-t-elle? ❘
— J'ai été ↓en garnison ↓à 'Caen, ❘ vers dix-neuf cent 'dix. ‖
— 'Moi, ❘ je suis des envi‾rons ↓de Li'sieux, prononça-t-elle. ‖
Et sa 'voix ❘ devint un 'chant. ‖
Elle nous décrivit ↓les prin'temps, ❘ lorsque la vallée ↓est toute
'blanche ❘ sous la floraison ↓des poi'riers ❘ et toute rose ↓avec les
po'mmiers ❘ sous le firmament 'gris. ‖ Et la 'brume. . . . ❘
— Vous voilà ly″rique, chère amie, coupa son mari. ‖ "Ne la
laissez pas conti'nuer : ‖ nous en au'rions ❘ jusqu'à demain ma'tin ! ‖
Nerveuse'ment, ❘ elle lança loin 'd'elle ❘ sa ciga'rette. ‖
— 'Moi, ↓raconta son mari, ❘ je me con'tente ❘ d'être Pari'sien. ‖
Mon clo'cher ❘ se nomme Notre-'Dame ❘ et mon 'mail ❘ les ‾Champs-
↓Ely'sées. ‖ Ce n'est déjà "pas si ″mal. ‖

Régine et Nous (Albert-Émile Sorel).
Tiré de la Petite Illustration.

19.

La petite 'ville ❘ du mi'di. ‖

La scène se passe ↓à 'Nîmes, ❘ par un clair ↓après-mi-di de
No'vembre. ‖ Monsieur ↓et Madame X ❘ vi‾sitent la
'ville. ‖

Madame. "Quel 'calme ! ‖ et quel "beau so'leil ! ‖ "Tout l'or de
l'au'tomne ❘ est sur les feu'illages. ‖ Sans ce'la, ❘ on ne se

croirait ‖jamais | au mois de No'vembre. ‖ Les fins d'au'tomne |
ont ici la dou'ceur | du prin'temps. ‖ J'ad'mire | ce jour
‖lumi‿neux et 'chaud | qui des'cend | d'un ciel 'bleu | im-
‖pe'ccable. ‖ On dirait une lu‿mière de 'rêve. ‖ C'est ‖presque
trop 'beau. ‖

Monsieur.   ‖Quel enthou″siasme, chère amie ! ‖ Mais ‖croyez
'bien | que je ne souris ‖nulle'ment | de votre ly″risme. ‖ Car
je par″tage votre admiration pour Nîmes. ‖

Madame.   Je l'espère pour ″vous. ‖ Vous ne seriez 'pas | pour la
vieille cité ↓gallo-ro'maine | un visiteur ‖digne 'd'elle | si vous
n'en compreniez 'pas | le ″charme. ‖ ‖Tout y est harmo'nieux, ‖
ne trouvez-vous 'pas? |

Monsieur.   ″Tout, ‖ en e'ffet. ‖ Je me rappelle ce 'square | que
nous ve‿nons ↓de traver'ser. ‖ Le jardin qui le 'pare | est
d'une ‖perfec'tion | cla'ssique. ‖ Il y a ‖par'tout | de beaux
'arbres. ‖ Je n'ai ‖jamais ‿vu a'illeurs | des jardins ↓aussi
agré'ables | que ceux ↓dont l'aspect ↓nous a enchan'tés | i'ci. ‖
C'est une ‖allé'gresse | et un re'pos | pour les 'yeux. ‖

Madame.   Ce qui est u'nique, | ce sont les monu‿ments ro'mains. ‖

Monsieur.   ′Oui.[1] | Le temps n'a ‖rien ô'té | à la majes'té | de leur
ar‿chitec'ture. ‖

Madame.   Au con″traire. ‖ Le cours des 'siècles | a donné ↓à leurs
vieilles 'pierres | la ‖seule pa'tine | qui leur con'vienne. ‖

Monsieur.   C'est ‖vrai ! ‖ Elles sont do'rées | à 'point. ‖

Madame.   Par ex'emple, | ce qui m'é'tonne, | c'est l'impression
↓de somno'lence | qu'on é'prouve | en en‿trant ↓dans la 'ville. ‖
Avez-vous remar'qué, | hier 'soir, | quand nous sommes
↓arri'vés? | Le si'lence | avait quelque ‿chose ↓d'impo'sant, ‖
‖même sur les boule'vards, ‖ et il n'était pourtant 'guère |
plus de neuf 'heures. ‖ Nous avons dit ‖presque en même
'temps, | comme si nous nous é‿tions ↓donné le 'mot : ‖ « On
di'rait | une ville 'morte ! » ‖ Vous vous rappe″lez, ‖ n'est-ce
'pas? |

Monsieur.   ‖Oh ! ‖ ‖très ″bien ! ‖ Il est évident ↓qu'au premier
a'bord, | ‖surtout quand on arrive d'une ville mouvemen‿tée
comme Mar'seille, | on est sur'pris | de trouver ici ‖tant de
'calme, ‖ de voir dans les rues ‖tant de flâ'neurs | qui

---

[1] For meaning of ′ see § 294 and footnote.

mu'sardent | tout le ⁻long du 'jour. ‖ Quand on vi'site | pour
la "première 'fois | "Nîmes la silen'cieuse, | on se de'mande : ‖
«"Suis-je dans Pompé'i | ou dans Hercula'num? ‖» C'est
une ci'té | endor'mie, ‖ au 'moins | pour ceux qui viennent
↓des villes industri'elles | et surpeu'plées. ‖

Madame. Voi'là | que vous exagé'rez, maintenant, mon ami. ‖
"Serait-ce déjà l'influence du soleil Nî‿mois qui nous vaudrait
cette em'phase? | "Fuyons-le pour le mo'ment, ‖ et allons
↓nous insta'ller | à la te'rrasse | de ce ca'fé. ‖ Je "meurs de
'soif ! ‖

Monsieur. Je ne serai pas fâché de 'boire, | moi non 'plus. ‖
"Qu'est-ce que vous allez 'prendre? ‖

Madame. Une limo'nade ! | Je 'crois | que c'est ce qu'il y a de
⁻plus ↓rafraichi'ssant. ‖

Monsieur. Gar'çon ! | "Deux limo'nades. ‖ (Au ⁻bout ↓de quelques
mi'nutes.) ‖ "Vrai'ment | ces gens du mi'di | me donnent
en'vie ! ‖ Ils ont l''air | de n'avoir au"cun sou'ci ! ‖ "Jamais
ils ne se 'pressent ! ‖ "Jamais on ne les voit cou'rir ! ‖ C'est
une 'vie | au ralen"ti qu'ils mènent ‖ et ils jouissent "pleine-
'ment | de toutes les dou'ceurs | qui les en'tourent. ‖ Il sem↓ble
que ce qui ne se fera pas aujour'd'hui, | se fera de'main. ‖
"A quoi bon se tourmen'ter? ‖ Et ils ont ⁻l'air heu'reux. ‖

Madame. C'est bien "vrai tout ceci, mon ami. ‖ Mais "croyez-
vous qu'ils n'aient pas leurs sou‿cis eux au'ssi? | Ils ne doivent
'pas | être épargnés non 'plus, ‖ a'llez ! | "Te'nez, ‖ "voyez
cette femme qui 'passe ! ‖ Croyez-vous ↓qu'elle n'ait pas eu ses
heures ↓de sou'ffrance? | "Voyez son vi'sage ! ‖ Mais au lieu
de faire ↓de la philoso'phie, | "si nous continuions notre
prome'nade ! ‖ "Qu'en dites-'vous? ‖

Monsieur. Vous avez rai'son, ‖ par'tons. ‖

Jacques Maurice Vallis *et* H. C.

20.
                 Va⁻cances ra'tées. ‖

'Pierre ↓et Su'zanne | se ren⁻con↓trent dans la 'rue. ‖
P. — Bon"jour, Suzanne ! ‖ "Comment allez-'vous? ‖
S. — 'Tiens ! | "Bon'jour Pierre. ‖ "Très 'bien, ‖ "mer'ci, ‖ et
'vous? |

P.   — Je vous croyais en'core | en va'cances. ‖ "Depuis quand
êtes-vous ren'trée? ‖

S.   — 'Oh! | Seulement depuis deux 'jours ; ‖ et je vous a'ssure |
que je n'en suis ⌐pas fâ'chée ! ‖

P.   — Pourquoi 'donc? ‖

S.   — Vous savez ↓que j'étais par'tie | avec une de mes a'mies, |
dans un petit village ↓du cen↓tre de la 'France, | à quelques
kilo'mètres | de La Bour'boule, ‖ n'est-ce 'pas? |

P.   — 'Oui,[1] | et "comme je vous en'viais ! ‖ lorsque vous m'avez
a'ppris | cette nou'velle. ‖

S.   — Eh 'bien, | nous avons eu un temps é"pouvan'table ! ‖
"Oh! mais a'lors, | quelque 'chose | d'é"pouvan'table ! ‖

P.   — "Vrai'ment ! | "Quel do'mmage ! ‖ Mais "dites-'moi, ‖ où
se trouve La Bour'boule? ‖ Vous dites dans le ⌐cen↓tre de la
'France, ‖ mais c'est assez "vaste il me semble, ‖ et je ne vois
pas ⌐bien où 'c'est. ‖

S.   — La Bour'boule | est en Au'vergne. ‖ C'est une ville 'd'eaux, |
à six kilo'mètres | du Mont-'Dore, ‖ "tout près du Puy de
San'cy. ‖ L'Au'vergne | est un pays "très pitto'resque, | qui
serait ab"solument ravi'ssant, | et "idé_al pour les prome'nades, |
par le beau 'temps. ‖ Naturelle'ment, | ce n'est ⌐pas ↓la haute
mon'tagne. ‖ Le Puy de San'cy | qui est le point "culmi_nant
du massif cen'tral, | n'a que "mil huit _cent quatre vingt six
'mètres | d'alti'tude. ‖ Mais "toute la chaîne des 'puys | a un
charme "tout particu'lier. ‖ Ce sont des vol⌐cans é'teints. ‖
Les trainées de 'lave | que l'on 'voit, | sont d'un "beau brun
rou'geâtre, | "quelque_fois viola'cé, | selon les ⌐heures ↓de la
jour'née. ‖ Malheureuse'ment, | nous n'avons eu que "deux
après-mi_di de beau 'temps, | pour 'jouir | de tout ce'la. ‖ Et
nous n'avons "jamais pu 'voir | le som⌐met ↓du Puy de San'cy ! ‖

P.   — Combien de temps êtes-vous restées là-'bas? ‖

S.   — "Huit 'jours. ‖ "Juste le temps de nous ennu'yer | à en
"mou'rir ! ‖

P.   — "Que faisiez-'vous, pendant la journée? ‖ Étiez-vous au
moins ↓dans un hôtel ↓confor"table? ‖

S.   — "Que me dites-'vous, Pierre? ‖ "Pas plus de 'chance | de
ce côté-'là ! ‖ Nous é'tions | dans une pension de fa'mille, |

[1] For meaning of ' see § 294 and footnote.

où nous avons été "bien malheu'reuses ! ‖ Je crois cepen'dant |
que "si le soleil avait dai⌣gné se mon'trer, | nous aurions
suppor'té | "plus a⌣llègre'ment, | les inconvé'nients | de la
mai'son. ‖ Comme il a plu à 'verse, | "presque ⌣sans a'rrêt, |
et 'que, | lorsqu'il ne pleuvait 'pas, | il faisait un brou'illard |
à ne "pas se 'voir, | à quelques mètres ↓de dis'tance, | nous
avons pa'ssé | la "plus grande par⌣tie de notre 'temps | dans
cette maison 'froide | et hu'mide. ‖ J'en "fri⌣ssonne en'core, |
"rien que d'y pen'ser ! ‖

P. — Cela n'a pas l'air "bien 'gai, ‖ en e'ffet, ‖ et je com'prends |
que vous vous so⁻yez ↓ennu'yées. ‖

S. — Figurez-'vous, | que nous en étions ré'duites, | pour nous
réchau'ffer, | "tant nous étions ge'lées, | à nous réfu'gier, |
"presque tous les a⌣près mi'di, | sous nos édre'dons ! ‖ "Car il
ne fallait pas son‶ger à sor‶tir ! ‖ Nous étions "priso‶nnières. ‖
Le te'rrain | qui entoure la mai'son, | et que l'on appelle :
« "foi'rail», | (sans 'doute | parce que c'est 'là, | que s'installe
la 'foire), | était "transformé en 'mare, | dans laquelle
"patau⌣geaient des 'oies | et des ca'nards, ‖ et la 'route | servait
de 'lit | à un "véri↑table ↑to'rrent. ‖

P. — 'Oh ! ‖ vous exagérez "sûre'ment Suzanne ! ‖ Mais je suis
heureux ↓de 'voir | que vous pouvez "déjà 'rire | de ⁻tous vos
ma'lheurs. ‖

S. — "Pas du 'tout, ‖ c'est "tel que je vous le 'dis. ‖ Il se passait
cependant "tous les ma'tins, | une petite comé'die | "fort
amu'sante. ‖ Mais vous êtes peut-être pre'ssé, Pierre, ‖ et je
vous re‶tiens, avec toutes mes histoires. ‖

P. — "Au con‶traire, ‖ cela m'intéresse "beau'coup. ‖ Je rentrais
chez 'moi, | et je suis "très heu'reux | de vous a⁻voir ↓ren-
con'trée. ‖ Je vous en ‶prie, Suzanne, ‖ "racon'tez. ‖

S. — Eh 'bien, | voi'ci : ‖ dans le vestibule ↓de la mai'son, |
accroché ↓près de la porte ↓de ma 'chambre | (car nous étions
↓au rez-de-chau'ssée), | se trouvait ↓un baro'mètre, | que "tous
les ma'tins, | "chaque pensio'nnaire | ve⁻nait ↓consul'ter. ‖
La procession ↓commen'çait | vers sept 'heures. ‖ Au ré'veil, |
désespéré ↓de ne pas voir ↓le so'leil, | et "dépri⌣mé par cette
pluie conti'nuelle, | chacun se diri'geait | vers le "malheu⌣reux
instru'ment, | et le ta'pait | avec "plus ou ⌣moins de vio'lence, |

espé⁻rant ↓le voir mon'ter. ‖ "Comme il s'obsti_nait tou'jours, |
il s'en suivait ↓à son a'dresse, | une ava⁻lanche d'in'sultes! ‖
Le vocabulaire ↓était "très va'rié, ‖ car il y avait 'là | un
commerçant de Pa'ris | avec sa fa'mille, ‖ 'riche, | mais c'est
"tout ce que l'on ↑peut 'dire. . . . ‖ un mécani'cien, | de Paris,
↓lui au'ssi, | avec un accent ↓faubou'rien | qui fai⁻sait ↓mes
dé'lices, ‖ "deux mé_nages d'institu'teurs, | une demoi'selle, |
employée de bu'reau, | qui nous donnait parfois ↓l'impre'ssion |
d'être un ⁻peu ↓détra'quée : ‖ elle est venue un 'soir | nous
chercher 'tous, | avec un air ↓d'il"lumi'née | pour nous faire
voir une 'source | qu'elle venait de décou'vrir | à la 'cave. . . . ‖
il s'agissait "tout _simple'ment | d'un ⁻robi'net! ‖ et en'fin, |
pour notre bo'nheur, | un ménage ↓de profe'sseurs | et leurs
en'fants, ‖ des gens "tout à fait char'mants, | avec les'quels |
nous avons passé "pas _mal de notre 'temps, | et qui ont
contri'bué | à nous ren↓dre la 'vie | un peu ⁻plus ↓agré'able. ‖

P.   — "Quel mé"lange! ‖ Et vous vous plaignez ↓de vous ê↓tre
ennu'yées! | Il me 'semble | que vous avez fait là-'bas | des
études "très intére"ssantes! ‖

S.   — 'Oh! "heureuse"ment! ‖ Sans ce'la, | la vie n'aurait "pas
été te"nable! ‖ Mais ce n'est ⁻pas fi'ni! ‖ La dernière lueur
d'espoir ↓é'teinte, | devant l'obstination ↓du baro'mètre, |
les réac'tions | se tradui'saient | d'une fa⁻çon ↓diffé'rente : ‖
Chez les 'uns, | c'était de la fu'reur, ‖ chez les 'autres, | un
mécontentement ↓plus conte'nu, ‖ chez cer'tains, | une es'pèce |
de résigna'tion. ‖ Il s'agissait ↓encore une 'fois | d'organiser
sa 'vie, | pour une "nouvelle jour'née | à res⁻ter ↓enfer'mé. ‖
Elles avaient été "si nom'breuses, | qu'il devenait "diffi"cile
de trouver une occupation! ‖ Les plus rési'gnés | parlaient
↓d'aller «"re'lire» | le jour⁻nal d'hi'er! ‖

P.   — "Comme c'est amu'sant, tout ça! ‖ Mais je comprends
'bien | quand 'même, | votre désappointe'ment, ‖ car vous
n'étiez pas partie ↓là-'bas, | pour faire des é⁻tudes ↓de
carac"tère. ‖ C'était le so"leil qu'il vous fallait, ‖ un ciel "bleu, ‖
le "grand "air. ‖

S.   — Figurez-'vous | que les gens du pa'ys, | 'eux, | n'avaient
"pas du tout 'l'air | d'être affec'tés | par ce mauvais 'temps. ‖
Il est 'vrai | qu'ils en ont sans 'doute | l'habi'tude! ‖ J'ai

vu "plus d'une 'vieille | abritée ↓sous un "grand para'pluie, |
assise ↓sur un petit 'banc | adossé ↓à une 'haie, | raccommodant
des 'bas, | ou tri↓co'tant, | "bien tranquille'ment, | sous cette
pluie "ba'ttante, | "tout en surve‗illant une 'vache, | en ‑train
de 'paître ! ‖ C'est une 'scène | que je n'avais "jamais 'vue |
et qui m'a à la fois a↓musée, | et im‑pressio'nnée. ‖ Mais cette
'fois, | je vous 'quitte, Pierre. ‖ Aurons-nous le plai'sir | de
vous voir bien'tôt? | "Venez diner à la mai↑son dimanche
pro'chain. ‖ C'est enten'du? |

P. — J'ac'cepte | avec plai'sir, Suzanne. ‖
S. — "Entendu pour di'manche, alors. ‖ A mi'di, ‖ n'est-ce
'pas? | Au re'voir. ‖

H. C.

21.

Jour de 'pluie.‖

[*Note.*—For meaning of ′ see §§ 294, 296.]

La scène se 'passe | dans un sa'lon | dont les fe'nêtres | ou↓vrent
sur une ave'nue | plantée 'd'arbres. ‖

Perso'nnages : ‖ une jeune 'femme | (Margue'rite), | une jeune
'fille | (Thé'rèse), | un vieil a'mi | ('Jacques), | en vi‑site
chez 'elles. ‖

Marguerite. — "Quel "temps a"ffreux ! ‖ Il 'pleut | depuis "huit
'jours ! ‖ Regardez donc ce ciel 'gris ‖ d'où 'tombe | un "nouveau
dé'luge. ‖ N'est-ce pas "deséspé'rant? |
Thérèse. — Voyez notre ave'nue : ‖ C'est une "vraie grenou'illère ! ‖
Marguerite. — 'Oui, ‖ et "comme c'est agré'able, de clapoter
là-dedans, ‖ quand on ‑fait des 'courses. ‖ C'est-à-dire ↓qu'on
se 'crotte | "jusqu'aux o'reilles ! ‖
T. — Et "dire qu'il y a des pays où le ciel reste 'bleu | "onze mois
de l'a'nnée ! ‖
M. — Ceux qui les ha'bitent | ne connaissent 'pas | leur bo'nheur. ‖
Jacques (sur un ‑ton ra'illeur). ‖
— "Quel ac"cès de mélanco"lie, mesdames. ‖ J'en suis "tout
é'mu. ‖ "Permettez-moi de présenter mes condolé↑ances à
vos deux tris↑tesses réu'nies. ‖

M.   — "Quand je vous dis que les ↑hommes n'ont pas de 'cœur! ‖
En voilà ↓un "nouvel ex'emple. ‖ "Co'mment! ‖ Je suis 'triste, |
ce temps a'ffreux | me met du gris ↓sur le 'cœur, | et au lieu
de me 'plaindre, | vous vous mo'quez! | J'es'père | que vous
n'êtes pas venu nous voir ↓aujour'd'hui | pour faire ↓de
mauvaises ↓plaisan"teries, ‖ n'est-ce 'pas? |

Jacques.   — "Là, ‖ "là, ‖ "chère Ma'dame, ‖ "ne nous fâchons
'pas. ‖ Considérez-'moi | comme é‑tant ↓à vos 'pieds. ‖ Je
vous demande in"finiment par'don. ‖ Je vous pro'mets |
d'écouter "respectueuse'ment | vos dolé'ances : ‖ "dites à votre
vieil a↑mi toutes vos tris'tesses. ‖ (Il se ‑met à 'rire.) ‖

M.   — Vous vo′yez? | Vous êtes de "moins en 'moins | sé'rieux. ‖
Vous êtes "décidé'ment | in"suppor'table! ‖

T.   — En'fin, ‖ cela vous a ′muse, | ′vous, Monsieur, | de voir le
'temps | larmoyer ↓comme une élé'gie | du ma‑tin au 'soir, ‖
et ce'la | pendant "huit ′jours? | Vous trouvez que c'est ′gai, |
la musique ↓de ces a'verses | qui tom'bent, | in"terminable-
'ment, | sur la ville ↓couleur de ′cendre? |

J.   — Je 'vois | que vous ressemblez ↓au po"ète : ‖ il pleure un
peu ↓dans votre "cœur quand il pleut sur la ville. ‖ "Mes
compli ′ments! |

M.   — "Comme c'est ga'lant, de votre part, ‖ ces iro'nies | dont
vous "cri'blez | notre mélanco'lie! ‖ Je le ré"pète, ‖ vous
n'avez "pas de 'cœur. ‖ Le voilà à 'rire | de nou'veau! ‖ "Mais
en'fin, ‖ vous trouvez que c'est si drôle que 'ça | de voir
pleu'voir | "sans a'rrêt | pendant une se′maine? . . . |

J.   — ′Drôle? | "Non, ‖ je ne vais 'pas | jusque "là. ‖ Mais je
re'fuse | de pren↓dre cet événe'ment | au tra"gique. ‖

T. (sarcas'tique)‖— ′Oui . . . | vous êtes un "déli↓cieux hu↑mo'riste. ‖
Et un "stoï'cien, | par dessus le mar'ché. ‖ Vous restez in-
"vulné'rable | aux tris'tesses | qui nous 'viennent | de la
cou‑leur du 'temps. ‖ Nous sommes ↓de "faibles "femmes,
nous. ‖ Vous êtes "bien au de'ssus | de tout ce"la, vous,
Monsieur. ‖ "S'émouvoir pour un peu ↑d'eau qui descend des
'nues! ‖ je vous demande ↓un 'peu | si c'est "raiso'nnable! . . . ‖
Mais c'est de l'enfanti"llage! ‖

M.   — "Ecoutez-'moi, mon ami, ‖ cette en'fant | se ‑moque de
'vous, ‖ mais vous ne l'avez ‑pas vo'lé! ‖

J. — ″Laissez-la se mo″quer, si ça doit la faire sourire, ‖ ″même
à mes dé″pens. ‖ J'en suis ″ra'vi. ‖ Pourquoi m'en fâche'rais-
je? ‖ Un sourire mo'queur, | pour une ″charmante jeune
‑fille comme 'elle, | c'est une grâce de ″plus. ‖

T. (qui é″clate de 'rire) ‖ — Oh! ″vrai'ment, | vous me com'blez ! ‖

M. — Il ne vous manquait 'plus | que de ⁻faire ↓des madri'gaux ! ‖
C'est ″com'plet. ‖ En'fin, | je vois 'que, | ″tout de 'même, |
vous savez culti'ver | la ⁻fleur ↓de rhéto'rique. ‖ On ne vous
connaissait 'pas | ce ta″lent. ‖ Vous nous voyez ″pétrifiées
d'admira'tion. ‖

T. — Mais, ⁻à pro'pos, ‖ je vous ai demandé ↓tout à 'l'heure |
si vous trouviez ↓amu'sant | de voir pleu'voir? . . . ‖

M. — ″Oui, au fait . . . ‖ nous atten'dons | que vous nous
chantiez les mé'rites | et les beau'tés | du temps de 'pluie. ‖

J. — Je vous ai répon'du | que je ne prenais pas la 'pluie |
au tra'gique. . . . ‖ c'est ″vrai. . . . ‖ Je n'ai pas 'dit | que je
la préfé'rais | à un beau jour ↓de so″leil . . . ‖ ″non . . . ‖ mais
je m'en acco″mmode. . . . ‖ Avouez que vous-'mêmes,
↓mesdames, | vous n'avez ″pas raison de vous ″plaindre, ‖
dans ce ″beau sa'lon | où 'brûle | un ″bon feu de 'bois. ‖ Vous
avez 'là, | dans ce petit meu↓ble élé'gant, | à portée ↓de votre
'main, | les 'livres, | romans ↓et poé'sies, | qui vous permettent
↓de dissiper ↓votre en'nui . . . | de partir ↓pour le pays des rêves
↓litté'raires. . . . | Vous pouvez ↓vous enchanter l'es'prit |
en lisant de bonnes 'proses | ou en chantant ↓de belles 'rimes. . . |

T. — ″Ça y 'est. . . . | C'est une ″confé'rence! |

M. — 'Oui, | nous prenons un ⁻bain ↓de littéra'ture. ‖ Oh! mon
a'mi, | c'est ″trop de bon'tés. . . . ‖

J. — ″Vous m'avez demandé mon opi↑nion sur la 'pluie. . . . ‖[1]
Je vous la ″donne. ‖ ″Tant pis pour ″vous : ‖ il ne fallait ⁻pas
me dé'fier. ‖ Je conti⁻nue ↓ma confé'rence, comme dit cette
aimable enfant. . . . ‖ Qu'est-ce que je disais 'donc, déjà? ‖

T. (d'un 'ton | plein de défé⁻rence co'mique). ‖ — Vous par⁻liez
de la 'pluie . . . ‖ et avec ″quel élan poé″tique, Seigneur ! ‖

J. — Quand il 'pleut, | au de'hors, | et que je suis ″bien au 'chaud, |
dans un salon accue'illant | comme le 'vôtre, | avec de
″charmantes a'mies | comme 'vous, | le ciel a ″beau s'ennuager

---

[1] See Appendix 3.

de ″spleen, ‖ je pense ″quand 'même | que la ‾vie est 'bonne. . . ‖
Par con'traste, | je m'api'toie | sur ceux qui courent ↓à leur
tra'vail, | dans la 'rue, | sous les ″froides a″verses. . . . ‖ et je
me dis a'lors | que le destin ↓ne s'est pas montré mau'vais |
à mon é'gard. ‖ 'Puis | je me peu↓ple l'imagina'tion | de choses
'gaies. . . . ‖ Te'nez, ‖ ″en ce mo'ment, ‖ je regarde ces 'bûches |
qui font une ″si belle flam'bée | dans la chemi'née. . . . ‖ Eh
'bien, ‖ que croyez-'vous? ‖ En les regardant brû'ler, | j'évoque
le 'temps | où elles étaient de ″grandes et belles 'branches | sur
quelque ‾ar↓bre de la fo'rêt. ‖ Je me 'dis : ‖ «″Combien de
prin↑temps les ont fait rever'dir? ‖ ″Combien d'au↑tomnes les
ont dépou↑illées de leurs 'feuilles?» ‖ Et je songe au'ssi | à
″tout le labeur qu'il a fa'llu | pour qu'elles arrivent ″jusqu'i'ci |
sous forme de ‾bois ↓à brû'ler . . . ‖ et pour qu'elles égaient
↓de leur 'flamme | ce ″morose après-mi'di | de dé'cembre. . . . ‖
Et pendant que je songe ↓ain'si, | la ‾pluie ↓peut tom'ber, ‖
je ne pense 'plus | qu'elle est une chose 'triste. ‖ Pourquoi ne
feriez-vous pas comme 'moi? . . . ‖ C'est si diffi'cile? |

M. — Dites-'moi, mon ami. . . . ‖ je suis un ‾peu in'quiète. . . . ‖
″Est-ce que vous avez l'inten↑tion de vous présen↑ter à
l'Académie fran'çaise? |

J. (qui se met à 'rire). ‖ —″Non, Madame. ‖ Je vous promets ↓que
cet accès ↓de littéra'ture | ne deviendra ‾pas chro'nique . . . ‖
il ‾reste ↓à l'état ai'gu. ‖ C'est une 'crise | qui n'aura ‾pas de
lende'main. ‖

T. — Quel ″do'mmage! ‖

M. — Mon a'mi, | voici qu'on apporte ″juste'ment | le 'thé. . . . ‖
Vous allez en prendre une 'tasse | avec 'nous. ‖ Les ora'teurs |
boivent toujours quelque ″chose, quand ils ont parlé. . . . ‖

T. — Un verre 'd'eau. . . . |

J. — Je suis gâ'té : ‖ j'au'rai | une tasse de 'thé. ‖ Je vais vous
adre'sser | un ‾hym↓ne de grati'tude. . . . . ‖

M. (effra'yée) ‖ — Oh! ″non, ‖ ″non. . . . ‖ Votre petit discours
↓sur la 'pluie | nous su'ffit. ‖

Jacques Maurice-Vallis.

22.
Une em'plette | ¬peu ↓ordi'naire. ‖

[*Note.*—For meaning of ' see §§ 294, 296.]

Perso'nnages : ‖ deux jeunes 'femmes | (Geneviève ↓et
Fran'çoise), | un petit garçon ↓(An'dré,) | quatre 'ans, |
le receveur du 'tram, | le concierge ↓des ateliers ↓du
P.L.'M., | un ouvri'er, | un employé ↓du bu'reau, | le chef
↓du bu'reau | (Monsieur 'L.). ‖

G. — Comment se rend-on à Ou'llins de Vénissieux? ‖
F. — Ou'llins? | Qu'est-ce que tu veux aller 'faire à Oullins? ‖
G. — 'Mais, | "acheter un va'gon. |
F. — Un va'gon! | a'lors, | tu penses tou'jours | à ton va¬gon
↓de chemin de 'fer. ‖ L'année der'nière, | dé'jà, | tu nous en
a¬vais par'lé. ‖
G. — Mais ↓bien "sûr, ‖ "plus que ja"mais, ‖ il devient une
"nécessi"té. ‖ C'est un "toit en ces moments de crise, ‖ où
l'on ne peut "plus se per'mettre | de passer ses va'cances |
dans un hô'tel. ‖ Un vagon de chemin de 'fer, | posé dans un
endroit "bien choi'si, | pourrait faire une "très agré↑able
maison de ↑cam'pagne ! ‖
F. — Serait-ce "si agréable que ce'la? | Ne vaudrait-il pas 'mieux |
acheter une maison de "bois, par exemple? ‖ Tu 'sais | qu'on
peut avoir quelque chose de "très co'quet, | pour "dix-neuf
↑mille 'francs. ‖
G. — "Dix-neuf mille 'francs ! | Tu n'y penses "pas ! ‖ Si tu
di'sais | "dix-neuf↑cents 'francs, ‖ ce serait plu'tôt | dans la
mesure ↓de mes mo"yens. ‖
F. — Dans ce 'cas, | cela vaut la 'peine | d'aller se rensei'gner |
sur les va'gons. ‖ Tu sais ↓où t'adresser ↓à Ou'llins? |
G. — 'Oui, | aux ateliers de construc¬tion du P.L.'M. |
F. — Eh 'bien, | cet après-mi'di, | nous i¬rons ↓à Ou'llins. ‖
An'dré. — Moi au"ssi, je veux y aller ; ‖ "j'aime les va"gons,
moi. ‖
F. — Mais "certaine"ment, mon petit, ‖ "on t'emmène'ra ! | Ce
n'est pas un va"gon qu' André aimerait acheter, ‖ mais un
train "tout en'tier, ‖ avec locomo'tive, ‖ ten'der, ‖ four'gon, ‖
et cæte'ra. ‖ Nous prendrons l'autobus ↓jusqu'à 'Lyon | et

le tram ↓pour Ou'llins | part ↓de la place Belle-'cour, | le
termi⁻nus ↓de notre auto'bus. ‖

Dans le 'tram. ‖

F. — Trois 'places | pour Ou'llins. ‖ "Où faut-il des'cendre |
pour a'ller | aux ate⁻liers ↓du P.L.'M.? ‖

Le Rece'veur. — Vous descendrez ↓à l'a'rrêt | après le 'pont, ‖
vous prendrez ↓la rue de la 'gare, | vous traverserez ↓le passage
à ni'veau, | puis vous verrez ↓une passe'relle | sur votre 'gauche,‖
et suivant ↓que vous désirez les machines ↓ou les voi'tures, |
vous tournerez à 'gauche | ou à 'droite. ‖

F. — "Très 'bien. ‖ Tu te rappelleras tout 'ça, | 'toi? | Cela me
parait un ⁻peu ↓compli'qué. ‖

G. — "Naturelle⁄ment, | pour un achat "si peu ordi'naire, | on
doit s'a'ttendre | à a↓voir un itiné'raire | non ⁻moins
↓compli'qué. ‖

F. — En'fin | j'es⁻père ↓que nous nous y retrou'verons. ‖

An'dré. — Mais "pourquoi tu veux acheter un va'gon, Geneviève?‖

G. — Pour en ⁻faire ↓une mai'son. ‖

An'dré. — Une mai⁄son . . .? |

Le rece'veur. — C'est i'ci | que vous descen'dez, Mesdames. ‖
Prenez cette 'rue, | allez ↓jusqu'au passage ↓à ni'veau, |
traversez 'le, | et vous ve↓rrez la passe'relle | "tout de suite
a'près. ‖

F. — Mer'ci. ‖

En 'route | vers les ate'liers. ‖

F. — Tu m'en fais ⁄faire des courses, avec ton vagon! ‖ Avoue
↓que c'est une emplette "peu ba⁄nale. ‖

G. — Nous voi'ci | au pa⁻ssage ↓à ni'veau. ‖

F. — Et voi⁻ci ↓la passe'relle, ‖ et de ce cô'té, | on ⁻va ↓aux
ma'chines. ‖ "Si le cœur t'en ↑dit de te payer une ma'chine! . . . ‖

G. — Et de ce cô'té, | les voi'tures. ‖ C'est "là | que nous i'rons. ‖
Je n'ai "pas changé d'i'dée, depuis tout à l'heure. ‖ Quelles
im"menses portes en 'fer! ‖

F. — Bien ⁄sûr, ‖ "pour laisser pa↑sser des voi↑tures de chemin
de 'fer! ‖[1]

[1] See Appendix 3.

G. — Mais il y a une petite 'porte | à cô'té. . . . ‖ Et une so'nnette !‖
"Tire la 'corde. ‖

F. — C'est plutôt une ″cloche ! ‖

Le Con'cierge. — Mes'dames? |

F. — Nous voudrions sa'voir | si on peut ache'ter | une voi⁻ture
↓de chemin de 'fer. ‖

Le Con'cierge. — Acheter ↓une voiture ↓de chemin de 'fer? |
'Mais. . . . | ″Co'mment? ‖

G. — Nous voudrions sa'voir | si c'est une ⁻chose po'ssible. ‖

Le Con'cierge. — Ma 'foi ! | je n'en ⁻sais 'rien, ‖ je dois vous
'dire | que je n'en ai ″jamais ‿vu sor'tir | par cette 'porte. ‖
Et 'puis | c'est ″cher, une voiture ; ‖ ″te'nez, ‖ celle-'ci | vaut
bien ″un mi'llion. ‖

G. — Mais ″oui, ‖ mais ce n'est ″pas ce que nous vou″lons ; ‖
nous voulons ↓une voiture ↓réfor″mée. ‖ Il parait ↓que la
compa'gnie | en ″vend aux particuliers. ‖

Le Con'cierge | *à un ouvri'er.* ‖ — Dis 'donc, ‖ ces 'dames | veulent
ache'ter | un va'gon. ‖ Tu 'sais | si la compagnie ↓en 'vend,
toi? |

L'ouvri'er. — Ma 'foi ! | 'Non. ‖

G. — En'fin, ‖ ne peut-on pas nous 'dire | quelque 'part | i'ci, |
si la chose ↓est fai'sable | ou ⁄non? |

Le Con'cierge. — ″Ah ‖ mais ⁄si ! | (A l'ouvri'er.) ‖ ″Tiens, ‖ ″va
donc au bu↑reau, demander si on vend des vagons réfor↑més
au pu'blic. ‖

L'ouvri'er. — ⁄Oui, | 'mais. . . . |

Le Con'cierge. — Mais ″oui, ‖ vas-″y. ‖ ″Tu me téléphoneras
la ré'ponse. ‖[1]

(L'ouvrier 'part, | pas très sûr ↓qu'on ne se joue pas de
'lui, | et se re⁻tourne ↓plusieurs 'fois.) ‖

Le Con'cierge. — Qu'est-ce que vous voulez donc 'faire de ce
vagon? ‖

G. — Une mai⁻son de cam'pagne. ‖

Le Con'cierge. — ″En e⁄ffet, | l'idée n'est ″pas mauvaise du ⁄tout. |
Et la maison est à ″moitié meu⁄blée. |

G. — Elle est du 'moins | pourvue de 'sièges. ‖

---

[1] See Appendix 3.

T

Le Con'cierge. — C'est qu'il y en a ↓qui sont confor″tables de ces voitures. ‖ Il n'y manque ″rien, ‖ ″même dans les voi'tures | de troisième 'classe. ‖ Et en'core, | nous ne voyons pas ↓les plus mo″dernes ici, ‖ car nous ne fai‾sons ↓que la répara'tion. ‖ Tout de 'même | le vagon-hôpi'tal | que la compagnie ↓a offert ↓à la ville de 'Lyon | est pa‾ssé ↓dans les ate'liers. ‖ Voi″là quelque chose de bien. ‖ ″Ah! ‖ mais voilà l'ouvri‾er qui re'vient. ‖ Je ″pa'rie | qu'il vient vous cher'cher. ‖

L'ouvri'er. — Monsieur le chef de bu'reau | désire voir cette 'dame | qui veut ache‾ter ↓un va'gon. ‖

An'dré. — On va aller ↓près des va'gons? |

L'ouvri'er. — Il est préfé'rable | que les en'fants | ne passent pas ↓parmi les voi'tures | qui sont ″consta'mment | en mouve-'ment. ‖

   (Geneviève ↓et l'ouvri'er | a‾rrivent ↓aux bu'reaux.) ‖

L'ouvri'er. — Veuillez attendre i'ci | un mo'ment. ‖

   (Un Monsieur en 'gris | descend ″majestueuse'ment | un esca'lier.) ‖

Le Mon'sieur. — Vous dési'rez, ↓Madame? |

G. — Je voudrais sa'voir | si la compa'gnie | vend des vagons ↓réformés | aux particu'liers. ‖

Le Mon'sieur. — Vous venez de la part ↓de 'qui? |

G. — 'Mais, | ″de per′sonne. | Je voudrais sa'voir | pour mon ″propre 'compte, | si la ‾chose ↓est po'ssible. ‖

Le Mon'sieur. — Il faudrait 'voir | le ‾chef ↓des bu'reaux, ‖ Monsieur 'L. ‖ ″Veuillez me 'suivre. ‖

   (Dans le bu'reau.) ‖

G. — Excusez-'moi, Monsieur, de vous déranger, ‖ mais, ″pourriez vous me 'dire | si la compa'gnie | vend des vagons ↓réformés | au pu'blic? ‖

Monsieur 'L. — ′Oui, | ″cela s'est déjà ′fait, | mais ″comment proposez-vous de l'emme'ner ce vagon, quand on vous le donnera? ‖ C'est ″grand, un vagon. ‖

G. — J'avais supposé ↓que la compagnie ↓pourrait me l'ame'ner | à la gare ↓la plus 'proche | de l'en'droit | où je veux le 'mettre; ‖ et puis a'lors, | ce serait ″naturellement à 'moi | d'en dispo'ser. ‖

Monsieur 'L. — Parfaite′ment! | ″Parfaite′ment! | Je vous pose ↓cette ques'tion, | car nous avons eu des 'gens | 'qui |

après avoir correspondu ↓avec Pa'ris, | "déba‿ttu les 'prix, |
ont été "fort embarra'ssés | quand nous leur avons 'dit : ‖
Voi⁻ci ↓votre va'gon, ‖ "prenez-'le. ‖ Et "où voulez-vous qu'on
vous l'expé'die? ‖

G.   — A Char'lieu. ‖

Monsieur 'L.   — Mais "c'est très ʹsimple. | Nous expédions ↓ces
jours-'ci | "quatre ou cinq voi‿tures refor'mées | à la Société
Ouest-↓Mé⁻taux ↓du Co'teau. ‖ Vous connaissez ↓le Co'teau? |

G.   — "Naturelle"ment. ‖

Monsieur 'L.   — Vous pourrez ↓vous arran'ger | avec 'eux. ‖

G.   — Et "combien à peu 'près | peut coû⁻ter ↓une voi'ture? ‖

Monsieur 'L.   — Nous en avons vendu ⁻huit cents 'francs. ‖

G.   — Je vous remer'cie Monsieur, ‖ et je m'ex'cuse | d'avoir
⁻pris |votre 'temps. ‖

Monsieur 'L.   — Mais "pas du ʹtout. | C'était "bien i‿ci qu'il
fallait vous adre'sser | pour ce renseigne'ment. ‖

Le Monsieur en ⁻gris ↓à l'ouvri'er. ‖   — Reconduisez Ma'dame. ‖
        (En pa⁻ssant ↓devant la 'loge.) ‖

Le Con'cierge.   — A'lors, ‖ vous avez fait a'ffaire? |

G.   — Mais ʹoui. |

Le Con'cierge.   — Eh bien "tant 'mieux. ‖

F.   — Tu as ton va'gon? |

G.   — "Pas en'core, ‖ mais ce-la ↓va s'arran'ger. ‖

F.   — Mainte'nant | tu n'as plus ↓qu'à comman'der | "huit
‿paires de 'bœufs, | pour le faire mon⁻ter ↓à Chan'don. ‖

V. Lacroix.

INTONATION OF *n'est-ce pas?*

(i) If *n'est-ce pas?* is really a question, the speaker requiring the answer "Yes" or "No" as he is not sure that his statement is true, the intonation is that which is typical of all other questions capable of being answered by "Yes" or "No":

sɛ pa ri ˈsi, ‖ nɛs ˈpɑ?|
nu zɑ̃ na vɔ̃ ˈkatr, ‖ nɛs ˈpɑ?|

Similarly in English:

It's ˈthis way, ‖ ˈis'nt it?|

We have ˈfour, ‖ ˈhaven't we?|

(ii) If the speaker is sure of the truth of his statement and yet wants to have it confirmed:

sɛ pa ri ˈsi, ‖ nɛs ˈpɑ?‖
sɛ bo ku ˈmjø, ‖ nɛs ˈpɑ?‖

Similarly in English:

It's ˈthis way, ‖ ˈisn't it?‖

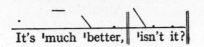

It's 'much 'better, ‖ 'isn't it?‖

(iii) If the speaker is quite sure of the truth of his statement and expects no reply at all, the words *n'est-ce pas* have little meaning, and the intonation is the same as that of final syllables of small significance :

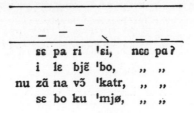

sɛ pa ri 'ɛi,   nɛɛ pɑ?
i lɛ bjɛ̃ 'bo,   ,, ,,
nu zɑ̃ na võ 'katr,   ,, ,,
sɛ bo ku 'mjø,   ,, ,,

In English, *isn't it? haven't we?* etc., in a similar context are pronounced as under (ii), the fall not being from a height great enough to suggest a real question, and the stress weak :

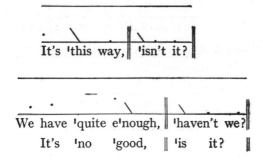

It's 'this way, ‖ 'isn't it? ‖

We have 'quite e'nough, ‖ 'haven't we?‖
It's 'no 'good, ‖ 'is it? ‖

APPENDIX 2

"Breaking" within a Sense-Group (in the Rising Part of an Intonation Group)

We have seen that breaks in the rising part of an intonation group are generally made by lowering the pitch immediately *after* pronouncing the final syllable of a sense-group. (See § 128.)

Breaks in the rising part of an intonation group are also frequently made by lowering the pitch immediately *before* the final syllable of a sense-group; so that the break occurs medially in a sense-group, often medially in a word.

Compare

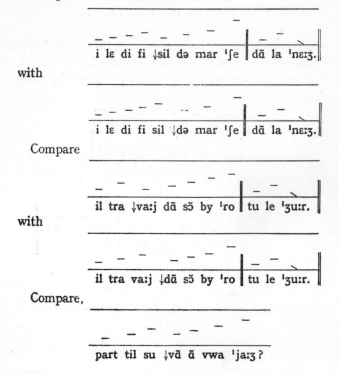

with

i lɛ di fi ↓sil də mar 'ʃe ‖ dɑ̃ la 'nɛːʒ.‖

i lɛ di fi sil ↓də mar 'ʃe ‖ dɑ̃ la 'nɛːʒ.‖

Compare

with

il tra ↓vaːj dɑ̃ sɔ̃ by 'ro ‖ tu le 'ʒuːr.‖

il tra vaːj ↓dɑ̃ sɔ̃ by 'ro ‖ tu le 'ʒuːr.‖

Compare,

part til su ↓vɑ̃ ɑ̃ vwa 'jaːʒ?

with

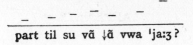

part til su vã ↓ã vwa ˈjaːʒ?

Compare il ɛ ridi↓kyl də sɔrˈtiːr │ ã s mɔˈmã ‖ with il ɛ ridikyl ↓də sɔrˈtiːr │ ã s mɔˈmã. ‖

Compare mɔ̃ pɛr a aʃ↓te yn meˈzɔ̃ │ a la kãˈpaɲ ‖ with mɔ̃ pɛr a aʃte ↓yn meˈzɔ̃ │ a la kãˈpaɲ. ‖

Compare il ɛ nese↓sɛːr d i aˈle │ ɔʒurˈdɥi ‖ with il ɛ nesesɛːr ↓d i ale │ ɔʒurˈdɥi. ‖

Compare il pasa la ↓tɛːt dã l uvɛrˈtyːr │ e nu ˈdi . . . ‖ with il pasa la tɛːt ↓dã l uvɛrˈtyːr │ e nu ˈdi. . . . ‖

It would seem that a break just before the final syllable of a sense-group is, in many cases, a step towards emphasis for intensity :

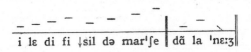

i lɛ di fi ↓sil də marˈʃe │ dã la ˈnɛːʒ‖

is nearer to the emphasis expressed in

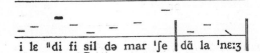

i lɛ ⁿdi fi sil də mar ˈʃe │ dã la ˈnɛːʒ ‖

than is

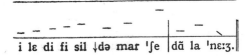

i lɛ di fi sil ↓də mar ˈʃe │ dã la ˈnɛːʒ. ‖

It is not necessary for English learners to make a break before the end of a sense-group in the rising part of an intonation group,[1] but it should be understood that this is very often done by French people.

[1] Except where the final syllable is ə. (See §§ 133, 140.)

APPENDIX 3

SENTENCES WITH AN IMPLICATION PRONOUNCED WITH THE FALLING INTONATION

Statements with an implication pronounced with the Rising intonation are given in Chapter VIII (see §§ 97, 98, 104), and in Chapter XX (see §§ 393, 394). Many such sentences may also be pronounced with the Falling intonation, the fall not being carried to a low pitch. This intonation often introduces a strong element of exclamation, interrogation, request, especially when each syllable is strongly stressed, as is often the case. There is a greater appeal to the reason of the hearer and a more definite attempt to overcome any scruples, incredulity, or hesitation he may feel.

The reader must imagine a suitable context for each of the following examples :

─ ─ ─ ─

╲

"pɥis kil nã vø 'pa.[1]

or

─ ─ ─ ─

might mean *Prenez-le, je vous en prie.   Pourquoi ne pas le prendre, voyons.*

─ ─ ─ ─

╲

"nu le za vɔ̃ 'vy.

or

─ ─ ─ ─

---

[1] To show the emphatic nature of sentences of this kind, and also the fact that the intonation falls from the beginning, the mark ‖ is placed before the first syllable (as for exclamations, commands, etc.).

might mean *Mon Dieu, pourquoi continuer à nous dire qu'ils ne sont pas rentrés?   Ne dites pas ça, voyons, puisque nous savons qu'ils sont rentrés.*

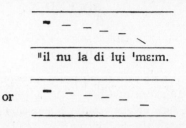

"il nu la di lчi 'mɛːm.

or

might mean *Pourquoi dire que ce n'est pas vrai?   Il ne peut pas y avoir de doute.*

Puisqu'il est libre with the intonation shown above might mean *N'hésitez plus.   Allez le voir.   Maintenant, vous pouvez bien y aller sans le déranger.*

APPENDIX 4

List of books recommended for the study of French and English
Intonation :

(a) FRENCH

Französische Intonationsübungen. H. KLINGHARDT and M. de
FOURMESTRAUX. (Schulze, Cöthen, 1911.)
Traité pratique de prononciation française. MAURICE GRAMMONT.
(Delagrave, 1914.)
French Intonation Exercises. H. KLINGHARDT and M. DE FOUR-
MESTRAUX. Translated and adapted for English Readers by
M. L. BARKER. (Heffer, Cambridge, 1923.)
Précis de Phonétique Comparée française et anglaise. P. GÉNÉVRIER.
(Didier, 1927.)
La prononciation française. MAURICE GRAMMONT. (Delagrave, 1930.)

(b) ENGLISH

Intonation and Emphasis. H. O. COLEMAN. (In *Miscellanea Phonetica*,
1912, published by the Association Phonétique Internationale.)
Übungen im englischen Tonfall. H. KLINGHARDT. (Schulze, Cöthen,
1920.)
English Intonation. H. E. PALMER. (Heffer, Cambridge, 2nd edition,
1924.)
A Handbook of English Intonation. LILIAS E. ARMSTRONG and IDA C.
WARD. (Teubner, Leipzig, and Heffer, Cambridge, 2nd edition,
1931.)
An Outline of English Phonetics, Chapter XXXI. DANIEL JONES.
(Teubner, Leipzig, and Heffer, Cambridge, 3rd edition, 1932.)